A nineteenth-century artistic impression of the princely state of Porbandar, in Gujarat, where Mohandas Karamchand Gandhi was born in 1869.

GANDHI

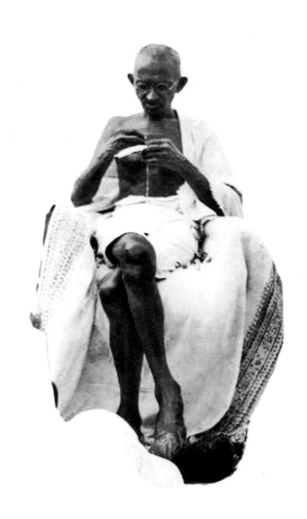

GANDHI

AN ILLUSTRATED BIOGRAPHY

PRAMOD KAPOOR

BLACK DOG
& LEVENTHAL
PUBLISHERS
NEW YORK

TO MAA AND PITAJI

Writing this book brought me closer to them

Black Dog & Leventhal Publishers
Hachette Book Group
1290 Avenue of the Americas
New York, NY 10104

www.hachettebookgroup.com
www.blackdogandleventhal.com

Originally published in 2015 by Roli Books in India.

First U.S. Edition: September 2017

Black Dog & Leventhal Publishers is an imprint of Hachette Books, a division of Hachette Book Group. The Black Dog & Leventhal Publishers name and logo are trademarks of Hachette Book Group, Inc.

The publisher is not responsible for websites (or their content) that are not owned by the publisher.

The Hachette Speakers Bureau provides a wide range of authors for speaking events. To find out more, go to www.HachetteSpeakersBureau.com or call (866) 376-6591.

Photo/art credits information is on page 328.

Library of Congress Cataloging-in-Publication Data has been applied for.

ISBNs: 978-0-316-55415-2 (hardcover), 978-0-316-55416-9 (ebook)

Printed in India

10 9 8 7 6 5 4 3 2 1

ACKNOWLEDGMENTS

When I began my research on Mahatma Gandhi, I contacted a number of scholars and thinkers who had made impressive contributions to the literature on him. Some were generous with their time and suggestions; others dismissed my request as a worthless exercise. While the former imparted knowledge, the latter generated an intense inner determination. Both contributed to my experiment with Gandhi, so to them my sincere gratitude.

First, a big thanks to my colleagues who helped in putting this book together. Without very able and diligent support from my colleagues this book would have taken much longer to publish. To Sneha, our most trusted designer, who has been part of our team for nearly 20 years and whom I consider to be the best in the business. To Priya, my editor, whose demanding but very valuable suggestions made this book what it is. And to Neelam Narula, Rayman Gill-Rai and Dipali Singh for their editorial support. Saloni Vaid, a very able photo researcher, followed the leads meticulously and produced images on demand.

Alison Moore, an accomplished editor from the United Kingdom, helped me adapt the Indian edition for international readers. I would like to acknowledge her valuable suggestions and diligent editing. Thank you, Ali.

My friendship with some of the best Gandhian scholars and historians of our time has been invaluable. Among them was Professor Mushirul Hasan, who got me going and encouraged me to pursue the subject. My gratitude also goes to Tridip Surhud, ever helpful and the finest mind on Gandhian literature; and to Dr. Ashis Nandy, who gave me hours of his time, especially at the beginning of the project, and helped me understand some of the most difficult parts of Gandhi's story. Thomas Weber was generous with his extensive knowledge and understanding. The piece on the Salt Satyagraha is largely inspired by his writing on the subject and I thank him with a deep sense of gratitude for reading the manuscript. At the very start I had the opportunity to share lunch with Dr. Sunil Khilnani and his wife, Katherine, in London. Their initial appreciation and subsequent critique helped shape the book. My thanks to John Falconer, lead curator, visual arts, at the British Library, for being such a good friend and helping with material I could have never have found without him. I also thank Shahid Amin and feel privileged to have the support of Dr. Vinay Lal, E. S. Reddy, Ken Robbins, Vikram Raghavan and many other scholar friends who have been part of this journey.

From time to time I sent short pieces to my friends and can be accused of using them as my sounding boards. T. N. Ninan, whom I consider the finest newspaper editor, read a couple of pieces. He trashed the first one and suggested ways to improve it—I remember how thrilled I was to read his message about the second one, which he called a "riveting read." S. Prasannarajan came up with the title *My Experiment with Gandhi*, which I have used as the title for the introductory chapter in the book. Krishna Prasad, then editor-in-chief, *Outlook*, who published excerpts of my stories in his magazine, was a constant source of encouragement. Tony Jessudasan, despite his extensive travel and professional commitments, acted as a model reader and came up with very useful suggestions. Then there was Dilip Bobb, a master craftsman with words who helped with rewriting passages and editing them. Thank you, Dilip, for all your hard work and help.

My wife, Kiran, has been an adviser and researcher and has accompanied me all over the world in search of archival material. She has the ability to find unique data and images that I have often overlooked. Thanks are also due to Kapil and Diya for reading the pieces from time to time and for bearing with me at times when I would talk for hours about Gandhiji and nothing else. There is no formal thanks for them—my affection says it all.

Non-Co-operation tree and Mahatma Gandhi.

Dissenting pamphlets and posters formed part of the propaganda used during India's struggle for freedom. Many families who sympathized with the struggle and Gandhi's call for civil disobedience hid printing presses in their basements. The non-cooperation tree in the pamphlet above represents two factions: the Swaraj Part (left side of the tree), which was against Gandhi's decision to withdraw the movement after instances of violence, and the No-Changers (right side of the tree), who agreed with his view. Barring this minor difference in thought, the two factions shared the same ideology and goal of "Purna Swaraj," or complete independence.

CONTENTS

MOHANDAS KARAMCHAND GANDHI: A LIFE

1869, October 2	Born in Porbandar, Gujarat.
1879–80	Primary schooling at Rajkot, Gujarat.
1882	Marries Kasturba.
1885	Father, Karamchand Gandhi, dies at 63.
1888, June	Birth of first son, Harilal.
1888, September 4	Sails for England for higher studies.
1888, October	Reaches Southampton, England.
1888, November 6	Joins Inner Temple, London.
1890, June	Passes the London Matriculation.
1890, September 19	Joins the London Vegetarian Society and becomes a member of the executive committee.
1891, June 10	Called to the Bar.
1891, June 12	Sails for India, and on reaching Bombay learns of his mother's death.
1892, May 14	Receives permission to practice in Kathiawar courts, but fails to establish a successful practice.
1892, October 28	Second son, Manilal, born.
1893, April	Sails for South Africa, becomes a legal adviser to Dada Abdullah & Company.
1893, May 26	Refuses to remove his turban; leaves the court.
1893, June 7	Thrown out of first-class carriage of train at Pietermaritzburg station. Vows to dedicate himself to active non-violent resistance.
1893	Reads Tolstoy's *The Kingdom of God Is Within You*.
1894, August 22	Founds the Natal Indian Congress in South Africa.
1896, June 5	Sails to India and addresses meetings on behalf of Indians in South Africa.
1896, November 30	Sails for South Africa with his family.
1896, December 12	Reaches Durban, South Africa.
1897, May 4	Third son, Ramdas, born.
1899, October 11	Establishes Indian Ambulance Corps during Boer War.
1900, May 22	Assists Kasturba in the delivery of fourth son, Devdas.
1901, October	Leaves South Africa for India.
1901–1902	Attends Indian National Congress session in Calcutta; opens law office in Bombay. Fails to establish a successful practice.
1902	Returns to South Africa without family, after urgent request from Indian community.
1903, February	Opens law office in Johannesburg.
1903, June 4	First issue of *Indian Opinion* published.

1904, October	Reads John Ruskin's *Unto This Last*.
1904, December	Establishes Phoenix settlement.
1906, July	Takes vow of brahmacharya (celibacy for life).
1906, September 11	Starts satyagraha at Empire Theatre in Johannesburg, where people take pledge to oppose Asiatic Registration Bill (the Black Act).
1906, October 1	Sails for England to present Indians' case to Colonial Secretary.
1908, January 10	Sentenced to two-month imprisonment in South Africa but released on January 31.
1908, January 30	Signs agreement with General Smuts on Voluntary Registration.
1908, February 10	Assaulted by Mir Alam and others.
1908, August 16	Addresses mass meetings in Johannesburg where registration certificates are burned.
1908, October 14	Arrested at Volksrust, sentenced to two months' hard labor, released on December 12.
1909, February 25	Again arrested at Volksrust and sentenced to three months, released on May 24.
1909, June 23	Sails for England from Cape Town, South Africa.
1909, October 24	Attends Dussehra festival in London with Veer Savarkar also in attendance.
1909, November 13–22	Sails for South Africa from London. Writes *Hind Swaraj* and translates Tolstoy's "A Letter to a Hindu" on board the *Kildonan Castle*.
1910, June	Establishes Tolstoy Farm with Hermann Kallenbach. Vows to give up milk and experiments with fruit-based diet.
1911, May 15	Differences with eldest son Harilal.
1912, October 22	Gopal Krishna Gokhale arrives in Cape Town. Gandhi accompanies him on a tour of South Africa.
1913, September 22–23	Kasturba arrested and given three months' rigorous imprisonment.
1913, November 11	Sentenced to nine months' imprisonment with his European co-workers, Henry Polak and Hermann Kallenbach; released early on December 18.
1914, January 13	Negotiations begin with General Smuts. Satyagraha campaign suspended pending agreement between them and C. F. Andrews, and with ultimate passage of Indian Relief Act.
1914, July 18	Sails for England, leaving South Africa for good.
1914, December 19	Sails for India from London.
1915, January 9	Reaches Bombay.
1915, February 17	Visits Rabindranath Tagore's Santiniketan, Bengal.
1915, May 20	Establishes Satyagraha Ashram at Kochrab, near Ahmedabad.

1915, June 26	Awarded "Kaisar-e-Hind" gold medal.
1915, September 11	First Harijan family moves into the Satyagraha Ashram.
1916, February 6	Speaks at the inauguration of Banaras Hindu University, upsetting Annie Besant, Lord Hardinge and the maharajas present on the dais.
1916, December 26	Attends Indian National Congress session at Lucknow; meets Jawaharlal Nehru for the first time.
1917, April 10	Travels to Patna in Bihar with Rajkumar Shukla to investigate condition of indigo farmers.
1917, April	Leads satyagraha campaign for rights of indigo farmers in Champaran, Bihar; arrested at Motihari but case withdrawn. Later joined by Mahadev Desai at Champaran.
1917, June	Establishes Sabarmati Ashram near Ahmedabad, Gujarat.
1917, November 7	Mahadev Desai becomes Gandhi's secretary.
1918, March 15	Starts indefinite fast (first in India) to resolve dispute between mill owners and mill hands of Ahmedabad, Gujarat.
1918, March 18	Breaks the fast in three days after compromise between workers and mill owners.
1918, March 22	Addresses meeting of 5,000 peasants at Nadiad, Gujarat; urges them not to pay land revenue.
1919, February 24	Satyagraha pledge against "Rowlatt Act."
1919, April 13	Jallianwala Bagh massacre at Amritsar; Gandhi announces three-day fast in Ahmedabad.
1919, September 7	First issue of *Navajivan* published.
1919, October 8	First issue of *Young India* published.
1920, August 1	Returns "Kaiser-e-Hind" award to British government. Commences non-cooperation movement.
1921, July 31	Presides over a bonfire of foreign cloth in Bombay.
1921, September 22	Resolves to wear a loin-cloth only in devotion to khadi and simplicity.
1921, November 19	Fasts for five days at Bombay because of communal riots, following visit of Prince of Wales.
1921, December 24	Mass civil disobedience. Gandhi invested with "sole executive authority" on behalf of Congress.
1922, January 29	Bardoli taluka in Gujarat resolved against payment of land revenue; civil disobedience.
1922, February 4	Riots at Chauri-Chaura, United Provinces.
1922, March 10	Arrested at Sabarmati on charge of sedition for article in *Young India*. Pleads guilty at the "great trial" in Ahmedabad. Sentenced to six years' imprisonment.
1922, March 21	Transferred to Yeravda Jail, Poona, Maharashtra.

1923, November 26	Starts writing *Satyagraha in South Africa* in Yeravda Jail.
1924, January 12	Operated on for appendicitis and unconditionally released from prison on February 5.
1924, September 17	Begins 21-day fast for communal harmony at Maulana Mohammed Ali's house, Delhi.
1925	Announces one-year political silence and immobility at Congress session at Cawnpore (Kanpur), United Provinces.
1925, November 7	Madeleine Slade joins Satyagraha Ashram, and is named Mirabehn.
1925, December 3	The serialization of *Autobiography or The Story of My Experiments with Truth* commences in *Young India*.
1928, February 3	Boycotts Simon Commission.
1928, December	Moves resolution in Congress session at Calcutta, calling for complete independence within one year, or else the beginning of another all-India satyagraha campaign.
1929, October 31	Viceroy Lord Irwin announces Round Table Conference in London.
1929, December 27–31	Congress session at Lahore declares "Complete Independence" (Purna Swaraj) and boycott of the legislature.
1930, January 26	Proclamation of the Indian Declaration of Independence.
1930, March 12	Begins historic Salt March from Sabarmati to Dandi in Gujarat with 79 volunteers.
1930, April 6	Breaks the salt law at Dandi seashore.
1930, May 5	Arrested and sent to Yeravda Jail; released on January 26, 1931.
1931, March 5	Signs Gandhi–Irwin (Viceroy) Pact. Civil Disobedience ends.
1931, September 7	Visits London to attend Second Round Table Conference. Stays at Kingsley Hall. Conference ends on December 1. During this period he visits universities, meets celebrities, and broadcasts to America.
1931, November 5	Attends (in his loin-cloth) the royal reception for the delegates of the Second Round Table Conference at Buckingham Palace at the invitation of King George V.
1931, December 6	Visits Romain Rolland in Switzerland.
1931, December 14	Sails to India from Brindisi, Italy, after meeting Mussolini in Rome on December 12.
1932, January 1	Congress Working Committee adopts the resolution of Civil Disobedience.
1932, January 4	Arrested in Bombay and detained without trial at Yeravda Jail. Sardar Patel is a fellow prisoner.
1932, August 18	Writes to Ramsay MacDonald declaring his intention to fast unto death against the Communal Award.

1932, September 20	Begins fast unto death in protest against separate electorates for untouchables.
1932, September 26	Concludes "epic fast" with historic cell scene in presence of Rabindranath Tagore after British accept the "Poona Pact."
1933, May 8	Begins self-purification fast in prison, and is released.
1933, June 16	Youngest son, Devdas, marries Lakshmi Rajagopalachari.
1933, August 1	Arrested at Ahmedabad and sent to Sabarmati Prison in Gujarat; later shifted to Yeravda Jail.
1933, August 16	Sentenced to one-year imprisonment at Yeravda. Starts fast against the refusal of permission to work against untouchability while in prison; taken to hospital on the fifth day, and unconditionally released on eighth day.
1933, November 7	Nationwide Harijan Yatra commenced.
1933	Kasturba arrested and imprisoned for sixth time in two years.
1934, June 25	A bomb is thrown by a Hindu at Gandhi's car in Poona.
1934, September 17	Declares intention to retire from Congress.
1934, October 30	Resigns from Congress.
1935, December	Margaret Sanger, pioneering American birth control activist, visits Gandhi at Wardha, Maharashtra.
1936, May	Eldest son, Harilal, converts to Islam.
1936, November 12	Travancore temples (in Travancore princely state, now in Kerala) open to Harijans.
1939, February 2	Kasturba arrested in Rajkot, Gujarat.
1939, March 3	Commences fast at Rajkot against the breach of trust. Breaks fast on March 7; Chief Justice Maurice Gwyer appointed arbitrator.
1939, July 23	Writes to Hitler for first time, and again on December 24, 1941. Both letters remain undelivered.
1940, October 11	Congress Working Committee meeting at Sevagram, Wardha. Launches limited, individual civil disobedience campaign against Britain's refusal to allow Indians to express their opinions regarding the Second World War.
1942	Meets Sir Stafford Cripps in New Delhi, calls his proposals "a post-dated check." Proposals ultimately rejected by Congress.
1942, January 15	Informs Congress Working Committee at Sevagram that Jawaharlal Nehru is his political heir.
1942, August 8	Congress passes "Quit India" resolution. Gandhi leads nation-wide satyagraha under the slogan "Do or Die."
1942, August 9	Arrested with Kasturba and other Congress Working Committee members in Bombay; imprisoned at the Aga Khan Palace Prison, Poona, Maharashtra.

1942, August 15	Death of Mahadev Desai; cremated at Aga Khan Palace Prison.
1943, February 10	Begins 21-day fast at Aga Khan Palace to end deadlock in negotiations between viceroy and Indian leaders. Later, on May 6, 1944, released unconditionally after decline in health.
1944, February 22	Death of Kasturba; cremated at Aga Khan Palace Prison.
1945, June 14	Lord Wavell calls for negotiations.
1945, June 15	Congress Working Committee members released from Ahmednagar Fort Prison. Ban on Congress lifted.
1946, March 23	Three-member British delegation reaches Delhi.
1946, June 25	Congress Working Committee adopts resolution to accept formation of the Constituent Assembly.
1946, July 4	Viceroy Lord Wavell forms an interim government.
1946, August 16	Communal riots in Calcutta.
1946, September 2	Twelve-member interim government formed, headed by Jawaharlal Nehru.
1946, October 10	Communal violence in Noakhali, Bengal.
1946, October 15	Muslim League representatives join the interim government.
1946, November 6	Leaves for Noakhali. On January 2, barefoot march to Noakhali commences.
1947, June 2	Opposes Congress' decision to accept division of country into India and Pakistan.
1947, August 13	In Calcutta with Shaheed Suhrawardy.
1947, September 1	Starts indefinite fast against communal violence in Calcutta. Breaks fast on September 4.
1947, September 9	Reaches Delhi. Visits refugee camps to stop rioting and killing.
1948, January 12	Fasts for five days in Delhi for communal unity.
1948, January 20	A bomb is thrown during prayer meeting.
1948, January 30	Assassinated at Birla House by Nathuram Vinayak Godse. Dies at 78.
1948, January 31	Cremated on the banks of the Yamuna by third son, Ramdas.

FAMILY TREE

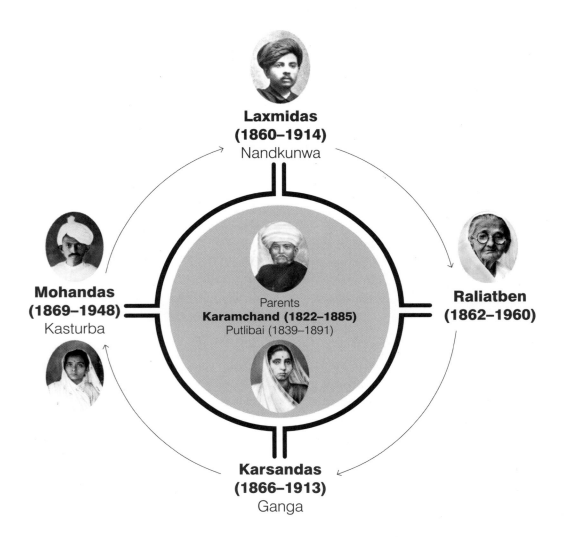

**Laxmidas
(1860–1914)**
Nandkunwa

**Mohandas
(1869–1948)**
Kasturba

Parents
Karamchand (1822–1885)
Putlibai (1839–1891)

**Raliatben
(1862–1960)**

**Karsandas
(1866–1913)**
Ganga

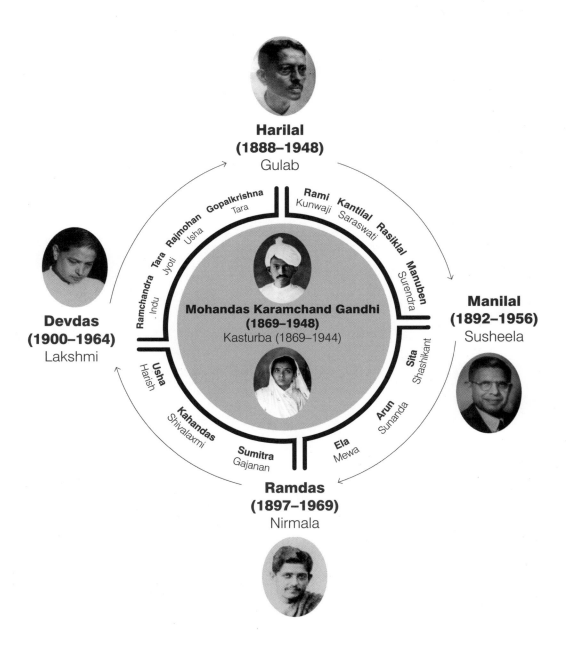

Harilal
(1888–1948)
Gulab

Ramchandra · Tara · **Rajmohan** · **Gopalkrishna**
Indu · Jyoti · Usha · Tara

Rami · **Kantilal** · **Rasiklal**
Kunwaji · Saraswati

Manuben
Surendra

Mohandas Karamchand Gandhi
(1869–1948)
Kasturba (1869–1944)

Manilal
(1892–1956)
Susheela

Sita
Shashikant

Devdas
(1900–1964)
Lakshmi

Usha
Harish

Kahandas
Shivalaxmi

Sumitra
Gajanan

Ela
Mewa

Arun
Sunanda

Ramdas
(1897–1969)
Nirmala

"Generations to come, it may well be, will scarce believe that such a man as this one ever in flesh and blood walked upon this Earth."

ALBERT EINSTEIN

My Experiment with Gandhi

Some years ago, I was surprised by the arrival of two policemen at my office. They announced: "Sir, we have come to take you with us."

As I had been in book publishing for most of my life, except for a short time when I was running a newspaper, I had become somewhat thick-skinned, but I must admit I was totally unprepared for such a situation. My heart skipped a few beats as I asked, "Why?"

"You have published a book that may incite the public," said one of them in a voice that lacked conviction but sounded well rehearsed.

Indeed, we had commissioned an interesting book on Dr. Bhimrao Ambedkar, a social reformer popularly known as the father of the Indian constitution, but it was more of a personal history than a political tome. When I signed up the book, I did so in the belief that if Ambedkar were alive he would have endorsed it. After all, he had included some of what I was going to publish in his own autobiography. However, not a single chapter had been submitted by the author at that point. So I composed myself and asked for a warrant. They did not have one. Sensing my refusal to be cowed, they left, but with a warning that if any of my actions disturbed public sentiment they had the right to arrest me. As it happens, the book was never published—the author died suddenly, leaving no manuscript. And now I am publishing *Gandhi: An Illustrated Biography*, which mentions Gandhi's sexuality and other personal details, but this time I do so without fear of a knock on my door. They don't generally issue warrants for publishing books on Gandhi.

A few years ago my Norwegian friend William Nygaard, with whom we had published a couple of non-political books, received six bullets that were meant for Salman Rushdie. He had dared to publish the Norwegian edition of *Satanic Verses*. Publishing has its risks. I had earlier faced a criminal suit and for close to 11 years had to be present at the Tis Hazari criminal courts in Delhi for publishing an illustrated edition of the Kama Sutra with visuals that were painted a few hundred years previously. Then some years ago, the youth wing of a political party demonstrated in front of an embassy merely because an author from that country had written an innocuous biography of their leader, which we intended to publish. I have neither read *Lady Chatterley's Lover* nor Wendy Doniger but every time books are banned, I am driven by an emotion difficult to describe, which has to do with freedom of speech and the written word, yet mixed with an apprehension of harassment. As long as works pass the test of authenticity, factual research and corroboration, publishers like me are excited about publishing books that provide new material or insights on the subject. That is why I did not have any fear while writing about Gandhi's personal life, which had darker shades too.

Writing about Mohandas Karamchand Gandhi was to me a privilege and a duty. He is Bapu, father of the nation, the Mahatma and a leader who has been analyzed, re-analyzed, criticized and applauded by several generations from the time the first book was written about him—Joseph Doke's *M. K. Gandhi: An Indian Patriot in South Africa*—in 1908, and his own first book in 1909 (*Hind Swaraj*). Although there have been rare instances of local or limited restrictions on books on Gandhi, such as Stanley Wolpert's *Nine Hours to Rama* and Joseph Lelyveld's *Great Soul: Mahatma Gandhi and His Struggle with India*, no one has protested against, or burned, books about him. So I hope the police will not return to my office, this time with the document they lacked earlier.

Gandhi called his life an open book and wrote and spoke about it with complete honesty. I did not live in that era, but I have read books and articles that show no one was more critical of his actions than he was. In publishing this illustrated book, I was driven by a passion and fascination, despite disagreeing with some of his actions and personal history. I plunged into the task of reading and researching the millions of words that have been written about Gandhi the man, the crusader, the husband, father, leader and politician, completely immersing myself in the project at the cost of everything else.

When I started, I had very little knowledge about Gandhi, except what I had learned in school or from anecdotes told by family members who supported him in the freedom movement. I took the plunge a couple of years ago, following my publisher's instinct.

To take the idea further, I discussed it with my old friend and author Mushirul Hasan. Without him realizing what he was pushing me into, and I equally ignorant of the ocean-like vastness of the subject, I started reading *The Collected Works of Mahatma Gandhi*, as he suggested. The next six months changed my life. I discovered many interesting real-life instances and stories, which would fascinate a lay reader but were perhaps too trivial for scholars to mention in their in-depth studies. After all, so much has been written on Gandhi that unless the vaults of private archives are unsealed or Gandhi's descendants decide to make public or auction their private papers, there is little left to discover. Yet, partly because of my fascination with what I was reading and partly because of my publisher's nose, I felt that his story needed to be retold for the present generation. I have tried to convey the stories as they happened without being overly judgmental. What makes this book different from all that has been published before is that each time I went digging for archival material, I stumbled across a piece of history or fascinating information considered irrelevant by historians. The more I dug, the more stories that emerged and the more my interest grew. It brought to life just how complex a character he had been, perhaps the greatest living statesman in history, a born leader and revolutionary, a man of extraordinary courage and vision, but also someone who was often at odds with his own teachings, at odds with the leaders and statesmen with whom he worked or negotiated, and at odds with many aspects of his own character, especially as a father and a husband.

Gandhi came to me early, as I suppose he does to many Indians, at school, where he was required reading. Like others at the time, my parents were deeply influenced by Gandhi and impatiently wanted their children to read Gandhi's autobiography even before they were mature enough to understand the book or the subject. Although we were not a "Gandhian" family, examples from his life were invariably quoted when we children did something wrong—in those days there was a little bit of Gandhi in everyone's life. My earliest visual memory is of a photograph of Gandhi, Nehru and Patel that hung alongside that of a revolutionary hero, Chandra Shekhar Azad, in our living room in Banaras. That was decades ago and many of those memories have faded. It was a family tragedy that has kept his name alive in my mind and it relates to his favorite bhajan—a devotional song— "*Raghupati Raghav Raja Ram, Patita Paavana Sitaram.*"

A day after my wedding, my mother suffered a stroke; she was paralyzed and lost her speech. She retained the ability to recite only one phrase: "*Patita Paavana Sitaram*," a Ram dhun—a hymn devoted to Rama—that Gandhi helped make a household hymn. She repeated it in times of happiness or distress. Perhaps this was a bit of Gandhi that remained in her mind, her only words till she died. Remembrances of her and her voice kept coming back as I worked on the book.

Gandhi is viewed and reviewed, analyzed and interpreted in a different manner every decade or so. What emerges from this revision and revaluation is the complexity of his character and the contradictions. A master of conflict resolution, he would forge agreements with his fiercest critics, but he could be extremely dictatorial when dealing with his closest relatives or his followers. He would often give in to his adversaries in seeking peaceful resolutions but would force his doting wife or staunchest followers to act against their wishes. At the height of the khadi movement, when Gandhi exhorted everyone to boycott foreign clothes, his wife, Kasturba, complained that she could not wear a khadi sari and cook—it was too heavy to do her chores—and asked for his permission to wear something lighter. Gandhi got so annoyed that he told his wife not to cook at all, for he would not eat food cooked by her while wearing unholy foreign cloth.

In 1915, as he embarked on a journey to discover India, the leaders he met, influenced or came into conflict with, and the mass of Indians who were fascinated by the man and his methods, eventually elevated him to the position of Mahatma ("great soul"). Gandhi himself approached his discovery of India and its people with childlike enthusiasm, talking to the people he met and shared space with. While Indian leaders were discovering Gandhi, he was familiarizing himself with India as an apprentice.

Lord Reading, viceroy of India, once remarked: "There is nothing striking about his appearance . . . I would have passed him by in the street without a second look at him. When he talks, the impression is different. He is direct, and expresses himself well in excellent English with a fine appreciation of the value of the words he uses." Gandhi would use that power of expression (after all, he was trained as a barrister) on the many crusades he undertook. One was to convert Indians who had become Westernized in their speech and dress. Using his persuasive powers and setting a personal example, he converted many Westernized Indians into adopting a "swaraj" (self-rule) lifestyle—one notable example was Motilal Nehru, who gave up his Savile Row suits for home-spun khadi.

As suggested by his mentor, Gopal Krishna Gokhale, Gandhi traveled extensively for the first few years after his arrival in India with his "ears open and mouth shut." He was emerging as a leader who would not only be a prime mover for India's independence but would give the world a unique armory called non-violence. By the early 1920s, Gandhi had been transformed into a leader with a massive pan-Indian following. His insistence on traveling third class kept him in touch with Indians of all classes. Thousands turned up to see him on railway platforms during his train journeys or walked miles to hear him speak at public meetings. Wherever he went, the cries of "*Mahatma Gandhi ki jai!*" (long live Mahatma Gandhi) were getting louder and reflected his fast-growing popularity and stature. He had clearly captured the imagination of the people through his novel methods of protest—non-violent and peaceful, but non-cooperative with the authorities. The acceptance of him and his methods, however, was not universal. Many political leaders and intellectuals questioned his non-violent satyagraha (insistence on truth) movement. In fact, a fierce debate broke out over this tactic. Many felt that while Gandhi used non-violent means, his ideas of protest were aggressive and often resulted in violent action by his followers. In fact, he called off his non-cooperation movement because it resulted in violence. Thousands of young men and women had by then sacrificed their education and jobs as they plunged into the freedom movement. Many of them felt let down. There was also criticism of the fact that he was undertaking life-threatening fasts in order to usher in peace. Leaders such as Annie Besant, M. A. Jinnah, M. R. Jayakar and even the radical Bal Gangadhar Tilak did not always agree with him. Jamnadas Dwarakadas, a close supporter of Tilak and Annie Besant, in his book *Political Memoirs*, has reproduced a wonderful dialog between Tilak and Gandhi that confirms this. At one stage during the conversation, Tilak said to Gandhi: "I am afraid that you are not a politician...you are a great saint...I should advise you to sit in your ashram... but leave it to us to go out to the world..." Gandhi in reply said: "I plead guilty to

the charge..." and questioned Tilak: "Don't you believe in non-violence as a suitable method...?" To this, Tilak replied: "I want swaraj. I want freedom for my country. Means is not a very important matter to me...but that is a hypothetical question." Gandhi could never agree to any compromise on the principle of non-violence.

The communists and those with left leanings, oddly enough, believed Gandhi was a supporter of the capitalists and openly opposed him. In London, where Gandhi had gone to attend the Second Round Table Conference, young communist leaders shouted slogans of "*Gandhi Murdabad*" (death to Gandhi).

It was not just the communists, but also some Western-oriented capitalists such as Burjor Padshah and Dinshaw Wacha, key directors of Tata Sons, who criticized him, perhaps irked by Gandhi's call for a boycott of mill-made cloth and in disagreement with his non-cooperation movement. Contrary to the general belief that industrialists G. D. Birla and Jamnalal Bajaj were early donors to Gandhi's cause, it was Sir Ratan Tata who had much earlier donated lakhs (100,000s) of rupees to Gandhi through Bal Gangadhar Tilak, in support of his fight against the apartheid regime in South Africa.

Gandhi's crusades would come to define India and impose it on the consciousness of the world. Gandhi never traveled to the United States, but he was revered by many across the Atlantic. The clergyman Dr. John Haynes Holmes called him "the greatest man in the world" in a 1921 sermon. And four years later, another American, the missionary Dr. Eli Stanley, inspired by Gandhi, wrote the bestselling book *The Christ of the Indian Road*; this in turn was to influence Martin Luther King Jr. Rather more surprisingly, perhaps, Gandhi visited Rome in 1931 to meet with the Italian dictator Benito Mussolini, whom he later described as looking like "a butcher."

What was fascinating about Gandhi and his methods was just how relentless he was in his pursuit of a goal, starting with freedom from British rule. He would come up with one novel idea after another in the fight for freedom—the Khilafat movement, non-cooperation, the boycott of foreign clothes, homespun khadi, the Quit India movement, the Salt Satyagraha. Gandhi often compared the latter to the Boston Tea Party that preceded the American War of Independence.

Nevertheless, when it comes to Gandhi, the contradictions remain. His name may now be synonymous with pacifism and non-violent struggle, but he was also an astute general who used the arsenal of moral authority to gain victory and he unashamedly milked that ability when friends turned foes, as in his dealings with many political leaders. British Prime Minister Winston Churchill was not a fan, and it fell on U.S. President Franklin Delano Roosevelt, amid the turmoil of the Second World War, to try reluctantly to intervene in Britain's "India affair," especially when Gandhi was dangerously ill on one of his life-threatening fasts.

Despite Gandhi's "order" to his friends to keep his life "an open book," the private papers of some of those very close to him (the Pyarelal papers being one such example), as well as his personal letters to his immediate family, are not in the public domain—they remain unpublished and inaccessible to most biographers, locked away in government and private vaults. It is to be hoped that one day they will be made public, if they survive.

When Gandhi returned to India, one of the first places he visited, along with his fellows from the Phoenix settlement in Durban, South Africa, was Rabindranath Tagore's university at Santiniketan. It was Tagore who gave Gandhi the title of Mahatma, and yet they disagreed on so many issues, especially the non-cooperation movement and on the boycott and burning of imported cloth. Both used their impressive writing skills to criticize each other in public. Tagore created a play, *Mukta Dhara*, to convey his disagreement, while Gandhi produced a wonderful piece, "The Great Sentinel," as a counter-critique. However, they still remained friends—Gandhi raised substantial money when Santiniketan was in a financial crisis and when Tagore passed away in 1941, Gandhi wrote one of the most moving obituaries.

While we will continue to admire his life and achievements, it is—for someone who did not live in his time or his mind—more difficult to explain his personal beliefs and how he treated his family and close friends. The treatment he meted out to his eldest son, Harilal, is an example. Harilal followed his father to jail in South Africa at a very young age and yet, inexplicably, Gandhi chose his nephew over Harilal when it came to financing higher studies in Britain. The man who earned fame for non-violence slapped his young wife, Kasturba, and then remarked that he had learned the first lesson of ahimsa (non-violence) from her silent tears. There are many other such instances of Gandhi's strange relationship with his family. They perhaps need a different psychological study. For him, his own family and the world at large was one institution and he treated both with equal objectivity. There was no difference between them.

One of the most complex aspects of Gandhi's life for me was the many women who were attracted to him, despite his vow of celibacy taken at the age of 37. Gandhi himself admitted to an American journalist that Sarala Devi Choudhurani, Tagore's beautiful and elegant niece, nearly destroyed his marriage. He was nearing 50 then. Gandhi's sexual life or sexuality has been the subject of much debate and criticism, especially his personal yagna (test of his resolve), which involved sleeping naked with a few close women followers, including his teenage grandniece, Manubehn. Many close to him wrote to him advising against this practice. This was at the peak of Hindu–Muslim riots in Noakhali, where he traveled as a pacifist in 1946–1947. Parasram, his personal secretary at the time, wrote an angry ten-page letter after witnessing this bizarre form of yagna, and quit his job. So did Prof. Sudhir Ghosh, his Bengali translator. To his credit, Gandhi made no attempt to hide their letters, often discussing the issue in public through letters and speeches. Yet, it seems the writings of those who either participated in the yagna or witnessed it are not readily available. I remember my first meeting with a senior social scientist. Before we could settle down in the chairs on the lawns of India International Centre in Delhi, I abruptly asked him what he thought of Gandhi sleeping naked with his teenage grandniece. His equally abrupt but truthful reply was that he, too, felt uncomfortable with this yagna. Of course, once we settled down he provided insights, explaining Gandhi's philosophy on sexuality.

While practicing and preaching non-violence, Gandhi knew of the risk he was taking with life and death. In fact, some of his most eloquent speeches and writings relate to death. On the death of his favorite teenage grandson, Rasiklal (son of his eldest and later estranged son, Harilal), Gandhi wrote an extremely moving obituary. Gandhi was very close to Rasiklal, who at the age of 17 had joined Jamia

Millia Islamia University in Delhi on his instructions to teach, but had then died of cholera. Gandhi wrote: "Truly speaking, death is God's eternal blessing. The body which is used up falls and the bird within it flies away. So long as the bird does not die, the question of grief does not arise." Gandhi clearly had a premonition about his own death. A few days before his assassination, he would repeat these thoughts to his close friends and followers as if he had foreknowledge.

In the court of Justice G. D. Khosla, Nathuram Godse, Gandhi's assassin, while justifying his heinous action, praised Gandhi intermittently in his speech, which lasted almost the entire day. His defense was so forceful, Khosla wrote in his memoir, that had there been a jury, it would have acquitted him. Perhaps Gandhi himself would have defended Godse. In the twilight of his life he had already pronounced a verdict on his would-be assassin: "If someone were to shoot me in the belief that he was getting rid of a rascal, he would kill not the real Gandhi, but the one that appeared to him a rascal." No wonder then, that I, and many more after me, will continue with the "experiment with Gandhi."

MOHANDAS KARAMCHAND GANDHI

1869–1948

1876

1883

1886

1907

1909

1913

1921

1924

1930

1888

1900

1906

1915

1917

1919

1936

1942

1948

"I must have been about seven when my father left Porbandar for Rajkot. There I was put into a primary school, and I can well recollect . . . the names and other particulars of the teachers who taught me. As at Porbandar, so here, there is hardly anything to note about my studies. I could only have been a mediocre student."

MOHANDAS KARAMCHAND GANDHI

1869-1914

Birth and Early Years in India
London–India–South Africa

FOURTH SON FROM HIS FATHER'S FOURTH WIFE

Mohandas Karamchand Gandhi was born on October 2, 1869, at Porbandar in western India. He was the youngest of four siblings. When asked about his mother, he would say: "The outstanding impression my mother has left on my memory is that of saintliness. To keep two or three consecutive fasts was nothing to her. During another Chaturmas [holy period], she vowed not to have food without seeing the sun. We children on those days would stand, staring at the sky, waiting to announce the appearance of the sun to our mother. And I remember days when, at his sudden appearance, we would rush and announce it to her. She would run out to see with her own eyes, but by that time the fugitive sun would be gone, thus depriving her of her meal. 'That does not matter,' she would say cheerfully, 'God did not want me to eat today.' And then she would return to her round of duties."

1869 Left: *Gandhi's mother, Putlibai (1839–1891), was a religious woman.*
Right: *Gandhi's father, Karamchand (1822–1885), was the chief minister of Porbandar state.*

1876 Left: *Gandhi, aged seven, in Porbandar. He was the fourth and last son from his father's fourth and last marriage. This is one of his earliest photographs.*
1886 Right: *Gandhi (right) with his elder brother Laxmidas. Both brothers were studies in contrast—while Mohandas valued frugality, Laxmidas favored comfort.*

The Gandhis apparently got into trouble often. Political intrigues forced grandfather Uttamchand out of the prime ministership of Porbandar and into exile in the nearby state of Junagadh. There he once saluted the ruling Nawab with his left hand. Asked for an explanation, he said: "The right hand is already pledged to Porbandar." Gandhi was proud of such loyalty: "My grandfather," he wrote, "must have been a man of principle."

"My books and my lessons were my sole companions. To be at school at the stroke of the hour and to run back home as soon as the school closed—that was my daily habit," wrote Gandhi. "I literally ran back, because I could not bear to talk to anybody. I was even afraid lest anyone should poke fun at me."

Gandhi's father married four times, after his successive wives died early. His first and second wives bore him two daughters and with his last wife, Putlibai, he had a daughter and three sons, Mohandas being the youngest. His elder brother Laxmidas practiced law and became a treasury official in the Porbandar government. Laxmidas spent money freely and liked to live lavishly, much like minor royalty of the time, even though he had a modest income. He married his daughters with great pomp and ceremony and owned two houses in Rajkot.

GANDHI GETS MARRIED

Despite the extremely high moral standards he set for himself, Gandhi would acknowledge that in his own life, he was guilty of one shameful act, of partaking in "the cruel custom of child marriage," as he would later castigate it. Gandhi was married, when he was not even 13, to Kasturba, who was also the same age. At the time, child marriage was an accepted custom. Gandhi says he was betrothed thrice without his knowledge. The first two girls chosen for him had died. The third betrothal took place when he was seven. Of his own marriage, he recounted every detail. The elders on both sides had agreed on the proposal, or proposals, since it was a "triple wedding." Gandhi would be married, along with his brother, two years older than him, and a cousin. It was a matter of convenience and economics. This would mean the family could spend lavishly on just one big celebration.

As he would write later in his autobiography, he could still picture himself sitting on the wedding dais, the rituals that followed, and then the first night, of "two innocent children unwittingly hurled into the ocean of life." At his age, it essentially meant "good clothes to wear, drum beating, marriage processions, rich dinners and a strange girl to play with." Carnal desire, he wrote, came later. He recalls that his eldest brother's wife had coached him on how to behave that first night, but later he would confess that no coaching is really necessary in such matters. Gandhi says he lost no time in assuming the "authority" of a husband. In his seminal book, *The Life of Mahatma Gandhi*, Jewish-American author Louis Fischer writes: "He loved Kasturba. His passion was entirely centered on one woman and he wanted it reciprocated, but the woman was a child." Gandhi was a jealous husband and Kasturba could not go anywhere without his permission. According to the joint family tradition of the time, enforced separations between young couples was common. During the first five years of their marriage, Gandhi and Kasturba spent only three years together.

For his wedding, the family had moved to Porbandar from Rajkot to take care of the preparations. His father, employed as a diwan (chief officer) to a local thakur (head of state), would follow later, in a horse-drawn coach, which toppled over during the journey. He arrived at the wedding heavily bandaged and in pain, but ensured that everything went smoothly. Gandhi, who was devoted to his parents, says he forgot about his father's condition in the "childish amusement of my wedding." When Kasturba was 15 and pregnant, Gandhi writes in his autobiography, while he was massaging his father's legs, "my mind was hovering about my wife's bedroom." One night, his uncle took over the massage duties and Gandhi rushed to his wife. A few minutes later, a servant knocked on the door and told him he was required urgently. Gandhi jumped out of the bed and rushed to his father's side, only to find he had passed away. Later, he would write: "If passion had not blinded me, I would have been spared the torture of separation from my father during his last moments…The shame of my carnal desire at the critical moment of my father's death is a blot I have never been able to efface or forget."

HONESTY PREVAILS IN CLASS

"There is an incident which occurred at the examination during my first year at the high school and which is worth recording," recalls Gandhi. "Mr. Giles, the Educational Inspector, had come on a visit of inspection. He had set us five words to write as a spelling exercise. One of the words was 'kettle.' I had misspelled it. The teacher tried to prompt me with the point of his boot, but I would not be prompted. It was beyond me to see that he wanted me to copy the spelling from my neighbor's slate, for I had thought that the teacher was there to supervise us against copying. The result was that all the boys except myself were found to

1888 An average student in school, Gandhi graduated from a high school in Rajkot, Gujarat. Shown are a high-school marksheet (above) and an application to his headmaster (right) signed by Gandhi, conferring his scholarship to another student.

have spelt every word correctly. Only I had been stupid. The teacher tried later to bring this stupidity home to me, but without effect. I never could learn the art of 'copying.' "

FIRST TRIP TO LONDON

At the age of 18, Gandhi set sail for London on September 4, 1888, having received a scholarship (worth 5,000 rupees) to study law. He had, as he later admitted, a secret desire to satisfy his curiosity about what London was like. He arrived in the third week of October after a long journey and proceeded to the Victoria Hotel, along with two other Indians he had met aboard the ship. His first impression of the hotel was that the porter there was better dressed than any of them. He was equally dazzled by the splendor of the hotel. "I had never in my life seen such pomp," he would recall later. After paying the bill of six shillings a day in advance, he followed the porter to the elevator, an invention Gandhi had never seen. He saw the boy press something, which he assumed was the lock of the door, which opened shortly after. Gandhi stepped inside and immediately thought they were in a room where they were supposed to sit for some time. It was only when the doors opened on the second floor that Gandhi realized that he had been in an elevator!

In London, Gandhi became quite a dandy. He was seen in photographs wearing a white tie, stiff French cuffs and a dress kerchief in his front pocket, with his hair neatly combed. Louis Fischer wrote that he used to spend 10 minutes each day combing and brushing his hair. His attempts to become a fashionable man saw him hiring a tutor to teach him French, another to teach him elocution and he even joined dancing classes, paying three guineas for an instructor. However, he gave up after six lessons since his feet could never coordinate with the music. Instead, he took up the violin, paying another three guineas to buy one, but soon realizing that it, too, was a futile investment. The music teacher then told him he would accomplish nothing by adopting the manners of a fashionable man about town.

1891 *Gandhi photographed as a young student in England.*

It was in London that Gandhi started to adopt some of the characteristics that would later define him as an ascetic who had given up the luxuries of life to attain self-discipline. He joined the Vegetarian Society of England and discontinued the practice of getting sweets and masalas, or spices, sent from India. In 1890, he became a member of the executive committee of the society and attended its annual conference in Portsmouth. It was a decision not without repercussions.

1891 *Gandhi (first row, sitting, right) with fellow members of the Vegetarian Society in London.*

As a committed vegetarian, he would have caused some problems in the Inner Temple kitchens during dining nights, though his refusal to drink alcohol made him quite popular, mainly because it left more wine for the other students!

After completing his term in Inner Temple, London, Gandhi came back to India toward the end of June 1892. In his application to the Bombay High Court on November 16, 1891, Gandhi wrote: "I am desirous of being admitted as an

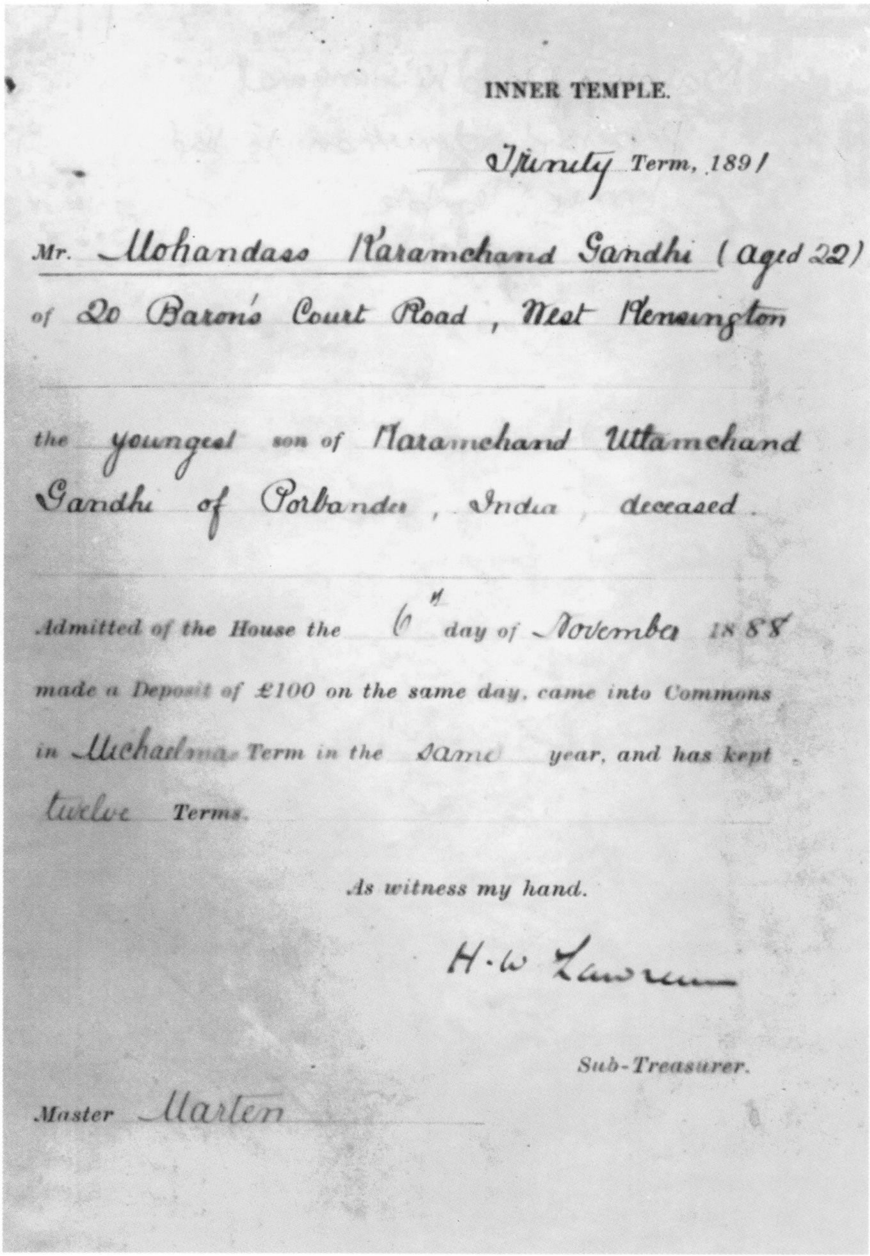

INNER TEMPLE.

Trinity Term, *1891*

Mr. *Mohandass Karamchand Gandhi* (aged 22)

of *20 Baron's Court Road, West Kensington*

the *youngest* son of *Karamchand Uttamchand*
Gandhi of Porbander, India, deceased.

Admitted of the House the *6th* day of *November* 18 *88*

made a Deposit of £100 on the same day, came into Commons

in *Michaelmas* Term in the *same* year, and has kept

twelve Terms.

As witness my hand.

H. W. Lawren

Sub-Treasurer.

Master *Marten*

1891 *Gandhi's years at Inner Temple, London, studying law, played a crucial role in shaping his life. Reproduced above is a certificate given to Gandhi from Inner Temple.*

1891 *W. D. Edwards, well-known author and practicing barrister in the Supreme Court of Judicature in England, wrote Gandhi a letter of recommendation for enrollment in Bombay High Court.*

advocate of the high court. I was called to the Bar in England on the 10th June last. I have kept twelve terms in the Inner Temple and I intend to practice in the Bombay presidency. I produce the certificate of my being called to the Bar. As to the certificate of my character and abilities, I have not been able to obtain any certificate from a judge in England, for I was not aware of the rules in force in the Bombay High Court. I, however, produce a certificate from Mr. W. D. Edwards, a practicing barrister in the Supreme Court of Judicature in England. He is the author of the Compendium of the Law of Property in Land, one of the books prescribed for the Bar final examination."

When Gandhi first decided to study in England, he was declared an outcast by the elders of the Modh Bania caste for his decision to study and live overseas. They

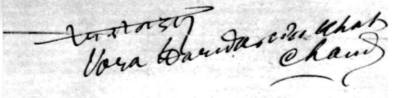

1891 *Facsimile of a resolution canceling Gandhi's expulsion from the Modh Bania caste (he was excommunicated due to his decision to study abroad), and (on facing page) readmitting him to it in 1891 in Rajkot.*

ordered him to stay in India, believing that an extended stay in London would lead him away from Hindu traditions. He was asked whether he was daring to disregard the orders of the caste, to which he replied: "I am really helpless. I think caste should not interfere in the matter." At this, the elders were incensed and they swore at Gandhi, who sat unmoved. Realizing that the young lad was determined to travel to England, they decided that Gandhi would be treated as an outcast from that day. They even declared that whoever helped him or even went to see him off at the docks would be punished with a fine of one rupee and four annas! However, they withdrew the order declaring him an outcast when Gandhi returned to India in 1891.

THE HEAD-DRESS INCIDENT

After spending less than two years in India and failing to establish a successful legal practice in Bombay, Gandhi arrived in South Africa toward the end of May 1893, to assist Abdullah Hajee Adam of Dada Abdullah & Co. (a legal firm with a Porbandar connection).

Soon after his arrival, he was reprimanded for wearing his turban in the courtroom by the magistrate of the Durban court. He describes the incident in his own words:

"It is true that on entering the Court I neither removed my head-dress nor salaamed, but in so doing I had not the slightest idea that I was offending His Worship, or meaning any disrespect to the Court. Just as it is a mark of respect among the Europeans to take off their hats, in like manner it is in Indians to retain one's head-dress. To appear uncovered before a gentleman is not to respect him. In England, on attending drawing-room meetings and evening parties, Indians always keep the head-dress, and the English ladies and gentlemen generally seem to appreciate the regard which we show thereby. In High Courts in India those Indian advocates who have not discarded their native head-dress invariably keep it on.

"As to bowing, or salaaming as you would call it, I again followed the rule observed in the Bombay High Court. If an advocate enters the Court after the judge has taken his seat on the bench he does not bow, but all the advocates rise up when the judge enters the Court, and keep standing until the judge has taken his seat. Accordingly, yesterday when His Worship entered the Court I rose up, and took my seat only after His Worship had done so."

"COLORED" MAN IN FIRST CLASS

One of the most famous, or infamous, incidents in Gandhi's life took place when he reached South Africa. On 7 June 1893, he boarded the first-class compartment of a train from Durban to Natal. When the train reached Pietermaritzburg, the capital of Natal, at around 9 p.m., a passenger entered the compartment and looked Gandhi up and down, clearly disturbed by the presence of a "colored" man traveling first class. The man left and returned with two railway officials. One of them told Gandhi to get down and accompany him to the freight compartment. Gandhi refused, saying he had a first-class ticket from Durban. The official said that did not matter and again insisted he move to the freight car. Gandhi remained obstinate, saying he had been allowed to travel in the compartment in Durban, and had no intention of getting off. Hearing this, the official threatened to call a police constable to have him evicted. Gandhi told him to go ahead since he had no intention of moving to the freight car. The official left and returned with a policeman, who grabbed him and pushed him out. His luggage was thrown out as well. Gandhi refused to get into the freight compartment and the train left without him. He sat in the waiting room and, the next morning, sent a long telegram to the General Manager of the Railways, complaining about the treatment. Today, the plaque at the station in Pietermaritzburg reads: "In the vicinity of this plaque, M. K. Gandhi was evicted from a first-class compartment on the night of 7 June 1893. This incident changed the course of his life. He took up the fight against racial oppression. His active non-violence started from that day."

1894 *Gandhi (standing, fourth from left) with co-founders of the Natal Indian Congress, Durban. This was Gandhi's first foray into public life, with the intention of helping resolve issues faced by Indians in South Africa.*

In 1894, Gandhi made his first official debut into India-related politics by spearheading the birth of the Natal Indian Congress. He had thought long and hard about a name for the organization. It had, he would write in his autobiography, "perplexed me sorely." The name "Congress" was anathema to the conservatives in Britain and yet, back home, it was the very life of India. He recommended "Natal Indian Congress" (NIC). It came into being on May 22, 1894, with Gandhi as its first Honorary Secretary. The president was Abdullah Hajee Adam of Dada Abdullah & Co. The objectives, as laid out, were to keep the people of India informed of its activities and to fight discrimination against Indians. In June, the Natal government introduced the Franchise Law Amendment Bill, which threatened the existence of Indians in South Africa by depriving them of their right to vote. Meetings were held in the offices of Messrs Dada Abdullah & Co. to consider what could be done to prevent the Bill from being passed in the Legislative Assembly.

1895 *Not many know of Gandhi's fondness for the game of cricket. This rare picture is of the Greyville Cricket Club, Durban. Gandhi (seated in the second row, fifth from left) is seen here with Parsee Rustomjee, a member of the Natal Indian Congress, on his right.*

During its formative years, the NIC introduced many petitions asking for changes to the proposed discriminatory legislation. The organization later allied itself with the African National Congress.

***

The above photograph is of Gandhi with members of the Greyville Cricket Club, Durban. Very few people would associate Gandhi with any sport—in his autobiography he described his aversion to physical exercise. Historian Ramachandra Guha researched this aspect of Gandhi's life and wrote an article for the *Hindu* in which he quotes a Gujarati journalist explaining that one of Gandhi's schoolmates remembered him as a "dashing cricketer" and an all-rounder, with an uncanny understanding of the game's uncertainties. During a match played between Rajkot city and Rajkot cantonment, Gandhi had a strong intuition that a certain player would be out, and that is exactly what happened.

1897 *Demonstration against Gandhi's disembarkation in Durban.*

On June 5, 1896, Gandhi set sail for India, where he addressed meetings on behalf of the Indian community in South Africa. His efforts to raise public opinion were widely reported in South Africa, with a great deal of exaggeration. He returned to Durban, along with 800 Indians, to an extremely hostile reception by the white population. They charged Gandhi with trying to flood Natal and Transvaal with unwanted, indentured, colored people. When the ship docked, Gandhi, accompanied by F. A. Laughton, a British legal adviser, disembarked and was recognized. In no time, a crowd gathered and started pelting Gandhi with stones and rotten eggs, while some others rained blows on his body. Fortunately,

the wife of the police superintendent, who was passing by, recognized him. The brave woman stood between him and the crowd. The police then escorted him to where he was staying. Even there, the house was surrounded by an angry mob. Superintendent Alexander sent Gandhi a message advising him to escape, in disguise. Gandhi wore an Indian policeman's uniform and slipped out, accompanied by two white policemen who had darkened their faces and dressed as Indians. They reached the police station, where Gandhi remained for three days until public anger had died down.

***

1899 Above: *Medals awarded to Gandhi for his services during the two campaigns in South Africa—the Boer War and Zulu Rebellion.* Left: *Gandhi (second row, sitting fifth from left) with the Indian Ambulance Corps during the Boer War.*

Gandhi's involvement in the Boer War in 1899 was a rare departure from his pacifist image. He set up a 1,100-strong Ambulance Corps, mostly comprised of Indian volunteers. At a critical moment, they were asked to serve inside the firing line. At Spioenkop, General Sir Redvers Henry Buller sent a message that though they were not required to, the government would be grateful if they could help shift the wounded from the battlefield. Gandhi and his corps immediately rushed to their rescue. In his autobiography, Gandhi wrote that they often marched 20 to 25 miles a day, bearing the wounded on stretchers.

1902 *Kasturba photographed in South Africa with three of her four sons—from left to right, Gandhi's sister's son Gokuldas, Manilal, Ramdas and Harilal. Kasturba was affectionately called "Ba" by her family members.*

During the birth of their youngest son, Devdas, Gandhi acted as Kasturba's midwife. He had studied a popular book on childbirth, which constituted a comprehensive course in obstetrics and infant care. On May 22, 1900, when Kasturba suddenly went into labor and it was too late to summon professional help, Gandhi stepped in and helped deliver the child. Later, he would declare that he was not nervous at all. Although Gandhi employed a nurse in South Africa after

1903 Gandhi (third from left) stands with his colleagues outside his law office at Johannesburg. Of his quest to find office space Gandhi said, "It was difficult for an Indian to secure rooms for an office in a suitable locality."

the birth of their third son, Ramdas, and again after the birth of Devdas, Louis Fischer wrote that he cared for the infants himself.

***

Said Gandhi of his quest to find a suitable office space to practice law in Johannesburg: "It was indeed doubtful whether I would be enrolled in the Transvaal Supreme Court. But the Law Society did not oppose my application and the Court allowed it. It was difficult for an Indian to secure rooms for an office in a suitable locality. But I had come in fairly close contact with Mr. Ritch, one of the merchants there. Through the good offices of a house agent known to him, I succeeded in securing suitable rooms for my office in the legal quarters of the city, and I started on my professional work."

INDIAN OPINION FOR SOUTH AFRICA

Gandhi's early writings and opinions began appearing in the publication he launched in 1903 called *Indian Opinion*. It was initially published in Gujarati, Hindi, Tamil and English, and talked about the difficult conditions faced by Indians in South Africa. Mansukhlal Naazar was the first editor, but Gandhi did most of the work and was, for all editorial matters, the person in charge. It was financed by him and he sank all of his savings into the project; he recalled a time when he was spending almost 75 pounds a month. It attracted a loyal readership among Indians and also introduced Gandhi to the principles of journalism. In the first month of its launch, he would recall later, he realized that the sole aim of journalism should be service. He understood the power of the press but also that an uncontrolled pen has the means to destroy.

1903 *First edition (center) of* Indian Opinion *published in 1903 "in the interest of the Indians in South Africa." This marked Gandhi's entry into the world of writing and journalism.*

  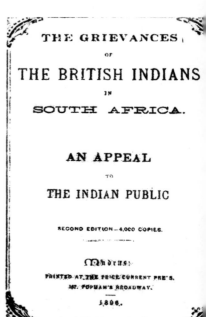

THE BOOK THAT INSPIRED GANDHI

Gandhi's life changed thanks to the book *Unto This Last* by social thinker John Ruskin. It inspired the establishment of the Phoenix settlement near Durban in South Africa. Gandhi read the book on a train journey and he could not sleep that night. He would later write that it made him determined to change his life in accordance with the ideals in the book. (He subsequently translated it into Gujarati, titling it *Sarvodaya*, meaning the "progress of all" in society.) Ruskin's book preached that the good of the individual is contained in the good of all, that a lawyer's work has the same value as a barber's—all have the same right to earn a living from their work. The book influenced Gandhi so deeply that he decided to move the *Indian Opinion* press to a farm on which everyone would labor, drawing the same living wage and attending to the journal in their spare time. The monthly allowance for each person was to be three pounds, irrespective of color or nationality. The only doubt was whether the ten people employed at the press would agree to settle on a remote farm for such a small allowance. Once they agreed, Gandhi advertised for a piece of land situated near a railway station around Durban. An offer came for a plot named Phoenix, which he inspected along with Albert H. West, one of his closest associates in South Africa. The 20 acres of land had a spring running through and a few orange and mango trees. Adjoining it was another parcel of land measuring 80 acres, with fruit trees and a dilapidated cottage, which they also purchased. The total cost was 1,000 pounds, amassed from donors and supporters.

UNTO THIS LAST BY JOHN RUSKIN

EDITED BY SUSAN CUNNINGTON

1904 *Gandhi as a barrister in Johannesburg. His suited figure here stands in stark contrast to the image of Gandhi that has prevailed in history.*

1904 *Gandhi (third row, standing fifth from left) with other settlers of the Phoenix settlement near Durban, South Africa.*

The Phoenix settlement was officially started in December 1904 and, despite numerous odds, *Indian Opinion* continued to be published from there. Gandhi attempted to draw relatives and friends who had come from India to Phoenix, although it was difficult for him to persuade many who had come to South Africa in search of a better life to move to a remote farm for minimum wages. He confessed to initial difficulties, found that changes had to be made, and that there were some hopes and disappointments.

Gandhi had become the recognized leader of the Indian community in South Africa and his movement of passive resistance was having an impact. British official and author Lionel Curtis, who served in South Africa, would say to him: "Mr. Gandhi, you are preaching to the converted. It is not the vices of Indians that Europeans in this country fear, but their virtues." Despite the

1906 *Gandhi (sitting, third from left) with his associates in South Africa.*

fact that tension between whites and Indians was growing, Gandhi decided to abandon the political arena and join the British Army during the Zulu rebellion in 1906 with a group of 24 Indian volunteers to serve as stretcher-bearers and sanitation aides. Gandhi said he joined because he believed that "the British Empire existed for the welfare of the world." By all accounts, he felt a genuine loyalty to the British.

1906 Gandhi (second row, sitting fourth from left) with members of the Indian volunteer Ambulance Corps of stretcher-bearers during the Zulu rebellion in South Africa.

The Zulu rebellion was a punitive expedition that descended into shootings and floggings. Since white physicians and nurses would not tend to the Zulus, the Indians took up the task and were witness to the horrors of black men being whipped till their skin was in strips. The Indian volunteers marched up to 40 miles a day, treating Zulus who were suffering and in acute agony. After a month, the ambulance service was disbanded. Gandhi came back with the rank of Sergeant

1906 *Sergeant Major Gandhi (Ambulance Corps) during the Zulu rebellion. He was appointed after taking an oath: "Be faithful and bear true allegiance to His Majesty King Edward."*

Major and was awarded a medal. On his return, he plunged into a cold war with the British, using his unquestionable moral force to engage in a battle that would make him a global icon and one of India's greatest leaders.

THE TERM "SATYAGRAHA"

Gandhi struggled to find the right phrase to describe his version of civil disobedience. There was the common English phrase "passive resistance," but he argued that this could be characterized by hatred and violence. It was clear, he would write later, that Indians needed to coin a new word to describe their non-violent struggle. In the *Indian Opinion* he announced a prize for the reader who came up with the best suggestion. It was Maganlal Gandhi, his nephew, who suggested the word "sadagrha," meaning "firmness in a good cause." Gandhi changed the word to "satyagraha" ("sat" for truth and "agraha" meaning firmness). The word would later become synonymous with Gandhi in South Africa and in India.

FROM SATYAGRAHI TO CELIBATE

While in the Ambulance Corps and rendering service in the Zulu uprising, Gandhi had occasion to think long and hard about the concept of brahmacharya (celibacy for life) and its implications, and how indispensable it was for self-realization. He pondered these issues for some weeks, including the vow of abstinence from sex. As he wrote in his autobiography, he could not live for both, the flesh and the spirit. Without the observance of brahmacharya, he was convinced, service toward the family would be at odds with service to the community. Once he was back from his Ambulance Corps service, he told Kasturba of his decision to abstain from sex. According to Louis Fischer's account, she made no protest. Gandhi himself would say she was never the "temptress" and it was he who determined the character of their physical relationship. Gandhi remained celibate from 1906, when he took the vow at the age of 37, till his death in 1948.

In his autobiography, he confessed that he did not realize the magnitude and immensity of the task he had undertaken. Yet he was equally convinced that it was the only path for him. He saw this self-purification as a preliminary act for "satyagraha," a concept that would define his life. To commit himself to satyagraha, Gandhi decided he needed to be fit and cultivate purity. He gave up cow's milk because he believed it stimulated animal passion. He then decided to live on a fruit diet and not only that, the cheapest fruit available. He practically did away with cooked food—raw groundnuts, bananas, dates, lemons and olive oil made up his normal diet.

"BLACK ACT" CONSIGNED TO ASHES

The Empire Theatre in Johannesburg was the stage for a mass meeting organized by Gandhi in September 1906. The meeting was in response to the Asiatic Registration Act, which required all male Asians, including Indians, to register with the authorities, to be fingerprinted and accept a certificate that they were required to carry at all times. A person who failed to register would lose the right of residence and could be imprisoned, fined or deported from the Transvaal. The Indian community branded it a "Black Act," and Gandhi declared that "even a crooked policy would turn straight if only we are true to ourselves." The Indians prepared for satyagraha. The prime minister of South Africa, Louis Botha, sent a message saying he "was helpless." Some Indians took out permits but most refused.

1908 Above and facing page: *Gandhi with other satyagrahis outside the Johannesburg prison after being released.*

They were ordered to register or leave the Transvaal. Failing to do either, they were brought before a magistrate on January 11, 1908. Gandhi was among them. He had attended the same court as a lawyer; now he stood in the dock. Gandhi told the judge that as their leader, he merited the heaviest punishment. He was handed down a sentence of two months' imprisonment. It was the first time Gandhi would experience jail and wear prison clothes: a loose coarse jacket marked with a broad arrow, short trousers, one leg dark, the other light, also marked with an arrow, thick gray woolen socks, leather sandals and a small cap not unlike the Gandhi cap he would make famous later. The cell could hold 13 prisoners and was clearly marked "For Colored Debtors." Soon, an emissary of General Jan Christiaan Smuts (who was minister of interior, mines and defense) came to Gandhi in prison with a formula for compromise. Gandhi in his prison uniform met General Smuts at his office in Johannesburg and agreed to Smuts' offer to repeal the Asiatic Registration Act if Indians registered themselves voluntarily. All of the prisoners, including Gandhi, were set free. Many Indians felt that Gandhi trusted Smuts too much. Pashtuns, in particular, felt betrayed because they had fought in the British Army, which defeated the Boers. Now they were being humiliated by the Boers and were being asked to give their fingerprints like petty criminals.

Gandhi arranged to register on February 10, 1908. As he walked to the registration bureau, a group of Pashtuns followed, and one of them attacked

1908 *Two thousand registration certificates going up in flames outside Hamidia Mosque, Johannesburg.*

him. Gandhi fainted. When he recovered, he was told that his assailants had been arrested. "They should be released," Gandhi said, adding that they believed in what they were doing and that he did not want to prosecute them. Though most Indians did register, Smuts denied that he had ever promised to repeal the Asiatic Registration Act.

Passive resistance was resumed and a meeting was called at Hamidia Mosque in Johannesburg on August 16, 1908. A huge iron cauldron was placed on a raised platform and more than 2,000 registration certificates collected from those gathered were thrown in and set alight. The crowd erupted in jubilation. The Indians were also joined by Chinese settlers. A *London Daily Mail* correspondent who was present compared it to the Boston Tea Party, when demonstrators in Boston had destroyed an entire shipment of tea sent by the East India Company, in defiance of the Tea Act of 1773.

Beloved Kastur,

I have received Mr. West's telegram today about your illness. It cuts my heart. I am very much grieved but I am not in a position to go there to nurse you. I have offered my all to the satyagraha struggle. My coming there is out of the question. I can come only if I pay the fine, which I must not. If you keep courage and take the necessary nutrition, you will recover. If, however, my ill luck so has it that you pass away, I should only say that there would be nothing wrong in your doing so in your separation from me while I am still alive. I love you so dearly that even if you are dead, you will be alive to me. Your soul is deathless. I repeat what I have frequently told you and assure you that if you do succumb to your illness, I will not marry again. Time and again I have told you that you may quietly breathe your last with faith in God. If you die, even that death of yours will be a sacrifice to the cause of satyagraha. My struggle is not merely political. It is religious and therefore quite pure. It does not matter much whether one dies in it or lives. I hope and expect that you will also think likewise and not be unhappy. I ask this of you.

Mohan Das

1908 *Toward the end of 1908, Gandhi's wife, Kasturba, fell ill. So obsessed was he with satyagraha that he paid little attention to his family and personal life. He was criticized by many for his relationship with his family, which bordered on indifference. In this letter to Kasturba, he explains his situation and how satyagraha was everything to him.*

1909 *At Verulam, 17 miles north of Durban, with Kasturba and a young boy.*

Following surgery in February 1909, Kasturba had become quite weak, to the extent that she could barely sit. To regain her strength, the doctor suggested that she should be given beef broth. Gandhi refused permission unless Kasturba herself consented to this. Gandhi immediately rushed to the hospital only to discover that the doctor had already given her the broth as she was in no condition to be consulted. Gandhi was very upset, but the doctor was unrelenting: "So long

1909 *Gandhi returned to London as a public figure, in contrast to his earlier position as a law student.*

as your wife is under my treatment, I must have the option to give her anything I wish." When Gandhi asked Kasturba, she said: "I will not take beef [broth]...I would far rather die in your arms than pollute my body with such abominations." Gandhi was "delighted." He always believed that the "body should not be dearer than the soul."

SPEAKING UP IN LONDON: GANDHI'S RAM, SAVARKAR'S DURGA

Gandhi sailed from South Africa on June 23, 1909 and reached London on July 10. He had gone mainly to lobby for Indians in South Africa but would cast a wider net. On October 24, he was invited to preside over Dussehra celebrations (a Hindu festival held to mark the victory of good over evil), organized by local Indians. He accepted the invitation, although the condition was that there should be no political content in the speeches. Veer Savarkar, a staunch Hindu nationalist who was studying law in London and had first met Gandhi earlier in 1906, was also invited as a speaker. In spite of their pledge, both Gandhi and Savarkar conveyed their political ideals concealed in religious speeches to the audience. While speaking about the festival, Gandhi praised the virtues of pacifist Lord Rama, and Savarkar extolled Goddess Durga who eliminates evil—both referred to their political ideologies, which were at variance when it came to methods, one peaceful and the other militant. The audience consisted of Hindus and Muslims and when Savarkar spoke, he declared: "Hindus are the heart of Hindustan," adding that just as the beauty of the rainbow is enhanced by its varied hues, Hindustan would appear more beautiful if it assimilated all that was best in Muslim, Parsi, Jewish and other communities. Gandhi agreed with his views, but his trip to London was more ambitious. He succeeded in making the "South Africa and India" issue a matter of Imperial concern. More importantly, for the first time, Gandhi began to involve himself in furthering the cause of India's independence. While in London he sought out Indians who represented all shades of political beliefs. It was to be the beginning of an epic journey.

1909 *Gandhi with a friend, Haji Ojer Ali, in South Africa.*

HIND SWARAJ: A BLUEPRINT FOR THE INDIAN REPUBLIC

With the trip to London not living up to his expectations, Gandhi, expecting to be arrested upon his return to South Africa, plunged feverishly into work while on the ship back, catching up with his correspondence, translating Count Leo Tolstoy's "A Letter to a Hindu" into Gujarati, writing a preface, and, most importantly, working on his first book. The book would be the most fruitful result of the voyage—it was *Hind Swaraj* (Indian Home Rule). Written at a frantic pace, Gandhi completed the 271-page hand-written manuscript in just nine days—being ambidextrous, he wrote almost 60 pages with his left hand when his right hand grew tired. The book constituted a series of dialogs between Gandhi, as an editor, and a reader, the typical Indian, who was loosely modeled on Indian pro-independence activist Veer Savarkar and his militant ideology. It questions whether there can be true home rule or self-government (swaraj) without self-rule. The book contained chapters on Congress, the partition of Bengal, the meaning of swaraj and Indian civilization, with the editor and the reader discussing the prevailing conditions in India through various issues, such as the railways, Hindu–Muslim relations, and the role of lawyers and doctors. Of all his books, *Hind Swaraj* was the one he liked best and, 40 years later, he would present it to Jawaharlal Nehru, explaining that it contained the blueprint for the Indian Republic. *Hind Swaraj* reaffirmed Gandhi's view that independence was possible only through passive resistance and that India would never be free unless it rejected Western civilization, which was unhealthy for India. The original, written in Gujarati, and first published in 1909, was banned by the British, but not the English translation, which, they felt, would have little impact on English-speaking Indians.

1909 *Handwriting using left hand.*
Above and facing page: *Hand-written pages from Gandhi's first book* Hind Swaraj.

1909 *Handwriting using right hand.*

COUNT LEO TOLSTOY

If Gandhi truly admired any one person, it was Leo Tolstoy, the celebrated Russian thinker and writer. While in London, Gandhi had been debating whether he should write to the great man, who had just celebrated his 81st birthday. He revered Tolstoy almost to the point of idolization. Count Tolstoy was a nobleman who had given up a life of luxury and power. He had no equal among European writers but lived a simple life and believed in his own version of non-violence. Gandhi read Tolstoy's works constantly and his bible was *The Kingdom of God Is Within You*, a book he recommended to almost everyone. He even presented a copy to the superintendent of the jail in Volksrust where he was imprisoned. Gandhi's ideas on peaceful resistance had been reinforced by Tolstoy's example. He finally wrote a letter to Tolstoy on October 1, 1909, in which he introduced himself, giving details of his campaign in South Africa and asking for the writer's blessings. In the letter, he asked for permission to reproduce a tract that Tolstoy had written and distribute 20,000 copies of it. The tract was titled "A Letter to a Hindu" and was written as a reply to a young Indian revolutionary who had asked Tolstoy whether the Indians had not the right to counter British rule by force and acts of terrorism.

Tolstoy's reply was that the situation the Indians found themselves in was their own fault because they had willingly accepted enslavement and collaborated with the British. If the Indians truly wanted to free themselves from the British, he suggested, they had a weapon more powerful than guns or terrorism, and that was non-cooperation. In a memorable passage, Tolstoy trashed the Indian obsession with their gods. "Cast aside all religious beliefs. Paradise, hell, the angels, the demons,

Left: *Leo Tolstoy.*
Facing page top: *The envelope of Gandhi's letter to Leo Tolstoy;* Below: *Sketch of Tolstoy by his daughter. She presented it to Gandhi when he visited Rome in December 1931.*

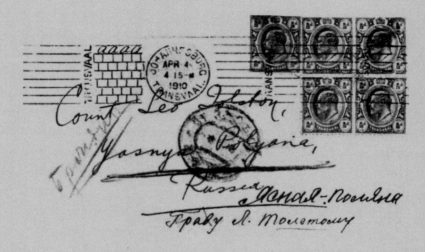

To dear Mahatma Gandhi a drawing I did from my father the last year of his life—Cordially, affectionately, and respectfully yours T. Koukhotine Tolstoy

reincarnation, resurrection and the concept of God interfering in the life of the universe—all these must be abandoned." In his letter to Tolstoy, Gandhi asked if he could omit the word "reincarnation" in the catalog of religious ideas denounced by Tolstoy. "Reincarnation or transmigration is a cherished belief for millions in India," he said, adding that it "explained the many mysteries of life." Gandhi's letter reached Tolstoy a week later, who noted in his diary: "Received a pleasant letter from a Hindu in the Transvaal." Two weeks later, he composed a reply. Gandhi would later write in *Indian Opinion*: "No one should assume that I accept all the ideas of Tolstoy. I look upon him as one of my teachers but I certainly do not agree with all his ideas. The central principle of his teaching is entirely acceptable to me." The two men would go on to exchange a number of letters. Tolstoy's last letter to Gandhi, dated September 20, 1910, reached its recipient after Tolstoy's death on November 20, 1910.

THE MAKING OF TOLSTOY FARM

When Gandhi returned from England to South Africa in 1909, political necessity led him to try and establish a cooperative where "civil resisters" would be trained to live a simple and harmonious life. Hermann Kallenbach's gift of a large piece of land outside Johannesburg, which Gandhi named "Tolstoy Farm," provided the necessary impetus. Tolstoy Farm would house an ideal community of satyagrahis—those living their lives in purity and prayer, working without complaint for the common good.

The 1,100-acre farm had over a thousand fruit trees, wells, a spring and a single house. More houses were added later. Kallenbach joined Gandhi and his family on the farm. Gandhi was the baker and jam maker and much more. He once wrote to a friend in India: "I prepare the bread required on the farm. We have just

AT TOLSTOY FARM
"I AM MOSTLY BUSY MAKING SANDALS THESE DAYS. I LIKE THE WORK AND IT IS ESSENTIAL TOO. I HAVE ALREADY MADE ABOUT FIFTEEN PAIRS. WHEN YOU NEED NEW ONES NOW, PLEASE SEND ME THE MEASUREMENTS. AND WHEN YOU DO SO, MARK THE PLACES WHERE THE STRAP IS TO BE FIXED—THAT IS, ON THE OUTER SIDE OF THE BIG TOE AND THE LITTLE TOE." (GANDHI TO HIS NEPHEW MAGANLAL)

Tolstoy Farm: main house, tent and the outhouses.

made marmalade from the oranges grown on the farm. I have learned to prepare caramel coffee…At present, we are working as laborers on construction work." Kallenbach had learned from German monks how to make sandals and he passed on his expertise to Gandhi. Being an architect, he also knew about carpentry. He taught Gandhi to make cabinets, beds and benches. Gandhi was also the general manager of Tolstoy Farm, which started with 40 young men, 5 women, 3 old men and around 30 children. Smoking and drinking were not allowed. At night, everyone slept together on an open platform. For Gandhi, it was an ideal situation, being able to live in a small community—of Hindus, Christians, Jews, Muslims and Parsis—devoted to the plans he had for them.

Once, an incident at the farm involving two girls and some boys gave him a sleepless night. The boys had exceeded the limit in expressing their love for the girls. In the morning, he decided that to keep such incidents at bay, the girls' heads should be shaved to "sterilize the sinner's eye." Such happenings filled him with guilt and he decided to perform an act of penance. He would go on a fast. It led to the discovery of a new form of protest, one for which he was ideally suited; it was an instrument he would use to great effect in the fight for Indian independence and thereafter.

GANDHI'S JEWISH FRIENDS

Gandhi had many supporters among South Africa's white population, the three most prominent being Henry Polak, Sonja Schlesin and Hermann Kallenbach. All three were Jews. On Kallenbach's recommendation, Schlesin joined Gandhi as a secretary and was put in charge of the Satyagraha Association's treasury and its collection of books. Polak, a journalist-turned-lawyer, became one of Gandhi's closest advisers. However, it was Gandhi's friendship with Kallenbach that endured the longest. Kallenbach, a wealthy German architect, was a tall, stocky man with a long handlebar mustache. Gandhi and Kallenbach met by chance, but a mutual interest in Buddhism forged a friendship. Till Gandhi returned to India in 1915, they were inseparable. Kallenbach had bought 1,100 acres of land outside Johannesburg and, in 1910, handed it over to the satyagrahis free of rent or charge. Gandhi named it Tolstoy Farm, after his favorite author.

***

On March 14, 1913, the Supreme Court of South Africa decreed that all marriages not celebrated according to Christian rites were invalid. Overnight, all Hindu, Parsi and Muslim marriages became illegitimate. Alarmed at the consequences, Kasturba and four

1910 *Albert West (top left), Hermann Kallenbach (with dog) and Gandhi (bottom right) in front of a tent at Tolstoy Farm.*

1913 *Gandhi and Kasturba in South Africa. Like her husband, Kasturba was an active satyagrahi.*

1913 *Gandhi and Kasturba as satyagrahis.*

On march through Volksrust.

1913 Above: *Gandhi's first history-making march through Volksrust, against the annual tax, ban on Asiatic immigrants, and invalidation of Hindu, Muslim and Parsi marriages.*

Below: *The Great March to the Transvaal, South Africa. The marchers were stopped at the border of Volksrust.*

Stopped at Border Volksrust.

other women participated in the satyagraha to protest. They were arrested at the Transvaal border and sentenced to three months' hard labor. The confrontation with the government started on November 6, 1913, when Gandhi led the march to the Transvaal.

Gandhi started his great march at 6:30 a.m. on November 6, 1913. He had communicated his intention to march to the Transvaal to demonstrate against the breach of trust by the Botha–Smuts government regarding the annual three-pound tax on indentured labor. He was joined by coal miners in the South African city of Newcastle, who had gone on strike in protest against the tax, and had been met with violence; some had died as a result of police gunfire. At Newscastle, women and children were accommodated in houses and the men slept on the grounds of the local mosque. Gandhi's army had swelled to 2,037 men, 127 women and 57 children. On November 6, 1913, Gandhi recalled later: "We offered prayers and commenced the march in the name of God."

Gandhi was arrested three times during the historic march through Volksrust, and just a few days after he was released from the Volksrust Prison he changed his appearance. He appeared at a mass meeting in Durban, abandoning his usual shirt and trousers. He now sported a knee-length white cotton tunic and a flowing dhoti that reached down to his ankles. His days of wearing Western clothing were over. He informed attendees at the meeting that he had assumed this new avatar in honor of those who had died during the anti-government campaign.

Gandhi handed each "soldier" a pound and a half of bread and an ounce of sugar. His instructions were clear: conduct yourself morally, hygienically and peacefully. Do not resist arrest. Indian merchants in Charlestown contributed rice, vegetables and kitchen equipment, and Gandhi appointed himself the head chef. A European baker at Volksrust undertook to supply bread every day, which he would send by rail to appointed spots along the route. Gandhi calculated that to reach their destination would take eight days, marching 20 miles a day.

ARRESTED THREE TIMES IN FOUR DAYS

Gandhi's proposed march to protest the discrimination against Indians had angered the whites in Volksrust, who held demonstrations to prevent him from entering the Transvaal. Some threatened to shoot any Indian who dared to cross the border. A heavy police presence prevented any violence and the guards allowed Gandhi, Kallenbach, Henry Polak and the protestors to pass, but shortly thereafter a police officer politely told Gandhi: "I have a warrant to arrest you." Gandhi was transported to Volksrust and arraigned in court. The prosecutor demanded his arrest but the judge released Gandhi on bail furnished by Kallenbach. The next day, the protestors halted at Standerton, where a magistrate informed Gandhi: "You are my prisoner." Gandhi replied: "It seems I have been promoted since magistrates take the trouble to arrest me instead of mere police officials." Five of his co-workers were sent to jail but Gandhi was again released on bail. Two days later, as Gandhi and Polak were marching at the head of the procession, a car drove up and the officer in it ordered Gandhi to accompany him. He had been arrested again. In four days, he had faced arrest three times. He was brought to trial, where he pleaded guilty. Since that was not enough to warrant his arrest, Gandhi asked Kallenbach and Polak to testify against him. Gandhi in turn testified against Kallenbach, following which Gandhi and Kallenbach did the same against Polak. Thus, all three were sent to prison.

Gandhi's arrest on his long march in November 1913 did not go as planned. When he began the march, he hoped to be arrested with all the marchers, creating a mass movement. However, when he was put under arrest, it upset his calculations. Gandhi's strategy was based on all of the marchers being arrested, but the government in Pretoria had sent instructions that none of the marchers should be arrested, only the leaders. His arrest had little effect on the movement since he had already made arrangements for a second line of leadership. It had not occurred to Gandhi that in the eyes of the government, he alone was guilty, deserving of punishment.

1913 *Policeman confronting Gandhi as he leads striking Indian mine workers from Newcastle to the Transvaal in protest of the Immigration Act, or the "Black Act."*

1913 *Gandhi (second from right) with Hermann Kallenbach to his right, and his secretary, Sonja Schlesin, on his left, just before their arrest.*

If his arrest was a setback to his plans, so was his unexpected release from prison on December 18, 1913, months before his full term, along with Kallenbach and Polak. Under pressure from the viceroy and the British government, a commission had been appointed to investigate the grievances of Indians in South Africa. The sudden release of Gandhi only gave credibility to the commission and the Smuts–Botha regime. Later, Gandhi would acknowledge that: "All three of us were disappointed upon our release." It did nothing for his cause.

***

1913 *Gandhi, Sonja Schlesin and Hermann Kallenbach, before the "Historic March" from Natal to Transvaal.*

Kallenbach treasured this photograph with Gandhi and his secretary, Sonja Schlesin, taken in 1913. He had it sewn into the collar of his jacket before traveling to England with Gandhi during the First World War. Being of German origin, he feared he might be interned and that the photograph would be confiscated, so he wanted to keep it safe. Kallenbach was interned, as he had feared, and prevented from traveling to India with Gandhi, but the authorities never discovered the hidden photograph.

1913 *Gandhi (extreme left) with Hermann Kallenbach (second from left) and others at Maritzburg station.*

Gandhi's first meeting with C. F. Andrews (facing page), missionary, social reformer and supporter of Indian independence, was interesting. Gopal Krishna Gokhale had sent Andrews and William Pearson, a teacher and friend of Andrews, both deeply knowledgeable about India and closely associated with Rabindranath Tagore, to mediate between the Indians and the government in Pretoria. When their ship docked in Durban, Gandhi, Polak and Kallenbach were waiting to receive them. Andrews bent down and touched the feet of this "small, slight figure wearing a coarse dhoti of an indentured laborer." Within a short time they became "Mohan" and "Charlie" to each other.

1913 *Gandhi (seated) with Reverend Charles Freer Andrews (left) and William Winstanley Pearson. This was the first time Andrews and Pearson met Gandhi.*

1914 *Gandhi addressing members of South Africa's Indian community in Verulam soon before he left for India.*

1914 *Farewell reception for Gandhi given by his followers at Verulam, South Africa.*

GENERAL SMUTS: "THE SAINT HAS LEFT OUR SHORES— I SINCERELY HOPE FOREVER."

The agreement at the end of the protracted negotiations between Gandhi and General Smuts in 1914 was regarded by the former as "The Magna Carta of South African Indians." Before the talks began, Smuts had told Gandhi: "This time we want no misunderstanding, let all the cards be on the table." In July 1914, the Indian Relief Bill officially came into force and signaled a major victory for Gandhi and his civil disobedience movement. Its main components were that Hindu, Muslim, Parsi and colored marriages were legal and the annual tax on indentured labor was abolished. The agreement paved the way for Gandhi's final departure from South Africa. Gandhi's mentor Gopal Krishna Gokhale had convinced him about the need to spearhead a similar kind of movement in India. In *Indian Opinion*, Gandhi wrote prophetically: "Civil resistance is a force which, if it became universal, would

1914 *Gandhi at the farewell meeting in Durban.*

revolutionize social ideals and…which fairly promises to overwhelm even the nations of the East."

On July 8, 1914, thousands of Indians and a number of Europeans assembled at the Town Hall in Durban to bid farewell to Gandhi, Kasturba and Kallenbach. Messages were read out from various organizations and a number of Gandhi's admirers paid emotional and glowing tributes. Gandhi attended the meeting dressed in a strange Indian outfit. He wore a kurta that looked more like a smock, a clumsily tied dhoti and sandals.

Cutting across religions and genders, members of the British Indian Association assembled to give a farewell banquet to Gandhi and Kallenbach at the Masonic Hall, Transvaal. C. K. T. (Thambi) Naidoo, a Tamil follower of Gandhi who had gone to jail several times, said: "On behalf of myself and my wife, I have the honor to present my four boys to be servants of India." For Gandhi, this was the most precious farewell gift. The four boys had been his pupils in the art of

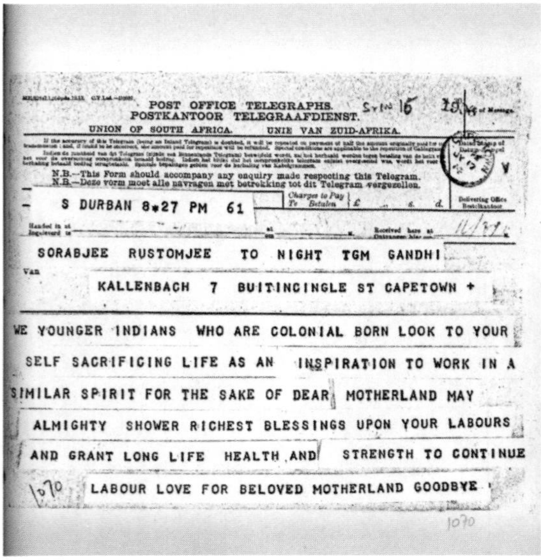

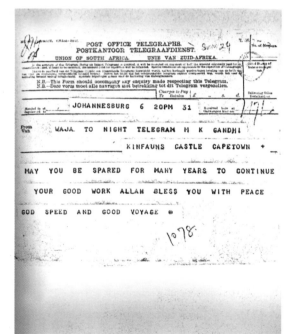

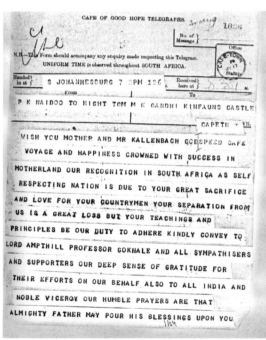

Top left telegram:

POST OFFICE TELEGRAPHS.
POSTKANTOOR TELEGRAAFDIENST.
UNION OF SOUTH AFRICA.   UNIE VAN ZUID-AFRIKA.

S DURBAN 8·27 PM 61

SORABJEE RUSTOMJEE TO NIGHT TGM GANDHI

KALLENBACH 7 BUITINCINGLE ST CAPETOWN +

WE YOUNGER INDIANS WHO ARE COLONIAL BORN LOOK TO YOUR

SELF SACRIFICING LIFE AS AN INSPIRATION TO WORK IN A

SIMILAR SPIRIT FOR THE SAKE OF DEAR MOTHERLAND MAY

ALMIGHTY SHOWER RICHEST BLESSINGS UPON YOUR LABOURS

AND GRANT LONG LIFE HEALTH AND STRENGTH TO CONTINUE

LABOUR LOVE FOR BELOVED MOTHERLAND GOODBYE

Top right telegram:

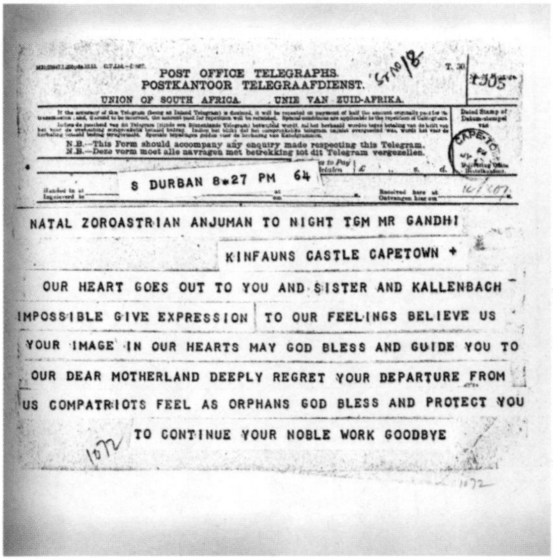

POST OFFICE TELEGRAPHS.
POSTKANTOOR TELEGRAAFDIENST.
UNION OF SOUTH AFRICA.   UNIE VAN ZUID-AFRIKA.

S DURBAN 8·27 PM 64

NATAL ZOROASTRIAN ANJUMAN TO NIGHT TGM MR GANDHI

KINFAUNS CASTLE CAPETOWN +

OUR HEART GOES OUT TO YOU AND SISTER AND KALLENBACH

IMPOSSIBLE GIVE EXPRESSION TO OUR FEELINGS BELIEVE US

YOUR IMAGE IN OUR HEARTS MAY GOD BLESS AND GUIDE YOU TO

OUR DEAR MOTHERLAND DEEPLY REGRET YOUR DEPARTURE FROM

US COMPATRIOTS FEEL AS ORPHANS GOD BLESS AND PROTECT YOU

TO CONTINUE YOUR NOBLE WORK GOODBYE

Bottom left telegram:

POST OFFICE TELEGRAPHS.
POSTKANTOOR TELEGRAAFDIENST.
UNION OF SOUTH AFRICA.   UNIE VAN ZUID-AFRIKA.

JOHANNESBURG 6 20PM 31

WAJA TO NIGHT TELEGRAM M K GANDHI

KINFAUNS CASTLE CAPETOWN +

MAY YOU BE SPARED FOR MANY YEARS TO CONTINUE

YOUR GOOD WORK ALLAH BLESS YOU WITH PEACE

GOD SPEED AND GOOD VOYAGE @

Bottom right telegram:

CAPE OF GOOD HOPE TELEGRAPHS.

N.B.—This Form should accompany any enquiry made respecting this Telegram.
UNIFORM TIME is observed throughout SOUTH AFRICA.

S JOHANNESBURG 7 2PM 126

P K NAIDOO TO NIGHT TGM M K GANDHI KINFAUNS CASTLE

CAPETN + VN.

WISH YOU MOTHER AND MR KALLENBACH GODSPEED SAFE

VOYAGE AND HAPPINESS CROWNED WITH SUCCESS IN

MOTHERLAND OUR RECOGNITION IN SOUTH AFRICA AS SELF

RESPECTING NATION IS DUE TO YOUR GREAT SACRIFICE

AND LOVE FOR YOUR COUNTRYMEN YOUR SEPARATION FROM

US IS A GREAT LOSS BUT YOUR TEACHINGS AND

PRINCIPLES BE OUR DUTY TO ADHERE KINDLY CONVEY TO

LORD AMPTHILL PROFESSOR GOKHALE AND ALL SYMPATHISERS

AND SUPPORTERS OUR DEEP SENSE OF GRATITUDE FOR

THEIR EFFORTS ON OUR BEHALF ALSO TO ALL INDIA AND

NOBLE VICEROY OUR HUMBLE PRAYERS ARE THAT

ALMIGHTY FATHER MAY POUR HIS BLESSINGS UPON YOU

1914 Farewell telegrams, expressing gratitude and goodwill from friends in South Africa.

passive resistance. Thambi Naidoo had earlier gone through the legal process and other ceremonies of adoption and had surrendered his paternal rights in favor of Gandhi. Expressing his heartfelt gratitude, Gandhi arranged for the "four pearls" to be sent to Tagore's Santiniketan with a group of other students led by Gandhi's nephew Maganlal.

FAREWELL, GANDHI

Gandhi's departure was preceded by a farewell tour of the country to say good-bye to the Indian community. Kasturba accompanied him on this triumphal tour, where they were honored by rapturous crowds. The eight-year struggle, Gandhi told them, had come to an end; the Indians had behaved courageously but so had the Europeans and it was time to let the wounds heal. Gandhi had thought of returning to India but first decided to sail to England to meet Gopal Krishna Gokhale. Kasturba and Kallenbach would accompany him. The three of them arrived in Cape Town and were taken through the city in a procession with a banner proclaiming: "Bon Voyage to the great Indian patriot M. K. Gandhi and his family, also Mr. Kallenbach. God be with you till we meet again." As a farewell gift, Kallenbach was given a pair of binoculars while Gandhi was presented with a gold watch, which he politely refused. Gandhi would never return to South Africa. In August 1914, as an advance party, Maganlal Gandhi, his nephew and close follower, left for India with some students and teachers from the Phoenix settlement, to join Rabindranath Tagore's Santiniketan.

Gandhi sailed for London on July 18, 1914. Before leaving, he gifted, through his aides, a pair of sandals he had made while in prison to General Smuts. Smuts reportedly wore them through the summers he spent at his farm. On one of Gandhi's birthdays, General Smuts sent a note to him that read: "I have worn these sandals for many a summer, even though I may feel that I am not worthy to stand in the shoes of so great a man."

Gandhi said he had come to India to settle here, and he would not go back to Africa unless necessary. Indians did not know him, neither did he know India well enough. His mentor Gopal Krishna Gokhale "commanded" that in the first year he should travel through India with "his ears open but his mouth shut."

1915–1929

Return to India
Non-cooperation Movement
Call for Complete Independence

1915 *Gandhi and Kasturba photographed upon their return to India.*

STRANGER RETURNING TO A STRANGE LAND

In December 1914, after spending a few months in London, Gandhi and Kasturba set sail for Bombay, traveling third class. As a German passport-holder, Kallenbach was not allowed to travel to India. Gandhi confessed in a letter to him that he was returning to India with no plans, no hopes and no certainties. He was a stranger returning to a strange land.

Gandhi arrived in Bombay on January 9, 1915, having been out of India for almost a quarter of a century. He was allowed to disembark at Apollo Bunder port, a privilege reserved for kings, viceroys and the most distinguished Indians. His political mentor, Gokhale, was on hand to receive him with a number of prominent Indians—including Sir Pherozeshah Mehta, Sir Cowasji Jehangir, B. G. Horniman, editor of the *Bombay Chronicle*, and Muhammad Ali Jinnah. He was invited to an audience with Lord Willingdon, the governor of Bombay. Harilal, Gandhi's eldest son, was also among those who received him. He was driven in a celebratory motorcade through the streets of Bombay and greeted in Hornby Street, Sheikh Memon Street and Peddar Road by large crowds who showered him with flowers and presented him with garlands.

A number of receptions were organized in Bombay over the next few days. In his book, *Political Memoirs*, Jamnadas Dwarakadas, a follower of Annie Besant and a close friend of Jinnah, says: "I remember how under the chairmanship of Mr. Jinnah a reception was held at China Baugh in Bombay under the auspices of the Gujerat Sabha, where speeches were made extolling Mr. Gandhi's services. Gold and silver caskets and even gold hand cuffs were offered to him as a token of appreciation. Gandhiji sold them all by public auction then and there. He had no use for gold or silver." Among the many receptions that were held to welcome Gandhi, one at Jehangir Petit's seaside palatial garden, popularly known as Petit Hall, remains memorable. Gandhi arrived dressed in a Kathiawari cloak, turban and dhoti, with Kasturba wearing a white sari in the Gujarati style. Everyone else was in Western attire and the ladies were in their finery. He was dazzled by the pomp and show. Yet the first thing he did, as he saw Sir Pherozeshah Mehta, was

1915 *Gandhi and Kasturba (seated in a horse-drawn carriage) were the focus of the celebratory motorcade that made its way across Bombay. They were greeted by throngs of people.*

to pay his respects by prostrating himself fully stretched on the ground in the traditional Indian way. In his autobiography, Gandhi wrote: "At a party given in my honor at Mr. Jehangir Petit's place, I did not dare to speak in Gujarati. In those palatial surroundings of dazzling splendor, I, who had lived my best life among indentured laborers, felt a complete rustic." Gandhi thanked all the leaders present, especially Gokhale, whose life he said was "an inspiration to him" and who had been "more than a brother" to him. Gokhale suggested that Gandhi spend a year traveling across the country, gaining experience.

Gokhale advised him against making speeches or answering questions from the public. Gandhi promised to follow the advice but was incapable of keeping quiet for long. He made close to 40 speeches that first year; most were responses to public questions. In an interview with the *Bombay Chronicle*, he said he was overwhelmed by the reception given to him and Kasturba. He added that he had come to India to settle here. India, he said, would be his future, but in what capacity, he was still to decide.

KATHIAWAR WELCOMES GANDHI

Shortly after his arrival in Bombay, Gandhi visited Porbandar to meet his sister, his brothers' widows and other relatives. He took a train to Rajkot, traveling third class. There was an outbreak of plague in Kathiawar at the time, and passengers in the third class were required to undergo medical tests. Gandhi was also told to report to the medical officer. Some people objected to this, including the medical officer, but Gandhi said that the inspector was only doing his duty. Wherever he went, he was afforded a grand welcome. The people of Rajkot held a reception in his honor, presided over by the diwan of Rajkot. At Porbandar, where he had spent his early childhood, and after many years, he met his family members in a great reunion.

1915 *The reception at Jetpur (Kathiawar) for Gandhi and Kasturba on January 21. Gandhi and Kasturba's relatives gave them a warm welcome.*

1915 *Gokhale passed away on February 19, barely 40 days after Gandhi returned from South Africa.*

GANDHI AND GOKHALE

Gopal Krishna Gokhale was someone Gandhi greatly admired and looked to for guidance. In his autobiography, Gandhi referred to Gokhale as his mentor and guide. From South Africa, Gandhi continually plied Gokhale with questions and requests. It was Gokhale who convinced Indian industrialists like Sir Ratan Tata to donate money for Gandhi's satyagraha. He was very active in collecting funds for the cause in South Africa, and was assisted by G. A. Natesan in Madras. Gandhi's affection and respect for Gokhale grew during the latter's visit to South Africa while Gandhi was still there. President of the Servants of India Society, a professor of English and economics and, more importantly, a close friend of Lord Hardinge, the viceroy of India, Gokhale visited South Africa in October 1912, on Gandhi's invitation, to assess the condition of the Indian community. He was treated as a special guest by the government and his visit was also celebrated by Indians. He had a two-hour meeting with Prime Minister Botha and General Smuts. He got them to agree to repeal the so-called Black Act and an annual tax imposed on indentured labor. Gokhale, along with Gandhi and Kallenbach, then sailed for Zanzibar. On board, Gokhale spoke at length about Indian politics, economics and the problems that lay ahead. He was introducing Gandhi to his future.

GOKHALE HAD HOSTED A FAREWELL FOR GANDHI BEFORE HE LEFT FOR SANTINIKETAN. THE TABLES WERE HEAPED WITH FOOD, THOUGH THERE WAS NO SIGN OF THE HOST. HE WAS EXTREMELY ILL BUT WAS SEEN TOTTERING ACROSS THE COURTYARD TO SAY GOOD-BYE TO GANDHI. THE EFFORT PROVED TOO MUCH AND HE FAINTED. IN A CONDOLENCE SPEECH AT SANTINIKETAN ON GOKHALE'S DEATH, GANDHI RECALLED: "A FEW DAYS AGO, WHEN HE WAS IN THE GRIP OF A PAINFUL AILMENT, HE CALLED SOME OF US AND BEGAN TALKING ABOUT THE BRIGHT FUTURE OF INDIA AS HE SAW IT. DOCTORS ADVISED HIM TO REST AND CEASE WORKING BUT HE DID NOT LISTEN. HE SAID: 'NONE BUT DEATH CAN SEPARATE ME FROM WORK' AND DEATH AT LAST HAS BROUGHT PEACE TO HIM. MAY GOD BLESS HIS SOUL."

Gokhale had founded the Servants of India Society to unite and train Indians of different regions and religions in welfare work and he wanted Gandhi to join the society and give it a boost. Gandhi also visited Gokhale, who was very unwell during those days, in Poona. From there, he left for Santiniketan. Though Rabindranath Tagore was away, Gandhi got to meet the students he had sent from Phoenix settlement, along with his two old friends from South Africa—C. F. Andrews and W. W. Pearson. He rushed back to Poona after receiving a telegram informing him of Gokhale's death.

SETTING UP SATYAGRAHA ASHRAM

After his return to India, Gandhi was faced with the question of where to settle. Many suggestions were made but his own preference was Ahmedabad in Gujarat. He was a Gujarati, spoke the language and had friends who were willing to finance the setting up of an ashram and a house for himself and Kasturba. Gandhi was also keen to revive the cottage industry of hand spinning, and Ahmedabad was a center of handloom weaving. He also hoped that financial help from its wealthy citizens would provide the funds needed to keep the ashram going. Jivanlal Desai, a barrister,

1915 Above: *Kasturba posed for a studio portrait soon after her return to India.*
Facing page: *Gandhi's first ashram in India, at Kochrab, 1915.*

offered to rent them his Kochrab bungalow. Other industrialists, too, pitched in and Gandhi was able to acquire additional bungalows to accommodate his followers, including some from the Tolstoy and Phoenix farms, the models for his new ashram, which he named Satyagraha Ashram. Gandhi drew up a constitution that made serious demands on the ashramites, including celibacy, truth, non-violence, a ban on wearing foreign cloth, and acceptance of untouchables. Gandhi was delighted to have brought in a family of untouchables to the ashram, even though it offended the businessmen who were financing the project. They withdrew their support from the ashram. Although the annual expenses amounted to 6,000 rupees, money was still trickling in from anonymous donors. Gandhi seemed content. In letters he wrote to Kallenbach and others, he mentioned agriculture, handloom weaving and carpentry as some of the ashram activities.

In September 1915, within four months of establishing the first ashram in Kochrab, the family of untouchables arrived—Dudabhai, a teacher, belonging to the untouchable Dhed caste from Bombay, came with his wife, Danibehn, and daughter, Lakshmi. Their arrival was not taken well by the other ashram inmates. Most of them rebelled and some even refused to eat. Kasturba, too, joined the chorus and threatened to leave the ashram. "I simply will not have untouchability in the ashram...go and live in Rajkot," said Gandhi to Kasturba. The argument went on well into the night. Finally, their teenaged sons, Ramdas and Devdas, had to intervene and after much discussion Kasturba relented. In times to come, she became so fond of the family that she asked for Gandhi's permission to adopt Lakshmi as their daughter since they did not have one.

"PLEASE STOP IT, GANDHI"

In South Africa, Gandhi had been a hero, the acknowledged leader of a successful movement, having taken on the might of a racist government. Back in India, though he was widely loved and respected, he still had to find his political feet and a substantial leadership role. There was no great movement to join, and since he had recently returned after spending many years abroad, he was not yet in the mainstream. On Gokhale's advice, he spent a year in observation and travel. Congress at the time was divided over its approach toward the British. It was more of a platform to express dissent than to actively protest. Ironically, it was an English woman, Annie Besant, who was paving the way with her Home Rule League, dedicated to Indian self-governance. A powerful influence on the country,

1916 *Gandhi with Kasturba during their stay at Banaras to participate in the inauguration ceremony of Banaras Hindu University.*

she was better known and respected than Gandhi at the time. She had founded the Hindu College in Banaras and, in February 1916, it was granted university status. To mark the occasion, the viceroy was to preside over a grand function, along with maharajas and educationalists from all over India. Gandhi, too, was invited and was asked to speak, with disastrous consequences. He was critical of the maharajas resplendent in their jewelry, saying that there was no salvation for India unless they stripped themselves of the jewelry and held it in trust for the poor. Many princes walked out.

Gandhi then commented on the heavy security in place for the viceroy, with policemen all around and posted on rooftops. "Why this distrust? Is it not better that even Lord Hardinge should die than live a living death?" He referred to the fact that India "in her impatience has produced an army of anarchists. I myself am an anarchist but of another type." He then went on to make a positive reference to bomb-throwers, at which point Annie Besant intervened and told him to stop.

The meeting ended in pandemonium. Besant would later say that her interruption was intended to protect Gandhi since his remarks may have influenced the students present, especially his statement about being an anarchist, a term associated with violence and bombs. Gandhi, in response, stated that but for Besant's interruption, he would have concluded his speech in a few more minutes and no possible misconception about his views on anarchism would have arisen.

The British commissioner was heard saying aloud: "We must stop this man from talking such rot." Madan Mohan Malaviya, a prominent Congress leader and one of the co-founders of the university, ran after the maharajas shouting: "Your Highness! Please come back, we have stopped him." But they moved on and not one returned.

CHAMPARAN: "BRITISH COULD NOT ORDER ME IN MY OWN COUNTRY"

Gandhi's association with Champaran, an obscure district in Bihar, was a turning point in his life. His Champaran revolution came about because of an uneducated indigo cultivator from the area, Rajkumar Shukla. He had arrived at the Congress session in Lucknow in December 1916 to try to acquaint the leaders with the plight of Indigo share croppers in Champaran. Thousands of poor, landless laborers and farmers had been forced to grow indigo instead of the food crops they needed for their survival. Terrorized by the militias of the British landlords, they were given a miserly compensation, leaving them in extreme poverty. In 1914, following a famine, the farmers in Champaran revolted.

Rajkumar Shukla approached many Congress leaders, but no one listened, not even Gandhi. When Shukla met him and narrated the story, Gandhi, never having heard of Champaran, paid little attention. Shukla persevered, following Gandhi everywhere he went and begging him to set aside one day to visit Champaran. Worn down by the man's persistence, Gandhi arrived in Patna accompanied by Shukla in April 1917.

In Patna, he was first taken to the house of Rajendra Prasad, who would go on to become independent India's first president. As Prasad was away, Shukla convinced the servants that Gandhi should be permitted to stay in the house in their master's absence. The servants, however, were reluctant. Gandhi's peasant-type dress had put them off and the servants refused to allow him to use the toilet inside the house or to draw water from the well, which they themselves used. They did not know Gandhi's background or his caste. Gandhi was upset and would write about Shukla in scathing terms: "The man who brought me here does not know anything. He has dumped me in some obscure place. The master of the house is away and the servants take us both to be beggars. They don't even permit us the use of the latrine, not to speak of inviting us for meals. I take care to provide for myself with the things I need so as to be able to maintain complete indifference." Gandhi's main concern, however, was that he may be unable to reach Champaran.

Gandhi then shifted to the home of Maulana Mazrahul Haq, a Muslim leader whom Gandhi had known in London. Mazrahul Haq sent a telegram to his friend J. B. Kripalani asking him to be at Muzaffarpur station to receive Gandhi, who was arriving from Patna at midnight. To Gandhi's astonishment, a large crowd was waiting for him and he was welcomed like a monarch. From Muzaffarpur, Gandhi traveled to Champaran.

The famine had created great distress and Gandhi was moved by the condition of the indigo workers. He had planned to spend a week there, but his stay in Champaran lasted seven months. Gandhi proposed a mass civil disobedience campaign and set up an ashram with supporters and volunteers from the region. He organized a detailed study and survey of the villages, recording the terrible suffering of the share croppers. His next step was to lead a clean-up of the villages, to build schools and hospitals and encourage the village leadership to abandon untouchability and the suppression of women.

He was joined by many young nationalists from all over India, including Rajendra Prasad, Braj Kishore Prasad (whose daughter Prabhavati later married Jayaprakash Narayan) and Acharya Kripalani. Gandhi was arrested on the charge of creating unrest and ordered to leave the province. Not one to bow down, Gandhi wrote back saying that he would not leave and would readily suffer the penalties of disobedience.

1917 *Rajkumar Shukla's persistence made Gandhi visit Champaran in Bihar.*

Thousands of locals protested, however, demanding his release. They subsequently let Gandhi go, and he met the lieutenant governor, Sir Edward Gait. An agreement was signed granting more compensation and control to the poor farmers of the region, and cancelation of revenue hikes until the famine ended. It was during this agitation that people started addressing Gandhi as "Bapu" (Father).

Rajendra Prasad, a young lawyer, would play a bigger role in Gandhi's life. He assisted Gandhi's group in Champaran, where they gathered statements from the exploited farmers. Prasad would later record that most of the group, including Prasad himself, were orthodox Hindus who would not eat food cooked by anyone except a Brahmin or a member of their own caste. They all had servants to do the washing, cooking and cleaning. Gandhi, as Prasad recalled, asked them if they really needed so many servants and urged them to adopt a simple lifestyle. Gandhi would carry his own luggage, clean the room he lived in and assist in cooking and serving food. Responding to his call, the servants were sent home except for one to wash the dishes. In the process, all caste barriers were broken down. The villagers who came to record their stories were astonished to see illustrious men cleaning their own clothes and rooms.

***

In the scorching heat of June 1917, the village of Kochrab, the site of Gandhi's bungalow-turned-ashram, witnessed a deadly plague epidemic. Gandhi moved to a new ashram that same year, the land for which had been acquired a few months earlier. Gandhi, with another Gujarati friend, had traveled around Ahmedabad scouting for land, which they eventually found on the banks of the river Sabarmati, not far from the Sabarmati Central Jail—a special attraction for Gandhi. They acquired 55 bighas of land (about 30 acres), and built on it with financial help from textile and shipping magnates who were Gandhi's friends. The ashram was established in 1917. Says Gandhi in his autobiography: "As jail-going was understood to be the normal lot of satyagrahis, I like this position." The ashram was started in a tent with a tin shed as the kitchen. "Some of the most active leaders of the independence movement began their political careers at the feet of the Mahatma in Sabarmati," says Louis Fischer.

1917 *Kasturba with her son Ramdas at Sabarmati Ashram.*

THE BUILDING OF SABARMATI ASHRAM
THE LAND WHERE SABARMATI ASHRAM WAS BEING BUILT WAS FULL OF SNAKES AND OTHER POISONOUS CREATURES. BUT THIS WAS NOT NEW TO GANDHI. SO OFTEN DID HE RISK HIS LIFE THAT THERE WAS USUALLY A CLASH BETWEEN MYTH AND REALITY. ONE OF THE BEST-KNOWN STORIES ABOUT GANDHI RELATES TO THE MOST VENOMOUS SNAKE IN SOUTH AFRICA AND A KING COBRA IN INDIA, BOTH OF WHICH WERE SAID TO HAVE CROSSED OVER HIS BODY WITHOUT CAUSING HIM HARM. SAID GANDHI: "IT'S TRUE THE GENTLEMAN CRAWLED OVER MY SHAWL AND LEFT."

1917 Clockwise from left: *Glimpses of the Sabarmati Ashram, where Gandhi and Kasturba lived between 1917 and 1930; "Raghupati Raghava Rajaram," Gandhi's favorite hymn, being sung by the inmates of the Sabarmati Ashram; (left to right) Purushottam Das Tandon, Jawaharlal Nehru, Ganesh Vasudev Mavalankar and Morarji Desai taking part in spinning; A prayer meeting in front of Hridaya Kunj, Gandhi's own home at the Sabarmati Ashram; Perspective shots of Hridaya Kunj.*

PATEL AND GANDHI

Vallabhbhai Patel was a leading lawyer and a prominent citizen of Ahmedabad. He was a blunt man who did not think twice before speaking his mind. There are many versions of his first sighting of Gandhi but they all refer to Patel sitting around a bridge table in Ahmedabad's Gujarat Club. This must have been around late 1916, by which time Gandhi had acquired a noteworthy reputation in India. When asked to listen to Gandhi as he was speaking at the club, Patel insisted on continuing with his game rather than listen to the Mahatma from South Africa.

That first reaction soon developed into one of the closest relationships any two people had during the freedom movement. When they became friends, Patel changed his dress from European suits to the dhoti kurta. According to Thomas Weber, a well-known Gandhian scholar: "The pompous lawyer became a pre-eminent fighter for the people in Gandhi's causes." Yet they agreed to disagree with reverence toward each other. They differed over the modality of the movement when Gandhi embarked on the Salt Satyagraha, over Nehru assuming presidentship in 1936, and their relationship with the Muslim League and its leader M. A. Jinnah. For over 15 months, beginning in January 1932, they were jailed together in Yeravda Jail in Poona. The prison term brought them even closer. According to Gandhi's biographer, Robert Payne, Patel "liked to prepare his (Gandhi's) drink of honey and lemon water, peel his fruits and look after the stick (neem datun) he used for cleaning his teeth." Gandhi had only one or two teeth left and it "amused" Patel to see Gandhi spend hours cleaning them. At Gandhi's behest, Patel improved his spinning skills and took lessons in Sanskrit. They spent time together in prison discussing temple entry for untouchables and Bhimrao Ambedkar's proposal for separate electorate for Harijans (Gandhi's name for the untouchables, meaning literally "children of God"). Gandhi announced his 21-day fast while in Yeravda, despite protests from Patel.

Patel was perceived to be pro-Hindu, though he tried many times to cast off this image. Barely five months after independence, at a public rally in Lucknow, he

Gandhi in a meeting with Sardar Vallabhbhai Patel at Birla House, New Delhi.

said: "I am a true friend of Muslims although I am dubbed as their greatest enemy. I believe in plain speaking…they must give practical proofs of their declaration." His forthright demeanor often got in the way of reconciliation with religious groups or political leaders opposed to his viewpoint. His credentials as a great administrator and negotiator came further to the fore when he persuaded all princely states, including those with a Muslim majority, to merge with the Indian Union. Gandhi had high respect for Patel's abilities in such matters, yet he nominated Nehru as India's first prime minister. It was Patel's political and administrative ability versus Nehru's charm and international popularity. And Gandhi chose the latter.

Patel was the last person to meet with Gandhi, minutes before his assassination. Gandhi had called him to discuss ways to resolve differences between himself and Nehru. Patel left as Gandhi was getting late for his evening prayer meeting. Soon after the prayer, Gandhi was to meet Nehru to discuss the same issue and bring about an agreement between the two. Barely had Patel reached home when he received the tragic news and rushed back. Nehru arrived a few minutes later. Wailing like a child, he embraced Patel as if two boys had lost their father. Overcome with sorrow, Patel said: "Others could weep and find relief from their grief in tears, I could not do that. But it reduced my brain to pulp."

PATEL'S ENVELOPES

WHILE IN YERAVDA JAIL WITH GANDHI, SARDAR PATEL PERFECTED THE ART OF MAKING NEW ENVELOPES REUSING OLD ONES. ON AUGUST 28, 1932, GANDHI WROTE TO HIS SECRETARY, PYARELAL, "NOBODY CAN EQUAL HIM (PATEL) IN THE ART OF MAKING ENVELOPES. HE MAKES THEM WITHOUT USING MEASUREMENTS AND IS GUIDED BY HIS EYES IN CUTTING THE PAPER, AND STILL HE DOES NOT SEEM TO TAKE MUCH TIME. HIS ORDERLINESS IS SIMPLY WONDERFUL." GANDHI CONSIDERED ENVELOPES MADE BY PATEL TO BE LUCKY, AS LETTERS SENT IN THEM WERE RARELY STOPPED BY THE AUTHORITIES.

JALLIANWALA BAGH: 1,650 ROUNDS FIRED...
379 MEN, WOMEN AND CHILDREN KILLED...
1,137 WOUNDED

On April 9, 1919, the Punjab government deported two Congress leaders from the province—Dr. Saifuddin Kitchlew, a Muslim, and Dr. Satyapal, a Hindu. It was on the day of Ram Navmi, a Hindu festival in which Muslims also participated. According to an official report, they shouted: "*Mahatma Gandhi ki jai*" and "*Hindu–Mussalman ki jai*" (Long live Hindu–Muslim unity), and protested against the deportation of the two leaders. They reinforced the slogan by drinking publicly from the same cup.

General Reginald Dyer, an officer of the Indian Army, issued a proclamation on April 12, 1919, banning all processions and public meetings in Amritsar. The next day, Dyer himself went around the city reading the proclamation out loud, although it seems clear that he did not cover all areas of the city.

Without giving the crowd gathered at the Jallianwala Bagh on Baisakhi day (April 13) any advance warning to disperse, which Dyer considered unnecessary since they had violated the proclamation, he ordered his men to open fire. According to some estimates, there were around 20,000 people in the enclosed park that afternoon—a park roughly 200 yards by 200 yards, flanked on all sides by high walls and overlooking balconies. It had just one narrow gate open for entry and exit.

The Hunter Commission, subsequently set up to examine the Jallianwala Bagh massacre and released later, would state: "The issue of the proclamation which was signed by the Brigade Major on General Dyer's behalf was left to the police; it does not appear what steps were taken to ensure its publication." It added: "From an examination of the map showing the different places where the proclamation was read, it is evident that in many parts of the city the proclamation was not read."

Under cross-examination by the Hunter Commission, Dyer revealed his state of mind and his purpose.

"Question: From time to time you changed your firing and directed it to the place where the crowd was thickest?

Answer: That is so.

Question: Supposing the passage was sufficient to allow the armored cars to go in, would you have opened fire with the machine guns?

Answer: Probably, yes."

The Hunter Commission report concluded that when examined, Dyer explained that his "mind was made up—if his orders against holding a meeting were violated, he was going to fire at once." Dyer himself testified: "I had made up my mind. I would do all men to death.... In all 1,650 rounds were fired by the troops...approximately 379 were dead plus 1,137 wounded...1,516 casualties with 1,650 bullets."

While the Hunter Commission was sitting, Jawaharlal Nehru found himself traveling from Amritsar to Delhi. In his autobiography, he writes that when he entered the train compartment, he discovered his fellow passengers were all British military officers. He adds: "One of them was holding forth in an aggressive and triumphant tone and soon I discovered that he was General Dyer, the hero of Jallianwala Bagh, and he was describing his Amritsar experience. He pointed out that he had the whole town at his mercy and had felt like reducing the rebellious city to a heap of ashes...I was greatly shocked to hear his conversation and to observe his callous manner. He descended at Delhi station in pajamas with bright pink stripes and a dressing gown."

THE MORAL FORCE NEVER FAILS

On March 19, 1919, Gandhi, who had gone to Madras for a meeting, was heard remarking to C. Rajagopalachari, his host: "Last night, the idea came to me in a dream that we should call on the country to observe a general hartal." This hartal (strike) was Gandhi's first call for civil disobedience in India. The provocation was the Rowlatt Act, which had come into force a day earlier. The First World War had ended in November 1918, but the emergency powers of arrest and suspension of civil liberties still continued, along with wartime press censorship. Britain had sent a committee headed by Sir Sidney Rowlatt to India to review the administration of justice. The committee recommended a continuation of wartime restrictions. Gandhi, recovering from a serious illness and still frail, began preparing for a nationwide hartal to force the government to withdraw the repressive legislation. He traveled to many cities, despite being so weak that his speeches had to be read by someone else. His letters to the viceroy, asking for a repeal of the unjust and subversive act, were ignored. Gandhi's call for hartal, for civil disobedience, spread across India like wildfire. It united a vast multitude of people in a common protest, giving them a sense of power. The hartal started on April 6 and paralyzed the economy. The deserted cities were proof that Indians united in peaceful protest could be a formidable force. Such a hartal had never been contemplated in India. In a letter, Gandhi wrote that he hoped to show the British that "physical force is nothing compared to moral force and that moral force never fails." There were outbreaks of violence, which Gandhi denounced, but could not stop. On April 18, he called off the campaign.

***

Gandhi's role as a newspaper editor came about by chance after the British authorities had ordered the deportation of B. G. Horniman, editor of the *Bombay Chronicle*. The directors of the paper asked Gandhi if he would take up the role of editor. The authorities, however, ordered the suspension of the *Bombay Chronicle*. The management also controlled another English publication, *Young India*, and asked Gandhi to become its editor instead. Gandhi was already handling the affairs of a Gujarati periodical, *Navajivan*. He faced the prospect of overseeing two weeklies published from different cities, Ahmedabad and Bombay. At his suggestion, *Young India* moved its offices to Ahmedabad. This gave Gandhi the opportunity to put across his views to a wider audience—both Gujarati- and English-speaking people.

1919 Left: *First issue of* Young India *(October 8, 1919);* Right: *First issue of* Navajivan *(September 11, 1919). Both were edited by Gandhi.*

INDIANS TO RENOUNCE ALL TITLES

On August 1, 1920, in protest of post-war developments that undermined the Congress-backed Khilafat movement involving Muslims in India, as well as the lack of action against General Dyer for the massacre in Amritsar, Gandhi returned three prestigious medals (the Boer War medal, Zulu War medal and Kaiser-i-Hind gold medal) awarded to him by the British Empire. He had been awarded these medals for his humanitarian and volunteer work in South Africa. In his letter

1920 Left and Right: *Gandhi returned the Kaiser-i-Hind gold medal (shown here front and back), awarded to him for his humanitarian work in South Africa.*

to the viceroy, Gandhi wrote: "I venture to return these medals in pursuance of the scheme of non-cooperation, inaugurated today in connection with the Khilafat movement. Valuable as these honors have been, I cannot wear them with a clear conscience as long as my Mussulman countrymen have to labor under a wrong done to their religious sentiments." His letter also mentioned that the government's attitude "on the Punjab question has given me additional sense for grave dissatisfaction." He concluded: "I can retain neither respect or have affection for such a government."

Addressing a meeting in Bombay, he called upon all Indians to renounce their titles, medals and honorary posts. He called on lawyers to give up their practice and asked parents to withdraw their children from government schools.

KHILAFAT AND NON-VIOLENT NON-COOPERATION MOVEMENTS

Toward the end of the First World War, the British had repeatedly assured Muslims in India that they would not harm the Caliphate's religious and temporal powers, an assurance they went back on once the war was over and the Ottoman Empire was defeated. Turkey represented the seat of the Caliph. The post-war treaties clearly left the Muslims feeling betrayed and cheated. The fear among Indian Muslims was that the Hajj and passage to the holy shrines in Arabia, which was under the Caliph, would be blocked. Sensing their anger and agitation, Gandhi saw an ideal opportunity to bring Muslims and Hindus together under a common umbrella. In September 1919, he organized a Khilafat Conference in Lucknow with

1920 *Maulana Mohammad Ali and Maulana Shaukat Ali, commonly addressed as the "Ali Brothers."*

the influential Ali brothers, Shaukat and Mohammad, along with Congress leader Maulana Abul Kalam Azad. The Ali brothers had led the way in raising Muslim sentiments against British rule. Gandhi followed up with another conference in Delhi, where he was elected president of the All India Khilafat Conference. He then suggested non-cooperation to the Khilafat Committee, provided it was non-violent. Many Muslim leaders objected, saying that non-violent non-cooperation was against the diktat of Islam. To break the stalemate, Gandhi met with Maulana Azad and the nationalist Muslim politician Hakim Ajmal Khan at the home of St. Stephen's College principal Susil Kumar Rudra in Delhi. An agreement was reached and at the Khilafat Conference in Meerut on January 20, 1920, Gandhi, for the first time, outlined his proposals for non-violent non-cooperation, which was passed with a majority. Legislatures would be boycotted, all titles and honorary positions would be renounced, lawyers would stop practicing and parents would take their children out of government schools.

Gandhi organized another Khilafat Conference in Delhi in November. It was a two-day event that started in the early afternoon and concluded at dawn. Gandhi was asked to contribute one pie (paisa). Since he never carried money, Khwaja Hasan Nizami, an important Muslim leader, paid the coin on his behalf. The coin was put to auction and fetched 501 rupees. A total of 2,000 rupees was raised on the spot. On January 19, 1920, a delegation of pro-Khilafat leaders including Motilal Nehru, Shaukat Ali, Madan Mohan Malaviya, Maulana Azad, M. A. Jinnah, Rambhuj Dutt Choudhury, Swami Shraddhanand, Hakim Ajmal Khan and Gandhi presented a demand to the viceroy to restore the spiritual and temporal powers of the Caliph and urged him to proceed to England to place their demands before the prime minister. Incidentally, Gandhi came up with the phrase "non-cooperation" in the absence of a better Hindi alternative, a language in which he was not very fluent at that time.

The Khilafat movement ended because the Ali brothers distanced themselves from Gandhi when he called off his non-cooperation movement after violence erupted in Chauri-Chaura in Gorakhpur district (United Provinces) in 1922, where a non-cooperation campaign was organized. They also criticized Gandhi's commitment to non-violence and later joined the Muslim League.

***

1921 *Hindus and Muslims protesting against British rule. Gandhi's charkha (spinning wheel) symbolized the end of this rule and propagation of everything "swadeshi."*

1921 *Participants of the non-cooperation movement pictured in the process of destroying foreign cloth. The purpose of doing away with foreign cloth was to encourage the production and the use of indigenous cloth and goods made within the borders of India.*

"A GIANT AMONG MEN HAS FALLEN"

LOKMANYA BAL GANGADHAR TILAK 1856–1920

Bal Gangadhar Tilak was also Gandhi's mentor in many ways and had personified the swaraj struggle in thought, word and deed. A Chitpawan Brahmin scholar and mathematician, he was editor of the *Kesari* and *Mahratta* newspapers. Considered by many to be the first revolutionary leader of India's independence movement, he was tried on charges of sedition in 1897 and again in 1908. Though Tilak and Gandhi differed in their political ideology, Gandhi looked up to him. Tilak died after a brief illness on August 1, 1920, in his Bombay home. It was the day Gandhi was to launch his non-cooperation movement. An argument had broken out between some of Tilak's supporters, who wanted to take the body to his hometown, Poona, for cremation, and some national leaders, who wanted him cremated with full

honors in Bombay. Dr. G. V. Deshmukh, Tilak's private surgeon, took his supporters to the balcony of Sardargruha building, where Tilak's body was kept, and showed them the huge crowd stretching the half-mile or so from Crawford Market to Dhobi Talao, indicating the futility of the idea of removing the body from Bombay. It was then agreed that the cremation should take place in Bombay, in Chowpatty. Gandhi was one of the pall bearers. After Tilak's death, Gandhi wrote in *Young India*: "A giant among men has fallen…We are purifying ourselves by discarding foreign cloth which is a badge of our slavery." At a

Tilak was cremated in the lotus position (sitting with legs crossed)—a distinction accorded to great souls in India.

BOYCOTT OF FOREIGN CLOTHES

BONFIRE OF FOREIGN CLOTHES

Shall take place at the Maidan near Elphinstone Mills Opp. Elphinstone Road Station on Sunday, 31st July, 1921.

THE CEREMONY WILL BE PERFORMED BY

MAHATMA GANDHIJI

All are requested to attend in Swadeshi Clothes of Khadi. Those who have not given away their Foreign Clothes are requested to bring them to the Meeting.

SPECIAL ARRANGEMENT IS MADE FOR LADIES AND CHILDREN

IN MEMORY OF

LOKMANYA TILAK

PUBLIC MEETING AT CHAUPATI, 1ST AUGUST 1921, AT 6-30 P: M.

Gandhi's appeal for a boycott of foreign clothes in the Bombay Chronicle.

mammoth meeting on Chowpatty beach, he said: "The best method of perpetuating Lokmanya's memory is the attainment of swaraj and swaraj is impossible without swadeshi [meaning of one's own country]. Here, out of the ashes, rose the force of non-cooperation."

On the eve of the first anniversary of Tilak's death, Gandhi lit a bonfire to destroy all of his clothes that were not made in India. The *Bombay Chronicle* described the event: "…and now a great shout, waving of arms, caps of which at least ninety percent were the plain white rough spun Gandhi caps which during the last few days have sprung like magic throughout the city, announced the arrival of the Mahatma." Kerosene was sprinkled on the pile and Gandhi lit the bonfire. He declared: "We are removing today a pollution from our bodies…. We attain today fitness to enter the temple of Swaraj."

HALF-NAKED FAKIR

There was a dramatic transformation in Gandhi over the years in terms of the clothes he wore, or didn't wear. While in South Africa, he was a lawyer impeccably dressed in the latest fashion, but he landed in India wearing Kathiawari dress. On Gokhale's advice, he wore the humble clothes of a peasant as he traveled across the country. He then adopted a more revolutionary look, donning a white skull cap made of khadi and a shirt and dhoti of the same homespun cotton. On September 22, 1921, in Madurai, he decided to strip himself of all clothes except a loin-cloth, of the type that poor farmers wear while plowing their fields. He announced his decision to the media, well aware that there would be a negative reaction among his supporters and other political leaders. Most thought he was going to turn an ascetic, and renounce the world. Dr. Rajagopalachari and many others present tried to dissuade him. Madan Mohan Malaviya exclaimed: "Brother, why this?" Later, Abbas Tyabji, a fellow freedom fighter, burst into laughter at Gandhi's appearance: "Look, Mahatma's not only lost his senses and turned mad, but he has devised a new way of making others mad also." The news spread and the people of Madurai got up early and lined the streets to have a look. They bowed in respect as the Mahatma left for Karaikudi. Gandhi reasoned that people wore too much finery and this would be a lesson to them. During winter months, he would don a shawl over his bare chest. In choosing to wear just a loin-cloth he had found a potent symbol, one that conveyed transparency. He would adopt this look for the rest of his life.

1921 *Gandhi with Annie Besant at a meeting in Madras.*

Gandhi with Rabindranath Tagore at Vanita Vishram during Tagore's visit to Ahmedabad for the 6th Gujarati Literary Conference in April 1920.

TAGORE AND GANDHI

Rabindranath Tagore and Gandhi first met in 1915. Tagore, a Nobel laureate, had already gained international acclaim for his creative genius and was regarded one of the finest poets ever, while Gandhi was still relatively untested in the Indian context. He had made his name in South Africa and had arrived in India barely two months before their meeting in Santiniketan, the "abode of peace" Tagore had set up in Bengal. The meeting had been arranged by C. F. Andrews, the English missionary who supported Indian independence and who had been asked to go to South Africa to help the Indian community, where he had met Gandhi, then a young lawyer.

Tagore and Gandhi would address each other as "Gurudev" (a teacher of the highest order) and "Mahatma," and their debates were greatly enriching, especially since this was a period when India was undergoing many dramatic social and political changes.

Gandhi with Kasturba during their visit to Santiniketan in 1940, just a year before Tagore passed away.

A close friend of both Gandhi and Tagore, Romain Rolland described their relationship as one "moved by admiration and esteem."

At Andrews' suggestion, 20 young members of the Phoenix settlement in South Africa were accommodated in Santiniketan. While there, Gandhi instilled in the institute's pupils and gurus habits such as cleanliness, and he had them do all the daily chores themselves—not relying on salaried servants as was standard. The Tagores, after all, were a feudal family. This was in March 1915, and Tagore not only accepted this practice, albeit diplomatically, but March 10 was celebrated as Gandhi Day every year (even now) when all the helpers and servants were given a holiday and the teachers and pupils did the cooking and cleaning.

For all his global acclaim, there is little doubt that Tagore recognized Gandhi as the supreme leader, even though their differences in opinion and attitude are familiar to students of modern Indian history. Tagore's famous letter to Gandhi at the beginning of the non-cooperation movement—condemning it as asceticism and an "orgy of frightfulness," which found "a disinterested delight in any unmeaning

The two eminent Indian personalities of the 20th century, both Gandhi and Tagore emphasized the need for India to become self-reliant.

devastation," and "an attempt at spiritual suicide"—has been quoted often enough as evidence of their very basic disagreement regarding the road ahead for India. He termed the propaganda of spinning as a big "political yarn." Tagore also openly disagreed with Gandhi's populist schemes, such as lighting bonfires of foreign cloth, having lawyers boycott courts or students stay away from schools and colleges.

One instance of their differences became evident in the first week of September 1921 at the height of the non-cooperation movement. Tagore and Gandhi had met at Tagore's Calcutta residence, Jorasanko, at the end of which the two parted "as friends who agree to disagree." The only other person present at this meeting was C. F. Andrews. While this meeting was taking place behind closed doors, Gandhi's supporters gathered outside Jorasanko and made a big bonfire of foreign cloth. Seeing this, Tagore took Gandhi to the verandah and said, "Look down there and see what your non-violent followers are up to. They have stolen cloth from the shops in Chitpore Road, they've lit a bonfire in my courtyard and are now howling round it like a lot of demented dervishes. Is that non-violence?" Tagore's article, published as "The Call of Truth" in the *Modern Review* in October 1921, stated: "Consider the burning of cloth, heaped before the very eyes of our motherland shivering and ashamed in her nakedness…the command to burn our foreign clothes has been laid on us. I, for one, am unable to obey it…"

Gandhi's strong rejoinder appeared in his journal, *Young India*, where he wrote: "The bard of Santiniketan has contributed to the *Modern Review* a brilliant essay on the present movement. It is a series of word pictures which he alone can paint…in burning my foreign clothes I burn my shame." Ultimately, their friendship and mutual respect transcended their differences.

Despite their public disagreements, Tagore and Gandhi remained close friends till the former's death in 1941. In 1921, Tagore wrote a play called *Muktadhara* in which the protagonist Dhananjay was loosely camouflaged as Gandhi, showing him as an ascetic who defies a cruel king and appeals to the king's subjects not to pay taxes. The play, though evocatively written, was never staged.

The Tagore–Gandhi relationship was deeply analyzed by Romain Rolland, the French essayist and philosopher and a close friend of both. Rolland had also won the Nobel Prize for Literature (in 1915). Tagore and Rolland met in March 1921, where they discussed Gandhi in great depth. Three years later, Rolland would write a much-acclaimed book on Gandhi, *Mahatma Gandhi*, and describe the relationship between Gandhi and Tagore as "the controversy between two great minds, both moved by mutual admiration and esteem."

FRIENDLY ADVICE
WHILE VISITING SANTINIKETAN, GANDHI SAW TAGORE EATING LOOCHIS (BENGALI PURIS) AND REMARKED THAT EATING WHITE FLOUR FRIED IN GHEE WAS "POISON," TO WHICH TAGORE REPLIED: "IT MUST BE A VERY SLOW POISON. I HAVE BEEN EATING IT FOR ALMOST HALF A CENTURY NOW."

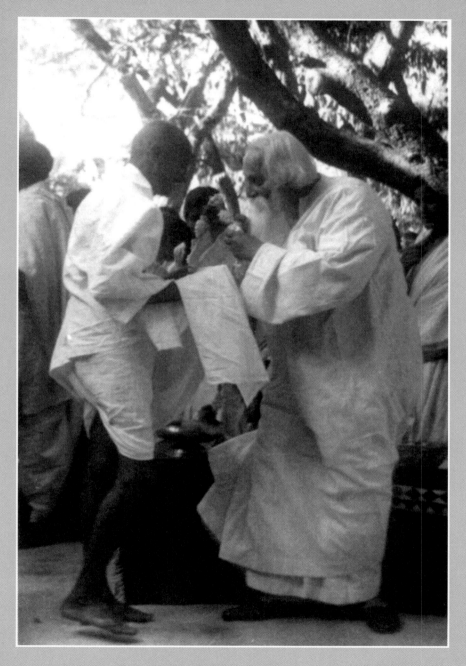

Tagore and Gandhi, despite being close friends and admirers of each other, often agreed to disagree.

PROMOTING KHADI

Encouraging women to participate in the swadeshi movement, Gandhi addressed various meetings specially organized for them. In one such gathering in Madras, he beseeched them to give up fine clothes, heavy food, jewelry and gossip. He suggested that they abandon ideas of high and low, touchable and untouchable, and treat all human beings the same.

Ever since he reduced his dress to an unstitched loin-cloth, khaddar (homespun cotton cloth) and spinning had become an obsession with Gandhi. In every public speech he made, he would go to great lengths to extoll the virtues of khadi, often teaching his audience ways to make yarn and spin the charkha.

THE PRINCE OF WALES ARRIVES...

Gandhi's call for a non-violent struggle would be tested on many occasions, among the most prominent being the visit of the Prince of Wales to India in November 1921. Gandhi had given a call for a general strike (hartal). The Prince of Wales landed to be met by an eerie silence. People stayed at home and businesses were shut. In Bombay, however, where Gandhi was, Eurasians, Parsis and Jews came out to welcome the royal visitor. Mobs attacked them and the violence turned into a large-scale riot. This was one of the rare occasions when Hindus and Muslims had joined hands against Parsis, Eurasians and all those who had opposed Gandhi's call for a boycott. Shops, buildings, trams and cars were set on fire and policemen were killed. Gandhi drove around the city trying to calm tempers and was horrified by what he saw. He came across two policemen dying of stab wounds while elsewhere mobs were attacking anyone wearing foreign clothes. He heard the rioters shouting: "*Mahatma Gandhi ki jai.*" He was shattered. "Never has the sound of those words grated so much on my ears," he later wrote. The rioting continued for several days, leaving 53 people dead. Gandhi was deeply disappointed and shocked at what his hartal call had turned into. The Bombay riots would expose the

1921 Above: *Gandhi at an all-women's meeting in Madras.*
Below: *Gandhi with a hand spindle (takli), addressing a public rally.*

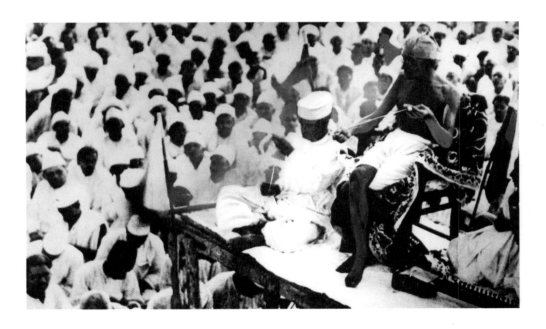

social, political and communal tinderbox that India was in danger of becoming. Gandhi declared that he would not eat or drink anything except water till peace was restored.

BOMBAY BURNS

The Bombay riots of November 1921 represented to Gandhi the failure of his non-violent non-cooperation campaign. His call for a boycott of the Prince of Wales' visit had gone horribly wrong and he needed to do penance in public view. He undertook a fast but it failed to have the desired effect. Communal tension was still evident in some pockets of the city. Gandhi would famously say: "I am a man of peace but I do not want peace that you find in the grave." Parsi temples had been violated and men and women killed. "I must refuse to eat or drink anything but water till the Hindus and Mussalmans of Bombay have made peace with the Parsis, the Christians and the Jews, and till the non-cooperators have peace with the cooperators." He remained in a state of depression for some days after the fast, which was followed by the arrest of several Congress leaders. Motilal Nehru and his son Jawaharlal, Lala Lajpat Rai and C. R. Das were arrested on charges of sedition and civil disobedience. Harilal, the son with whom Gandhi had a difficult relationship, courted arrest too. A proud father, Gandhi sent him a telegram: "Well done, God bless you. Ramdas, Devdas and others will follow you." In the last week of December, Congress met for its annual session and backed Gandhi's call for peaceful, non-violent civil disobedience against the government. The movement spread literally like wildfire with the burning of foreign cloth in every city.

CIVIL DISOBEDIENCE: A NEW BEGINNING

In December 1921 and January 1922, nearly 30,000 people were imprisoned after the Bombay riots. When the Indian National Congress convened in Ahmedabad in December 1921, 20,000 Indians had been arrested. Congress appointed Gandhi as its sole executive authority, which posed its own challenges. Within Congress there was growing pressure on Gandhi to intensify the mass civil disobedience movement. A mass struggle was, in Gandhi's view, the most effective as well as the most dangerous weapon. The All-India Congress Committee had already authorized its Provincial Congress Committees to refuse to pay taxes. However, Gandhi cautioned them to wait and watch and implement non-payment of taxes only in selected areas. His idea of mass civil disobedience was "a sort of general upheaval on the political plane—the government ceases to function, the police stations, the courts, offices etc. all cease to be government property and shall be taken charge of by the people." Gandhi's plan was to launch civil disobedience in one district; if it succeeded he proposed to extend it to the adjacent district and so on. He gave a warning that if violence broke out in any form, the movement would lose its character as a movement of peace, "even as a lute would begin to emit notes of discord the moment a single string snaps," said Gandhi.

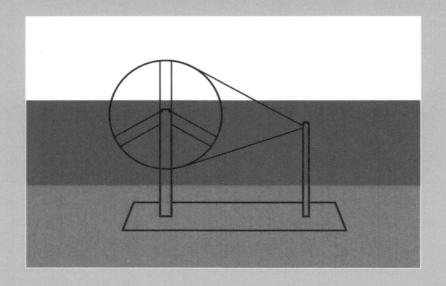

THE INDIAN FLAG IS BORN

Some time in early 1921, Gandhi decided that the time was right to create a national flag for the country. "A flag is a necessity for all nations...millions have died for it...it will be necessary for us to recognize a common flag to live and die for." Various designs had been offered but one man was persistent in his effort to design the flag. He was a young geologist called Pingali Venkayya, who had attended every Congress session to present his design. Gandhi wanted a flag that would instill patriotism and motivate the people. At the 1921 Congress session in Bezwada, Pingali presented his design to Gandhi. It had two colors, red and green, representing the two major communities, Hindus and Muslims. Gandhi wanted the addition of a white strip to represent the other communities, and the spinning wheel to symbolize swaraj. This design became the tiranga, or the tricolor. As soon as the design was announced, Gandhi was flooded with suggestions. The Sikhs wanted to include black (associated with combat), and there were also suggestions about the symbol, but Gandhi insisted that "there must not be any religious symbols and we must find a clear and permanent rallying object. That is the spinning wheel..."

CHAURI-CHAURA POLICE STATION SET ON FIRE

Gandhi launched a no-tax campaign to weaken the British government's stranglehold in Bardoli in Gujarat. In early February 1922, he communicated the steps he was contemplating and his reasons in a letter to the viceroy. The entire country was waiting to see what would happen. However, some 800 miles away, another event would derail Gandhi's plans and cause him great anguish and pain. In a remote part of the United Provinces, two villages called Chauri and Chaura in Gorakhpur district were to create dubious history. A procession of non-cooperatives, as they were known, staged a peaceful march past the local police station on February 4. It would turn into one of the darkest chapters in pre-independence history. A public meeting was arranged in Chauri-Chaura, where Congress and Khilafat leaders were to speak. Large crowds had gathered to hear them. They had embarked on a procession, but were beaten up by the police. The station officer, Gupteshwar Singh, observed the procession passing by and started hurling abuse. The police fired in the air—no one was injured. "Gandhi's power has turned bullets into water!" shouted the protestors. Rumors spread that some people had been killed, though. Immediately, the crowd started throwing stones at

AMRITA SHER-GIL AND CHAURA

A UNIT OF SATYAGRAHIS WAS SET UP IN A VILLAGE BARELY A MILE AWAY FROM CHAURI-CHAURA POLICE STATION, WHICH WAS LOCATED UNDER A PROSPEROUS ENCLAVE OF SARAYA ESTATE. NOT MANY KNOW THAT IT IS ASSOCIATED WITH ONE OF INDIA'S MOST CELEBRATED ARTISTS, AMRITA SHER-GIL. HER ANCESTORS HAD BEEN GIVEN THIS LAND AROUND THE MID-19TH CENTURY BY THE BRITISH, PRESUMABLY FOR SERVICES RENDERED TO THEM BY THE FAMILY. HER FATHER, UMRAO SINGH MAJITHIA, LIVED IN SARAYA ESTATE AND HER HUSBAND DR. VICTOR EGAN ALSO PRACTICED MEDICINE THERE. SHE HERSELF SPENT MANY YEARS IN SARAYA ESTATE AS A YOUNG GIRL AND PAINTED SOME OF HER FAMOUS RURAL PAINTINGS HERE. UMRAO SINGH ACTUALLY HAD HOLDINGS IN CHAURA TOO.

1922 *Victims of mob violence in Chauri-Chaura.*

the policemen. This time, they fired into the crowd and three protestors were killed. The crowd went wild and surged toward the police station, locking the doors from outside, dousing the building with kerosene and setting it alight. The charred bodies of 23 policemen were found in the debris, while those who had committed the incendiary act vanished to other locations. It was a huge blow to Gandhi's non-cooperation campaign. On February 9, Congress dismantled the volunteer groups in the villages around Chauri-Chaura. Devdas, Gandhi's youngest son, rushed

CHAURI CHAURA SENTENCES.

(FROM OUR CORRESPONDENT.)
ALLAHABAD, MAY 4.

The Governor in Council has accepted the recommendations to clemency of the Allahabad High Court in its judgment in the Chauri Chaura case, and orders reducing the sentences have been issued accordingly.

*** There were 170 appeals to the High Court of persons who had been convicted and sentenced to death in connexion with the murder of the inmates of the police station at Chauri Chaura, a village in the United Provinces, by Gandhi " volunteers " on February 4, 1922. The death sentence on nineteen of the ringleaders was confirmed, while 110 persons found guilty of murder had their sentences commuted to transportation for life, with a recommendation to mercy in the case of all except fourteen. Thirty-eight persons were acquitted and the remainder had their sentences modified.

Left: A newspaper report of May 4, 1922, regarding acceptance of recommendations for clemency of the Allahabad High Court in the Chauri-Chaura case.
Below: A rubber stamp impression of Mahatma Gandhi on the Register of Volunteers, Gorakhpur Congress Committee.

to Gorakhpur and Gandhi himself issued a statement proposing a suspension of the mass civil disobedience campaign. Gandhi's statement read: "I am violently agitated by the events in Gorakhpur district. The civil disobedience in Bardoli can make no impression on the country when disobedience of a criminal character goes on in other parts of the country." On February 12, Gandhi started a five-day fast by way of atonement. "I could not have done less, could I?" he wrote in a letter to Devdas.

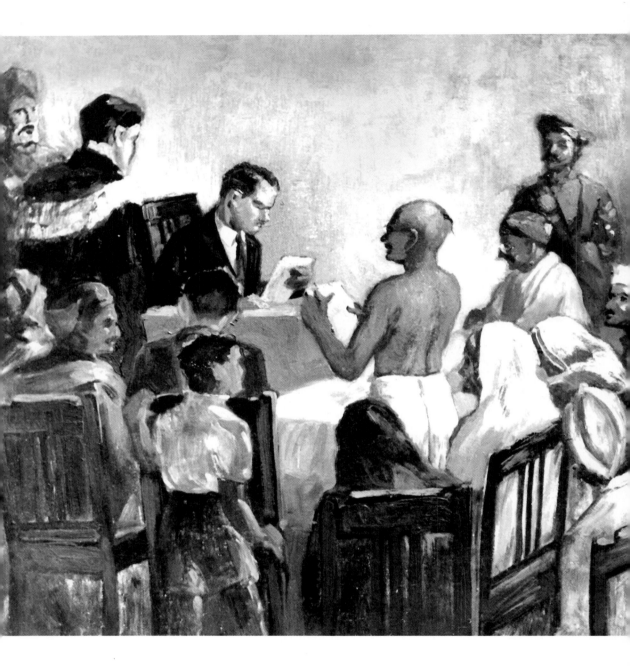

1922 *An artist's sketch of the Great Trial at the Government Circuit House, Ahmedabad.*

THE GREAT TRIAL—THE JUDGE BOWS TO THE PRISONER

It was to be a trial that transfixed the world. On March 1, 1922, Lord Reading ordered Gandhi's arrest. In a dramatic moment, Gandhi was arrested on March 10 at 10:30 p.m. The police parked their car some 80 yards from Gandhi's hut at the Sabarmati Ashram and sent word that Gandhi should consider himself under arrest and come to the waiting car when he was ready. Gandhi called a large group of ashramites to join him in prayer and the singing of a hymn. They applied a tilak on his forehead (a mark worn for religious reasons). He then walked to the car in an upbeat mood and was taken to jail. At the preliminary hearing, the day after his arrest, Gandhi gave his profession as "farmer and weaver" and pleaded guilty to the charge of writing seditious articles in *Young India*. He was kept in prison pending the trial. The "Great Trial," as it came to be known, was held in the Government Circuit House at Ahmedabad on March 18, 1922, in the court of Justice C. N. Broomfield. Gandhi and S. G. Banker, the publisher of *Young India* who had also been arrested, refused legal representation. Heavy military guards had been posted around the courthouse and surrounding streets. The trial began in a packed courtroom. After the indictment was read, the judge asked Gandhi if he wished to make a statement. Gandhi had prepared a written statement. It read: "I have no desire to conceal from this court the fact that to preach disaffection toward the existing system of government has become almost a passion with me...I do not ask for mercy. I do not plead any extenuating act. I am here, therefore, to invite and cheerfully submit to the highest penalty that can be inflicted on me for what in law is a deliberate crime

Sessions Case No. 45 of 1922.

I m p e r a t o r

Vs.

1. Mohandas Karamchand Ghandhy.
2. Shankerlal Ghelabhai Banker.

C o u r t :- Well I can only say that I do not agree. I have,
undoubtedly, a full discretion to convict the accused on their
plea if I think proper to do it, and in this particular case
I cannot see what advantage can be gained by going once more
through the evidence that was recorded before the Committing
Magistrate. As regards the point that the charge should be
investigated as fully as possible, the evidence recorded ---
before the Committing Magistrate, and as far as I know nothing
more would be recorded now -- would be evidence going to show
that Mr. Ghandhy is responsible for these particular articles.
And in the face of his plea it seems to me that it would be
futile to record further evidence on that point. As regards
the question of sentence, it goes without saying that from
the time that I have known that I should have to try the case
I have thought very carefully over the matter of sentence in
case of a conviction and although I am, of course, prepared
to hear everything that you and Mr. Ghandhy may have to say,
ik I honestly do not believe that the mere recording of all
the evidence and proceeding with the trial would make any
difference to the sentence one way or the other. I, therefore,
propose to accept the plea of the accused. Nothing, therefore,
remains but to pass sentence. Before doing that I should like
to hear what the Advocate General has to say on the question
of sentence.

18/3/1922.

W H Broomfield

Sessions Judge.

1922 *The Great Trial: a facsimile of the judgment in the court of C. N. Broomfield, district and session judge of Ahmedabad.*

and what appears to me to be the highest duty for a citizen." In conclusion, Gandhi asked for the severest penalty.

When Gandhi finished, Justice Broomfield, in an unusual gesture, bowed to the prisoner and pronounced his sentence. "The determination of a just sentence," he said, "is perhaps as difficult a proposition as any judge in this country could have to face . . . It would be impossible to ignore the fact that you are in a different category from any person I have ever tried or am likely to ever have to try . . . Even those who differ with you in politics look upon you as a man of high ideals and of noble and even saintly life." The judge then pronounced his sentence—jail for six years—adding that if the government were to reduce the sentence, "no one would be better pleased than I." He then bowed to the prisoner again. Gandhi heard the sentence, smiled and seemed cheerful. He rose to his feet and stated that the sentence was "as mild as any judge could inflict on me, and so far as the entire proceedings are concerned, I must say that I could not have expected greater courtesy." The trial had lasted exactly 100 minutes. To the embarrassment of the police, the crowds rushed toward Gandhi, presenting him with gifts, seeking his blessings and touching his feet. He was taken to Sabarmati Jail. Two days later, he would be taken by a special train to Poona and lodged in Yeravda Jail.

SURGERY UNDER THE HURRICANE LAMP

While in Yeravda Jail, Gandhi developed acute appendicitis. He was quickly moved to Sassoon Hospital in Poona on January 12, 1924. Indian physicians were put on a train for Poona from Bombay but before they could get there, Colonel Maddock, a British surgeon, informed Gandhi that they would have to operate immediately. While the operating theater was being prepared, V. S. Srinivas Shastri, head of the Servants of India Society, and Dr. Pathak, Gandhi's friend from Poona, were called and told to draft a public statement stating that Gandhi had been given the best treatment, and if anything were to go wrong there should be no anti-government agitation. Everyone realized that if Gandhi were to die, India would go up in flames. While signing this statement, Gandhi said to Maddock: "See how my hand trembles.

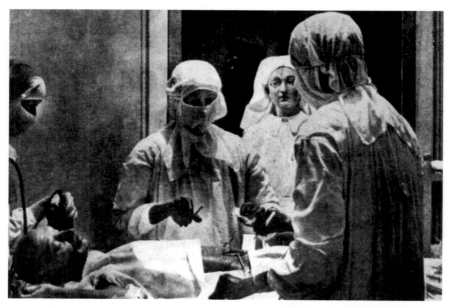

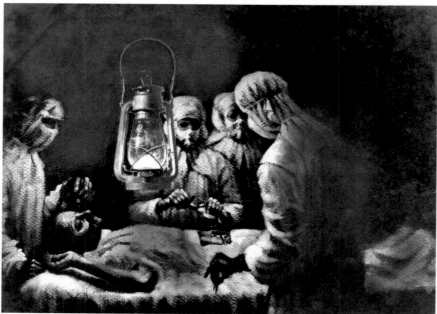

1924 *A photograph (above) of Gandhi being operated on at the Sassoon Hospital, Poona. The painting (below) shows how, when the electricity went off during the operation, the doctors had to continue by the light of a kerosene lamp.*

You will have to put this right." Maddock replied: "Oh, we will put tons and tons of strength in you." During the operation, which lasted 20 minutes, the electricity went off and the operation had to be conducted by the light of a hurricane lamp. A few hours' delay could have been dangerous for Gandhi. The operation was a success but the recovery was taking time, so the government decided to release him unconditionally. Gandhi was now free to go where he pleased. Released on February 5, his six-year sentence had lasted 22 months. To recuperate he stayed with Shanti Kumar Morarjee, an industrialist friend in Juhu, Bombay.

IT SEEMS GOD HAS BEEN DETHRONED...REINSTATE HIM IN OUR HEARTS: GANDHI ON 21-DAY FAST

Starting on July 11, 1924, a series of communal clashes between Hindus and Muslims broke out across the subcontinent, first in Delhi and then spreading rapidly to Gulbarga in the Nizam's dominions (in Hyderbad state) and Kohat in the North West Frontier Province, where Hindus were forced into a mass exodus to Rawalpindi. On September 12, riots broke out in Lucknow, which left many dead from both communities, and spread to Shahjahanpur, Allahabad and Calcutta. Gandhi, anguished by the growing militant divide between Hindus and Muslims, decided to undertake a fast. He first spoke of a 40-day fast but finally decided it would last 21 days. He began his fast on September 17 and wrote to C. F. Andrews, Motilal Nehru, Jawaharlal Nehru, Dr. Rajagopalachari, Annie Besant and some others, informing them of his decision. Gandhi was in Delhi, staying with Mohammad Ali, younger of the two Ali brothers of the Khilafat movement, to stress Hindu–Muslim unity. Before starting the fast, he issued a press release that stated: "Recent events have proved unbearable for me. My religion teaches that whenever there is distress which one cannot remove, one must fast and pray...it seems that God has been dethroned. Let us reinstate him in our hearts." A panel of doctors monitored his health and apart from some anxious moments, he withstood the fast well. Two Muslim physicians were on constant duty and C. F. Andrews opted to serve as a nurse.

1924 *Gandhi being weighed after the 21-day fast. Before the start of the fast he weighed 112 pounds (51 kilograms) and within seven days of the fast he had lost 7 pounds (3 kilograms), but he regained it quickly.*

On the last day, October 8, Andrews recalled that they were called for prayers at 4 a.m. He remembered Gandhi being wrapped in a dark shawl and he asked him whether he had slept well. "Yes, very well indeed," Gandhi replied. At about 10 a.m, Andrews writes, Gandhi asked the imam to recite the opening verses of the Koran. He then asked Andrews to sing his favorite Christian hymn: "When I Survey the Wondrous Cross." Finally, he asked Vinoba Bhave, a close associate from 1916, to recite from the Upanishads and to sing the Vaishnava hymn. It was time for the fast to be broken.

***

In 1926, Gandhi decided to retire from active politics. But his decision to retire increased his mass appeal. It was the kind of blind adulation he was not comfortable with. Wherever he went he was mobbed by frenzied hordes. His deification was complete. The role of Mahatma had become exaggerated. Even educated people believed he had divine powers. On occasions, the crowds were so large and unruly he was in danger of being crushed to death. Women turned up in large numbers, so much so that Gandhi would write: "The army of my sweethearts is daily increasing."

***

Gandhi was an incurable fund-raiser. He used his mass adulation as a convenient tool to get people to donate to his cause. He would convince the rich with whom he sat and dined to contribute to a cause for the poor, and even women and children were cajoled into donating their jewelry. Sporting a radiant smile, Gandhi would ascend the stage and make his appeal. The more expensive items offered by the crowd would be auctioned on the spot. "I have come to do business," he would state unabashedly, even charging for autographed photographs of himself.

1924 *A special meeting to honor Gandhi during one of his visits to Rajkot.*

1924 *Gandhi giving his presidential speech at the Belgaum Congress session on December 23.*

1924 *A rare moment: Gandhi at a garden party.*

Louis Fischer, in his biography *The Life of Mahatma Gandhi*, writes: "'Bania,' Gandhi's friends called him with amazement [referring to the business caste]. He was the shrewd, successful businessman, but his income and profits were never for himself. An American friend asked me to get him the Mahatma's photograph with a personal inscription. I found a photograph in the ashram, explained the request and asked him to sign. 'If you give me twenty rupees for the Harijan Fund,' Gandhi said with a smile. 'I'll give you ten.' He autographed it. When I told Devdas, he said, 'Bapu would have done it for five.'"

1927 *Gandhi portrait.*

"GO BACK SIMON"

Lord Irwin, the new viceroy, arrived in India in April 1926. For 19 months, he made no attempt to meet Gandhi, India's most influential leader. Finally, in October 1927, Gandhi received a message that the viceroy wanted to meet him to discuss the impending arrival of an official British commission, led by Sir John Simon, to make recommendations for political reforms in India. At the meeting Gandhi asked Irwin: "Is this the only business for our meeting?" When the viceroy replied in the affirmative, Gandhi got up and left without a word. Gandhi would later write to C. F. Andrews: "He is a good man with no power." About the same meeting, Irwin commented: "I have broken the ice and met Gandhi. He struck me as singularly remote from practical politics. It was rather like talking to someone who had stepped off another planet on to this for a short visit."

There was to be no Indian member, yet the Simon Commission's purpose was to decide the fate of the country. Every political party and organization decided to boycott it. When members of the commission arrived in Bombay, they were met with black flags and slogans saying "Go Back Simon." No Indian leader of any stature appeared before the commission. Instead, there was a protest in which the crowds that gathered were beaten mercilessly. Jawaharlal Nehru was assaulted with lathis (batons) in Lucknow and in a shocking incident in Lahore, Lala Lajpat Rai, a 64-year-old leading political figure in Punjab, was struck with a police lathi and died shortly afterward. In December 1928, some weeks after Rai's death, a senior police officer, Superintendent John Saunders, was assassinated. Gandhi called it a "dastardly act," but the assassin, Sardar Bhagat Singh, became a legend.

In the end, the Simon Commission produced a report, but Irwin's treatment of Gandhi had rendered it a failure.

1926 *Gandhi as Chancellor of the Gujarat Vidyapith (university) in Ahmedabad.*

1927 *Gandhi spinning at Chilaw in Sri Lanka, where he was invited by the famous freedom fighter Charles Edgar Corea. This was Gandhi's first visit to the island country.*

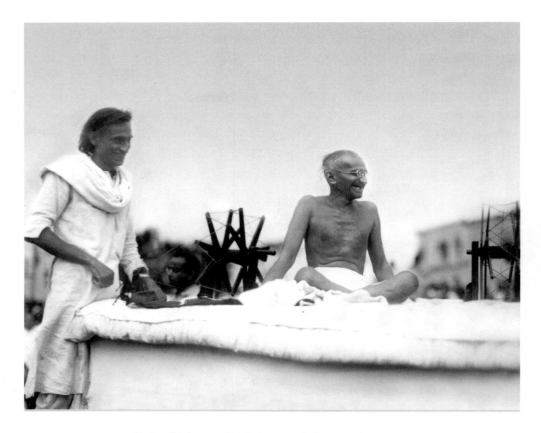

1928 *Gandhi, in one of his lighter moods during a demonstration.*

1929 *Gandhi seated with Sardar Vallabhbhai Patel (seated left on the diwan) at a public meeting in Surat.*

GANDHI AND BOSE

Born in 1897 in Cuttack, Subhas Chandra Bose was 28 years younger than Gandhi. After graduating in philosophy from Calcutta University, he attended Cambridge University and appeared for the Indian Civil Service examination in 1920. He placed fourth in the order of merit but resigned even before he became a probationer. He was deeply influenced by Bengal's tallest freedom fighter, Chittaranjan Das, and by Mahatma Gandhi, who had given a clarion call for the non-cooperation movement.

Bose arrived in India from England on July 16, 1921, and that very afternoon called upon Gandhi. He admired Gandhi tremendously, but his sentiments were to change drastically in the next decade. In 1931, Bose criticized Gandhi for not demanding complete independence at the Round Table Conference in London. Earlier in 1927, when Gandhi and other leaders were talking about dominion status for India, a young and impatient Bose shouted: "Bharat shall be free, the only question is when." In 1938, Bose won the presidentship of Congress. A year later, disregarding Gandhi's suggestion not to seek reelection, Bose contested and won again, this time defeating Gandhi's nominated candidate, Dr. Pattabhi Sitaramayya. Gandhi took this badly and announced it as his own loss. A distressed Bose resigned and formed his own party—the All India Forward Block. His disagreement with Gandhi continued.

During the Second World War, while Gandhi thought a weakened Britain would be forced to grant independence to India, Bose felt otherwise and advocated armed struggle. He was detained and put under house arrest in Calcutta. On January 17, 1941, Bose escaped to Europe

Subhas Chandra Bose with a guest at a reception held in his honor at St. Pancras Town Hall, London, on January 11, 1938.

via Afghanistan. He lived in Kabul, Moscow and Berlin, and was in Rome when Germany attacked Russia in the war. He formed his famous Azad Hind Fauj (Indian National Army) in Germany, and with the help of Hitler (whom he met once in 1942) he sailed to Japan, this time in a submarine. After an arduous journey he surfaced in Sabang, a small island in Sumatra, and was flown to Tokyo. On December 29, 1943, he unfurled the Indian tricolor in Andaman Island, thus being the first Indian to hoist the Indian flag on free Indian territory. In August 1945, he took a flight from Rangoon to Tokyo, changing planes at Saigon on August 18. On August 23, Tokyo Radio announced that the plane had crashed while taking off from Taihoku in Taiwan. Bose went missing and was thought to have been killed in the crash. According to his biographer and nephew Sisir Kumar Bose, in his last message to Gandhi conveyed through Radio Rangoon, Bose reported the great successes of his army and concluded: "Father of our nation! In this holy war for Indian liberation we ask for your blessings and good wishes."

A DIET PLAN FOR BOSE FROM GANDHI

1. Tea or coffee I do not consider to be essential to health. They often do harm. They may remain harmless, if tea is weak and straw color and coffee drunk with plenty of milk with only a spoonful or two of coffee.
2. If received fresh from the udder well cleaned and from a healthy cow, milk drunk fresh unboiled unwarmed is the best food.
3. Leafy vegetables must always be taken, better if taken as salads. All leaves are not edible in the raw state. Onion, pumpkin with the skin, pandora, brinjal, lady's finger, turnips, carrots, parsnips, cabbage, cauliflower are good additions to leaves. Potatoes and starchy tubers should be taken sparingly.
4. Dates are a fine food for a healthy stomach. Raisins are more digestible.
5. Garlic and onion in a raw state are strongly recommended in the West. I take raw garlic regularly for blood pressure. It is the best antitoxin for internal use. It is also recommended for tubercular patients.
   I think the prejudice against these two harmless vegetables is due to the odor which is the essence of them and it arose with the rise of Vaishnavism. Ayurveda sings the praise of both unstintingly. Garlic is called poor man's musk and so it is. I do not know what villagers would do without garlic and onion.
6. Yes, lemons and gur [jaggery] or honey are a good substitute for sweet oranges.

While under house arrest in 1936 at his brother's house near Darjeeling, where he was shifted from the prison because of his failing health, Bose was not allowed to correspond freely with the outside world. However, Gandhi's letter prescribing a diet and natural cure for Bose was delivered to him.

1930 *A huge procession through the streets of Bombay, composed largely of women, carrying banners advocating the boycott of foreign goods. This demonstration was carried out at the time when an unfair tax on salt caused bitter resentment among the people of India.*

PURNA SWARAJ: JANUARY 26 AS INDEPENDENCE DAY

The Simon Commission's approach had made the Indian political leadership determined to achieve complete independence. The Purna Swaraj declaration, or Declaration of the Complete Independence of India, was promulgated by Gandhi on behalf of the Indian National Congress on January 26, 1930. The people of India were asked to observe January 26 as Independence Day and the flag of India was hoisted publicly across the country. Gandhi envisioned a massive non-violent uprising. He wrote to Lord Irwin, warning him of the impending protest and seeking a way out: "I must not be misunderstood. Though I hold the British rule in India to be a curse, I do not intend harm to a single Englishman.... I know that in embarking on non-violence, I shall be running what might be termed a mad risk. But the victories of truth have never been won without risk." The letter was carried by an English follower, Reginald Reynolds, who arrived at the viceroy's house wearing a Gandhi cap and shorts made of khadi. From then on, Reynolds was affectionately called "Angad," after the monkey who carried Lord Rama's message to Ravana. The viceroy's reply was an expression of regret that the protest would bring Gandhi in conflict with the law, to which Gandhi responded: "I repudiate the law and regard it my sacred duty to break the mournful monotony of the compulsory peace that is choking the heart of a nation." Gandhi decided the protest this time would be characteristically symbolic—he proposed to overthrow an Empire with a fistful of salt!

"...policemen rushed upon the advancing marchers and rained blows on their heads with their steel-shod lathis. Not one of the marchers raised an arm to fend off the blows. They went down like nine-pins. Those struck down fell sprawling...with fractured skulls or broken shoulders.... The survivors, without breaking ranks, marched on until struck down. When the first column was laid low, another advanced. In 18 years of reporting in 22 countries...I have never witnessed such harrowing scenes..."

WEBB MILLER
REPORTING FOR UNITED PRESS OF AMERICA

1930-1939

Salt Satyagraha
Round Table Conferences, London

1930 *Revolution in India. Gandhi and followers march to Jalalpur in Surat district, where Dandi was situated. The salt law was to be contravened there.*

"I DO ASK YOU TO RETURN HERE ONLY AS DEAD MEN OR WINNERS OF SWARAJ"

On February 27, 1930, Gandhi wrote an editorial in *Young India* headlined "When I Am Arrested" and explained the evils of the salt tax. The British had suppressed production of salt in India in favor of imports from Britain. The Salt Act imposed a hefty tax that dramatically increased the price of salt. In protest, Gandhi announced his plan for a Salt Satyagraha, a march to Dandi, on the sea coast in Gujarat, where he intended to break the salt law, which made possession of salt from sources other than the British monopoly a punishable crime. He saw it as a symbolic act of protest that would appeal to those most affected by the hugely burdensome tax and he knew that salt, an essential ingredient in Indian homes, would strike a chord with the people. Gandhi emphasized the basic qualification of volunteers who would march with him—a proven commitment to non-violence. His initial list included those who had gone through the rigid discipline of the ashram. As he put it: "The first sacrificial offering was to be of the purest possible character." Gandhi had planned the Salt March as a point of no return. "For my part, I have taken the pledge not to return home," he said, "but I do ask you to return here only as dead men or winners of swaraj . . . even if the ashram is on fire, we will not return."

"ON BENDED KNEES I ASKED FOR BREAD AND I RECEIVED STONE INSTEAD"

Gandhi's Salt Satyagraha was to be a watershed moment in the civil disobedience movement. Gandhi described the salt tax as "the most inhuman poll tax that human ingenuity could devise." The wholesale price of salt was 10 pies (paisa) a maund (equivalent to 84 pounds/38 kilograms) while the tax on it was 20 annas (16 annas = 1 rupee), or 2,400 percent tax on the sale price. In his letter to Lord Irwin on March 2, 1930, Gandhi said that British rule had "impoverished the dumb millions by a system of progressive exploitation and by a ruinously expensive military and civil administration," which the country could ill afford. The administration, he said, was demonstrably the most expensive in the world. He then added: "Take your own salary. It is over Rs [rupees] 21,000 per month, besides many other indirect additions. The British Prime Minister gets £5,000 per year; that is over Rs 5,400 per month at the present rate of exchange. You are getting Rs 700 [11,200 annas] per day against India's average income of nearly 2 annas per day. Thus you are getting much over 5,000 times India's average income...I know that you do not need the salary you get...but a system that provides for such an arrangement deserves to be summarily scrapped." The letter announced his decision to launch a non-violent agitation. Lord Irwin did not reply to Gandhi's letter. Instead, his secretary expressed his regret regarding Gandhi's plan, which sounded more like a warning to Gandhi. "On bended knees I asked for bread and I received stone instead," said Gandhi. The die had been cast. Gandhi's civil disobedience movement, the Salt Satyagraha, announced in March 1930, would shake the Empire to its foundations.

MARCHER WITH A DIFFERENCE: KHARAG BAHADUR SINGH

Gandhi commenced his epic march, accompanied by 79 volunteers, of 241 miles to Dandi, a distance he covered in 24 days. The youngest marcher, Vitthal Liladhar Takkar, a student from Ashram School, was 16 years old, and the oldest was Gandhi, at 61. The volunteers marched in columns of three led by Gandhi carrying a bamboo stick, with Pyarelal, his secretary, behind him carrying Gandhi's and his own bags. The marchers were generally ashramites or those associated with the ashram.

The marchers also included, strangely enough, a man charged with murder. His name was Kharag Bahadur Singh, a commerce graduate and secretary of the Gurkha Samaj, an association of Gurkhas. He had stayed at the ashram earlier, but on February 26, 1927, had made headlines for stabbing a rich Marwari, Hiralal Agarwalla, in Calcutta. The provocation was a young Nepali girl who had been sold into sex slavery. She was kept in Hiralal's house for five months while he and his friends allegedly raped her every night. She managed to escape and her story came to the notice of the Samaj. Kharag Bahadur met her in the hospital and was so incensed by the brutality to which she had been subjected that he decided to avenge her. He went to Hiralal's house disguised as a trader. Once there, he pulled out his khukri (a Nepalese knife) and stabbed Agarwalla. He died and Kharag Bahadur was tried for murder.

In his defense, he told the court he had followed the doctrine of non-violence practiced by Mahatma Gandhi from 1918 when he was barely 13. He asked the judge to "hear the causes that led me to travel so long a distance, from 'ahimsa' to 'himsa' in so short a time." Like a true Gandhian he pleaded for a maximum sentence. He was, however, freed after two years for good conduct, and he wrote to Gandhi to allow him to join the march. He wanted to atone for the sins committed by Gurkhas who opened fire at Jallianwala, killing hundreds of fellow Indians. Despite protests from some marchers about his past, Gandhi let him be a part of the Dandi March. Kharag Bahadur continued with his agitation and took an active part in various other movements led by Gandhi. He was arrested in Ahmedabad, where he refused to enter the jail unless the main gate was fully open, enabling him to carry the national flag upright.

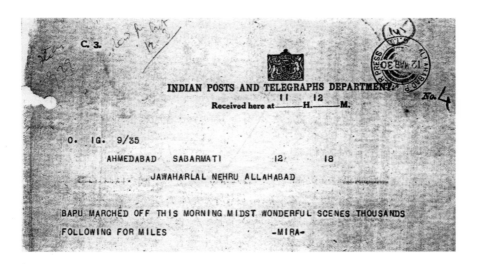

1930 *Telegram to Jawaharlal Nehru sent on March 12 by Mirabehn (who became one of Gandhi's closest followers) informing him of the departure of protesters for the Dandi March.*

Kasturba (extreme right) with Kamaladevi Chattopadhyay (center) during the Salt Satyagraha, photographed with a fellow supporter.

"WE ARE WARRIORS' WIVES"

Kasturba (Ba) Gandhi came into her own during preparations for the Dandi March. Three generations of her family took part in the march—her husband, her son Manilal and grandson, Kanti, who was 19 years old. She was inspired by the powerful symbolism of the march but naturally worried for her family. Gandhi had made it clear to the marchers: "You must be prepared to die. The British may use guns but you must not fight back."

Ba had woken before 4 a.m. on March 12, the day the march commenced, and dressed quickly. She had a lot to do that day. She was also aware of the crowd of journalists and photographers who had camped overnight outside the ashram. Ba made her rounds, waking everybody for early prayers, and also overseeing preparations for the food that the marchers would carry with them. As they gathered, the wives of the marchers, who would be left behind, had mixed emotions. Susheela, Manilal's wife, burst into tears while saying good-bye to her husband, and ran into Ba's arms. Nearly every woman was in tears, not knowing the fate of the men to whom they were bidding farewell.

Ba then came forward, according to her biographers—her grandson Arun and his wife, Sunanda—who gave the following account in their book published in India, *The Untold Story of Kasturba: Wife of Mahatma Gandhi*:

"'Our men are warriors,' Kasturba declared. 'We are warriors' wives. We must give the men courage. If we are brave, they will be brave.' Ba stood looking into her husband's eyes for a long wordless moment. In her left hand was a small brass plate, filled with a waxy mixture of ghee and vermillion which she had prepared earlier that morning. Slowly, solemnly she dipped the middle finger of her right hand into the bowl, then lightly touched Bapu's forehead imprinting on his brow the familiar red kumkum dot.... It was an invocation of good fortune for the departing traveler and prayer for his safe return.

"Ba was not through. She began moving down the column of marchers, carefully anointing every brow with a kumkum dot. As she passed, each man's face revealed what a priceless farewell gift he had just received."

THE "BATTLE OF RIGHT VERSUS MIGHT"

The marchers left Sabarmati accompanied by a large media contingent. The route was strewn with flowers, and villagers lined up to greet them with India's national colors as they passed. It was a grueling challenge. There was a horse meant for Gandhi, though he never used it, and two bullock carts. "Less than twelve miles a day in two stages with not much luggage is child's play!" said Gandhi. They got up at 4 a.m. and after the daily routine of prayer and breakfast left the ashram at 5 a.m. sharp. Gandhi would halt for the night but continue to spin for an hour and write by moonlight, jotting notes and updating his diary. Gandhi developed blisters on his feet and his rheumatism started acting up. He refused to be carried or stop walking, knowing the accompanying British media would play up any weakness. They passed through Aslali, where some marchers were forced to travel by bullock carts because of blisters. One cart also doubled as a shop selling khadi (cloth) and the other carried Gandhi's commode and charkhas (spinning wheels)—both necessities whenever he traveled. On March 20, five days before Gandhi's expected arrival in Jalalpur, the British had hired workers to remove natural salt deposits from the area. An extraordinary confrontation was building. At Dandi, Gandhi bathed in the sea, then stepped on the seashore, where salt was deposited by the incoming tide. He then scooped up some salt. In doing so, in one dramatic moment he broke the law prohibiting the possession of indigenous salt.

When asked for a message by an American correspondent, Gandhi wrote: "I want world sympathy in this battle of Right versus Might."

1930 *Gandhi and his entourage marching during the Salt Satyagraha.*

"IN 18 YEARS OF REPORTING IN 22 COUNTRIES…I HAVE NEVER WITNESSED SUCH HARROWING SCENES"

Gandhi's son Manilal ran ahead of the marchers as they were approaching the salt flats at Dharasana, 20 miles away from Dandi. The flats were well secured with barbed wire and guarded by 400 policemen.

The bloody confrontation between Gandhi's salt marchers and the British forces in Dharasana was dramatically captured by Webb Miller, a correspondent for the United Press of America, who was present at the scene. "In complete silence, the Gandhi supporters halted a hundred yards from the stockade. The officers ordered the marchers to retreat. They continued to advance…. Suddenly, at a word of command, scores of native policemen rushed upon the advancing marchers and rained blows on their heads with their steel-shod lathis. Not one of the marchers raised an arm to ward off the blows. They went down like nine-pins. From where I stood, I heard the sickening whack of clubs on unprotected skulls… Those struck down fell sprawling, unconscious or writhing with fractured skulls or broken shoulders. The survivors, without breaking ranks, silently and doggedly marched on till struck down." Another group of 25 men came forward and sat down. Webb Miller recorded that the police "continued savagely kicking the men in the abdomen and testicles." Still another group took their place. Miller wrote: "Enraged, the police dragged them by their arms and feet and threw them into the ditch. One was dragged into a ditch where I stood and the splash of his body doused me with muddy water…. Hour after hour, stretcher-bearers carried back a stream of inert, bleeding bodies." Miller observed that 25 native riflemen were posted on a knoll overlooking the compound. The satyagrahis were aware that any minute, the order might be given to open fire. Miller counted 320 wounded marchers in the field hospital. "In 18 years of reporting in 22 countries…I have never witnessed such harrowing scenes," he wrote. His report was flashed around the world and Dharasana would cast a long, dark shadow over the British Raj.

1930 *The violence meted out toward Gandhi and his volunteers during the Salt Satyagraha stirred the wrath of the nation, and unrest escalated everywhere.*

1930 *Gandhi, with his back toward the camera, photographed after taking a bath in the sea at Dandi on the morning of April 6—this was akin to ritual bathing after a long pilgrimage.*

1930 *Gandhi (rear left) with other marchers and followers, breaking the salt law. The first fistful of salt was lifted at Dandi on April 6.*

1930 *Gandhi at a public meeting at Bhimrad, Surat district. It was here on April 9 that Gandhi, with other satyagrahis, violated the salt law again.*

1930 Above: *Gandhi's secretary, Mahadev Desai, addressing a large crowd of 100,000 men and women near Elis Bridge in Ahmedabad before the Dandi Yatra.*
Facing page: *Gandhi volunteers photographed in Kapadwanj, in Kheda district of Gujarat, watching fellow members of their band march toward their destination and make salt.*

"HAVE YOU COME TO ARREST ME?"

Following the Dandi March, rumors circulated that Gandhi's arrest was imminent. The decision to arrest him was finally taken on May 3, 1930. Gandhi was at Karadi, a village near Dandi, along with 40 of his followers. Shortly after midnight on May 5, some 30 armed policemen entered the camp led by two British officers. Gandhi was asleep in a small reed hut while the others were sleeping under trees. He was awakened by flashlights shining on his face.

He sat up and asked: "Have you come to arrest me?" The officer replied, "Yes," and inquired whether his name was Mohandas Karamchand Gandhi. At this, Gandhi requested permission to clean his teeth. He was told to make it quick. Gandhi then asked if he was being arrested under Section 124A of the Indian Penal Code. The officer replied in the negative, showing a written order. "Would you mind reading it to me?" asked Gandhi. The order stated that Gandhi was being arrested under Regulation XXXV of 1827 and he was to be immediately sent to Yeravda Jail. Regulation XXXV had been enacted at the time of the East India Company's dominance and was used against rebellious princes.

The police officers were nervous and wanted to get the arrest over quickly, fearing trouble. Gandhi remained calm, calling his followers to sing "*Raghupati Raghav Raja Ram*," before he walked toward the waiting police truck. By early morning, the news of his arrest had spread across India. However, on January 26, 1931, India's Independence Day, Lord Irwin unconditionally released Gandhi and other Congress leaders.

1930 *Gandhi photographed before his arrest reading a newspaper at Dandi.*

(True Copy)

"Dilkhusa"
Panchgani.

July 17th 1944.

Dear Prime Minister,

You are reported to have the desire to crush the 'naked faqir', as you are said to have described me. I have been long trying to be a faqir and that naked - a more difficult task. I therefore regard the expression as a compliment, though unintended. I approach you then as such and ask you to trust and use me for the sake of your people and mine and through them those of the world.

Your sincere friend

Sd. (M.K.Gandhi)

Winston Churchill contemptuously called Gandhi a "half-naked fakir" in 1931. Thirteen years later, Gandhi replied to Churchill with this letter in an effort to reach out to him, as the move toward the transfer of power was building up in India.

GANDHI-IRWIN PACT

On his release from Yeravda Jail, Gandhi wrote to Lord Irwin, asking for face-to-face discussions. The First Round Table Conference had taken place in London in November 1930, but no Congress leader had attended it. Lord Irwin and Gandhi met on February 27, 1931. According to Louis Fischer: "On 1 March, Gandhi came to Irwin at 2:30 p.m. The discussions continued till his dinner time. Miss Slade had brought his dinner—forty dates and a pint of goat's milk—to the palace and Gandhi ate it in the presence of the Viceroy..." At about 6 p.m. Gandhi left for Congress leader Dr. Mukhtar Ansari's house in Daryaganj, but he returned, on foot—a walk of five miles—later that evening. He remained with Irwin till past midnight. He got back home at 2 a.m. to a waiting Congress Working Committee. Finally, after much discussion and tough bargaining, the Gandhi–Irwin Pact was signed on March 5. The details of the pact were announced on the same day. The essential agreements were that civil disobedience would be called off, political prisoners released, salt manufacturing permitted in specific coastal areas, and that Congress leaders would attend the Second Round Table Conference in London. There was no mention of independence or dominion status. Gandhi declared: "The goal...complete independence. India cannot be satisfied with anything less."

In London, Winston Churchill would show his contempt for Gandhi and Irwin when he thundered: "It is alarming...nauseating to see Mr. Gandhi, a seditious Middle Temple lawyer now posing as a fakir...striding half naked up the steps of the viceregal palace, while he is still organizing and conducting a campaign of civil disobedience, to parley on equal terms with the representative of the King Emperor..." He did not know it then, but the "half-naked fakir" would be coming to London, to attend the Round Table Conference as the sole representative of Congress.

Thirteen years later, Gandhi replied to Churchill's outburst with a letter (facing page). But the letter was never delivered, and it was only a year later that Gandhi made it public. However, it was too late as Churchill had already been voted out by the British public.

1931 *Gandhi photographed before departing for London to attend the Second Round Table Conference. Also in the picture are (front row, left to right) Madan Mohan Malaviya, Sarojini Naidu (face back to the camera) and Kasturba Gandhi (extreme right).*

At noon on August 29, 1931, Gandhi boarded the *SS Rajputana* in Bombay to sail to London to attend the Second Round Table Conference. He was accompanied by Madan Mohan Malaviya, Sarojini Naidu and his son Devdas, as well as Mirabehn (Madeleine Slade), who considered Gandhi her spiritual father, and the industrialist G. D. Birla. A huge crowd had gathered to see them off. "There is every chance I will return empty-handed," he told them, but once on board, he seemed in a jovial mood, joking with the captain about being his prisoner, and was seen enjoying himself on the ship's bridge.

1931 *Gandhi bidding farewell to his countrymen before his ship set sail for England.*

Gandhi and his party were booked into second-class cabins. On an inspection tour, he noticed that Mahadev Desai and some others had brought a large number of leather suitcases and the cabins were heaped with expensive luggage. There was even an American-made folding camp bed that someone had gifted for Gandhi to use as a deckchair.

"What is all this?" Gandhi asked. Mirabehn explained that these things had been collected in the haste of last-minute preparations for the voyage, to which Gandhi retorted: "If you want to travel with such luggage, you should live with those who like that." He personally saw to it that seven suitcases and trunks were offloaded at Aden, to be shipped back to Bombay.

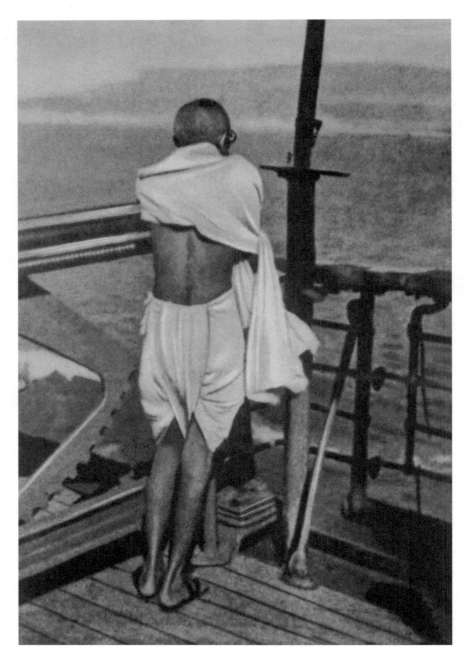

1931 *Following his routine of writing letters, spinning and reading, Gandhi spent most of his days on the deck of the ship.*

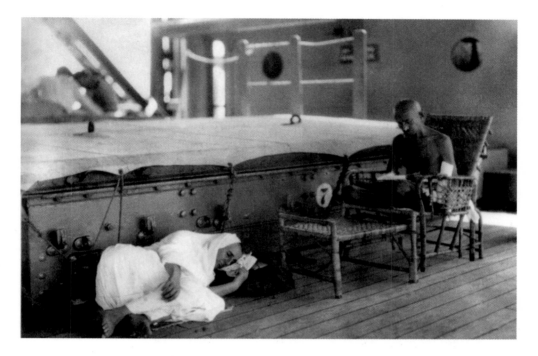

1931 *Gandhi at work on the sun deck during his voyage to England. Mirabehn is seen taking a nap.*

On board the *SS Rajputana*, Gandhi had insisted that he and his party should travel by the lowest class, which was classified as second class. However, since he was such a famous passenger, the captain invited him to the bridge, where he examined the sextant and Gandhi even steered the ship for a brief period. He spent all of his time on the ship's deck, meeting other passengers, playing with children and choosing one corner where he could receive visitors and dictate letters.

Aboard the ship, his routine was exactly like it was at the ashram. He would rise early for prayers, then spend time on deck spinning, writing letters and eating food that had been brought especially for him, mainly fruit and goat's milk. At Suez, he received a telegram from Nahas Pasha, leader of the Egyptian Wafd Party, addressed to "The Great Leader Al Mahatma Gandhi." Once the ship docked, a horde of Egyptian cameramen came on board and took photographs showing him in a relaxed mood, as if he did not know he was being photographed.

MEET THE KING

1931 *A cartoon and a portrait of Gandhi breaking bread with the king. Seated (L to R) in the portrait are: Sarojini Naidu, Queen Mary, King George V and Madan Mohan Malaviya, with Gandhi holding the king's hand.*

Gandhi Sips Boiled Goat's Milk at Tea Given by King

LONDON, Nov. 5.—(AP)—Wearing a loincloth and shawl, Mahatma Gandhi attended a formal reception today at Buckingham palace and stood before the king from whom he has been trying for years to wrest the vast Indian empire.

It was the first time the humble little Nationalist leader, who claims to represent 60,000,000 untouchables and 300,000,000 other Indians, had met George V., and he seemed to like it immensely.

"The king and queen were most friendly and gracious," he said. "I also liked the prince of Wales."

Wales Flies to Party.

The prince had come by airplane from Liverpool to attend the stately tea party at the royal palace to which about 600 guests were invited.

Before the function was half over Gandhi abruptly left the palace, for he has no patience with social gatherings and the conversation usual on such occasions bores him.

The mahatma showed none of the signs of awe frequently manifested by the subjects of the king. Rather, he comported himself with the oriental placidity that is so strong a factor in his character.

The guests were not required to make any obeisance before the king and queen. Such a gesture would have been distasteful to the Nationalist leader. When the king, dressed in morning attire, offered his hand Gandhi shook it heartily and, after bowing reverently, raised both his hands in front of his chest in the manner of a Buddhist priest—the most decorous form of Indian greeting.

Furnishings Daze Gandhi.

The reception took place in the famous picture gallery of the palace. Gandhi appeared dazed as his bespectacled eyes swept over the regal furnishings of the gallery and its galaxy of kings, queens, and other notables of the past whose portraits looked down upon him.

The mahatma's shawl was gossamer, and it had been freshly washed by Miss Madeline Slade, his British born disciple, but his dress contrasted strangely with the dazzling silken robes of India's ruling princes, who also were among the guests. The bejeweled turbans, diamond earrings, pearl necklaces, and [bracelets?] of the princes rep[resented] inc[al]culable wealth.

While the others [par]takes, and ice cream [he could be a real ro] humbly clad guest, [provided with a bowl] milk. Both the king a[nd] chatted with him brie[fly]

After the party wa[s] intimated that the co[nversation be]tween himself and the [king con]sisted mostly of plea[sant ques]tions an answers abou[t ...] and its effect on a m[inority?] come from India.

Asked if the king [had given] encouragement to his h[opes for] Independence, the mah[atma] ward heaven, put his palm and said, "Only [en]couragement, not king[...]"

Chicago Tribune   Oct. 31, 1931

Gandhi to Go to King's Party in Loin Cloth

BY JOHN STEELE.

[Chicago Tribune Press Service.]

[Pictures on page 3.]

LONDON, Oct. 30.—Mahatma Gandhi, loin cloth and all, is going to see the king and queen. He has received a "command" from the lord chamberlain to attend a party at Buckingham palace next Thursday. India's "holy man" has announced that he will wear his "habitual dress of loin cloth, shawl and sandals."

In the event King George objects to the loin cloth, the mahatma stated that he would refuse the royal invitation.

Indians and others are wondering whether he will repeat his performance of 1921 when he met the prince of Wales in India. He was conferring with Sir Tej Bahadur Sapru, moderate Indian leader, when the prince called. Gandhi threw himself at the prince's feet, praying, "Be good to India!"

1931 *The British press could not get enough of the curiosity that was Gandhi.*

Gandhi reached London on September 12, 1931, for the Second Round Table Conference. While in London, he was invited to Buckingham Palace for tea with King George V and Queen Mary. He arrived wearing a dhoti, sandals, a shawl and his dangling watch. Later, when asked whether he was wearing enough clothing, he replied: "The king had enough for both of us." King George was a gruff character, clearly not amused at the letters he had been receiving from his viceroys about the "little upstart" Gandhi. He expressed his disapproval to Gandhi, especially about the

1931 *Gandhi with the great Hollywood actor and showman Charlie Chaplin.*

boycott of his son, the Prince of Wales, during his visit to India. Gandhi replied: "I did not boycott your son, Your Majesty, but the official representative of the British Crown." The king then told Gandhi: "I won't have you stirring up trouble in my Empire." Gandhi maintained a dignified silence. Visibly annoyed, Gandhi, when asked about the meeting, said it had been a boring affair.

Gandhi was also invited by Britain's wartime prime minister, David Lloyd George, to his estate in Surrey, where they had a three-hour conversation. Some years later, Gandhi's biographer Louis Fischer wrote about the visit with some interesting insights. Fischer had met Lloyd George in 1938 and asked him about Gandhi's visit. Lloyd George said that all of the servants had come out to meet Gandhi, something they had never done for any of his other visitors. He also mentioned a black cat that no one had seen before, and which mysteriously appeared and sat on Gandhi's lap. When Gandhi left, it, too, vanished. The cat never showed up again.

1931 *Gandhi recording for Columbia Broadcasting Company at Kingsley Hall, London.*

Charlie Chaplin was keen to meet Gandhi. Gandhi had never heard of Chaplin or seen his movies, but when told that Chaplin came from a poor family, Gandhi agreed to meet him. They had a friendly argument about machinery, which Chaplin felt was a great boon to mankind, but Gandhi's view was that it made India dependent on Great Britain and the only way to reduce that dependency was to boycott all machinery. Gandhi sold the idea of the spinning wheel and homespun cloth to Chaplin.

The Columbia Broadcasting Company, one of the premier music and recording companies of the time, requested that Gandhi record a speech for posterity. He agreed to the recording, but only if it were non-political in nature, and chose to read one of his old published articles on God—an "unseen power that defied proof."

INDIAN
ROUND-TABLE CONFERENCE
1930-31

Cartoon of the First Round Table Conference, 1930, at which the Congress was not represented.

1. Rt Hon. Ramsay MacDonald
2. Lord Sankey
3. Rt Hon. J. H. Thomas
4. Sir Samuel Hoare
5. Earl Deel

6. Marquess of Zetland
7. Hon. Oliver Stanley
8. Sir Robert Hamilton
9. Marquess of Reading
10. Marquess of Lothian

29. Sir Ghulam Hussain Hidayatullah
30. Sir Shah Nawaz Bhutto
31. Khan Bahadur Hafiz Hidayat Husain
32. Dr. Shafa'at Ahmad Khan
33. Nawab Sir Sahibzada Abdul Quiyum
34. Sir Sayed Sultan Ahmed
35. Mr. M. A. Jinnah
36. H. H. The Aga Khan
37. Sir Muhammad Shafi
38. Nawab Sir Ahmad Said Khan
39. Mr. Fazl-Ul-Huq
40. Captain Raja Sher Muhammad Khan
41. Maulana Muhammad Ali
42. Mr. Zafrullah Khan
43. Begum Shan Nawaz
44. Mrs. Subbarayan
45. Mr. B. V. Jadhav
46. Diwan Bahadur Ramaswami Mudaliyar
47. Sir A. P. Patro
48. Raja of Parlakimedi
49. Kunwar Bisheshwar Dayal
50. Maharajadhiraja of Darbhanga
51. Dr. Narendra Nath Law
52. Sir Cowasji Jehangir
53. Mr. H. P. Mody
54. Sir Provash Chandra Mitter
55. Sir Bhupendra Nath Mitra
56. Mr. J. N. Basu
57. Mr. C. Barooah
58. Diwan Bahadur M. Ramachandra Rao
59. Mr. C. Y. Chintamani
60. Sir C. P. Ramaswami Aiyar
61. Sir Pheroze Sethna
62. Sir Chimanlal Setalvad
63. Sir Tej Bahadur Sapru
64. Rt Hon. Srinivasa Sastri
65. Rt Hon. A. Henderson
66. Rt Hon. W. Wedgwood Benn
67. Mr. O. De Glanville
68. U Ba Pe
69. U Aung Thin
70. Mr. M. M. Ohn Ghine
71. Mr. C. E. Wood
72. Sir Hubert Carr
73. Mr. T. F. Gavin Jones
74. Lieut. Col. H. A. J. Gidney
75. Rao Bahadur A. T. Pannir Selvam
76. Mr. K. T. Paul
77. Dr. B. R. Ambedkar
78. Rao Bahadur Srinivasan
79. Mr. N. M. Joshi
80. Mr. B. Shiva Rao
81. Sardar Sahib Ujjal Singh
82. Sardar Sampuran Singh
83. Raja Narendra Nath
84. Dr. B. S. Moonje
85. Mr. S. B. Tambe
86. Mr. M. R. Jayakar

11. Mr. Isaac Foot
12. H. H. The Maharaja of Alwar
13. H. H. The Maharaja Gaekvar of Baroda
14. H. H. The Nawab of Bhopal
15. H. H. The Maharaja of Bikaner
16. H. H. The Maharaja Rana of Dholpur
17. H. H. The Maharaja of Jammu and Kashmir
18. H. H. The Maharaja of Nawanagar
19. H. H. The Maharaja of Patiala
20. H. H. The Maharaja of Rewa
21. H. H. The Chief Sahib of Sangli
22. Sir Prabhashanikar Pattani
23. Sir Mahubhai Mehta
24. Sardar Sahibzada Sultan Ahmed Khan
25. Nawab Sir Muhammad Akbar Hydari
26. Sir Mirza Muhammad Ismail
27. Colonel K. N. Haksar
28. Mr. A. H. Ghuznavi

THE ROUND TABLE CONFERENCES

TO THE CONFERENCE

By 1930, the British government, following the report submitted by the Simon Commission in May that year, felt it was necessary to look at administrative and constitutional reforms in India. To get a feel of whether India was ready for dominion status under the British monarchy, three Round Table Conferences were initiated and organized by the government. The First Round Table Conference was inaugurated by Lord Irwin on November 12, 1930. Among others, it was attended by 16 British representatives led by Prime Minister Ramsay MacDonald. Almost 60 Indians, including two women, representing various religions, castes and classes, regions and governments, attended the conference. The Indian delegation was led by Aga Khan III without any representation from the Indian National Congress. Gandhi at the time was in Yeravda Jail. The conference proved inconclusive.

Following the Gandhi–Irwin Pact in March 1931, Gandhi was persuaded to attend the Second Round Table Conference in September as the sole representative of Congress. This conference had 112 delegates, with the usual mix of representatives of the British government, rajas and maharajas. Sarojini Naidu, Madan Mohan Malaviya, Mahadev Desai, Pyarelal, Madeleine Slade, G. D. Birla and Gandhi's son Devdas were Gandhi's special invitees. Dr. B. R. Ambedkar, the

Dalit leader, challenged Gandhi's right to speak for the "untouchables." Ambedkar demanded a separate electorate and reserved seats for Dalits. The Muslim delegates also demanded a separate Muslim electorate. Ambedkar and leaders of other groups formed a unified front of anti-Congress minorities at the conference to prevent any endorsement of Gandhi's views. Gandhi later told journalist William Shirer that he had never been more humiliated. Issues that should have been debated at home were bitterly discussed in the open in London. The British seized this opportunity to tighten their grip on India instead of loosening it, which was the main objective. Gandhi came back disappointed and empty-handed.

The British went ahead with a Third Round Table Conference starting in November 1932, which lasted close to six weeks and was a non-starter.

Gandhi flanked by Lord Sankey and Pandit Madan Mohan Malaviya at the Second Round Table Conference at St. James' Palace, London, in 1931. Other prominent Indians (clockwise after Pandit Malaviya) are: Rangaswami Iyer, Tej Bahadur Sapru, M. R. Jayakar, Srinivas Sastri, P. C. Mitter, Dr. B. R. Ambedkar, B. S. Moonje, Shafat Ahmed Khan and Zafrulla Khan.

"FAREWELL AND BEWARE. I CAME A SEEKER AFTER PEACE. I RETURN FEARFUL OF WAR."

The Second Round Table Conference concluded on December 1, 1931. The 11 weeks it lasted had been an ordeal for Gandhi and he was exhausted and depressed at what had taken place. He crossed the English Channel to France, where he told the *Bristol Evening News*: "My last words to England must be: 'Farewell and beware. I came a seeker after peace. I return fearful of war.'" Over the years, he had received numerous invitations to speak—from the USA and from Sweden, Norway, Denmark, Germany, Holland, Switzerland and other European countries. An invitation from a Berlin-based institute offered him 1,000 Deutsche Marks for

1931 *Gandhi with Romain Rolland at Villeneuve-Montreux, Switzerland, in December. Rolland's book* Mahatma Gandhi *was published in 1924.*

each lecture—a huge sum at the time. A public meeting was held in the largest cinema house in Paris and it was packed to capacity. He had canceled all his European engagements except one: a meeting with Romain Rolland, the French polymath and Nobel laureate who was living in Switzerland. Says Louis Fischer: "Before Gandhi's arrival on 5 December, Rolland had received hundreds of letters connected with the Mahatma's visit: an Italian wanted to know from Gandhi what numbers would win in the next national lottery; a group of Swiss musicians offered to serenade Gandhi under his window every night; the Syndicate of the Milkmen of Leman volunteered to supply 'the King of India' with dairy products during his stay." Gandhi and his party were Rolland's guests for six days, during which time he and Gandhi met and talked for several hours each day. During their stay, Pyarelal recalled Rolland playing a movement by Beethoven on the piano for Gandhi. It was, he said: "a spiritual experience."

GANDHI AND MUSSOLINI

The Italian government invited Gandhi to visit. He traveled to Rome, opting to stay with General Moris, a friend of Romain Rolland's. On the day of his arrival he was invited to meet with Benito Mussolini, "Il Duce." Accompanied by Mirabehn, Mahadev Desai and General Moris, Gandhi reached Mussolini's office, where they were met by an usher. Then the huge doors opened and Il Duce got up from his massive desk and met Gandhi halfway before escorting the group back to his desk. While Gandhi and Mirabehn sat down in the two chairs provided for them, General Moris and Mahadev were left standing. Mussolini started asking Gandhi questions. He asked about the Round Table Conference and India's economic situation. He also asked if East and West could meet, to which Gandhi replied: "Why not? West has been exploiting East. The moment exploitation stops, the door will be open for cooperation between the two." The meeting lasted about 15 minutes. Once outside, Gandhi commented to Mahadev: "His eyes are those of a cat, did you notice?" Mahadev replied: "More like the eyes of Satan." Later, when asked about his impressions of Mussolini, Gandhi answered: "He looked like a butcher."

According to a secret report filed by New Scotland Yard on December 23, 1931, Gandhi was very keen to obtain an audience with the pope. This was not granted due to insufficient time being given to Vatican authorities. The report goes on to say that the real reason, as ascertained from reliable sources, "was that His Holiness vetoed a meeting, on the ground that the scanty attire of the Mahatma did not meet Papal obligation."

Gandhi later visited the Vatican galleries and the Sistine Chapel. Standing before the figure of Christ, nailed to the crucifix and dying, Gandhi wept. "Tears sprang to my eyes as I gazed," he recalled later.

"MR. GANDHI, IT IS MY DUTY TO ARREST YOU"

Gandhi, with Pyarelal, returned to Bombay on December 28, 1931. A huge crowd had gathered to welcome him home. Kasturba was there as well, looking frail and anxious, her main worry being how long he would be allowed this freedom. Kasturba's fears were not unfounded. The new viceroy, Lord Willingdon, was ill-disposed toward Gandhi. There were serious discussions between the viceroy and his advisers about banishing Gandhi to the Andaman Islands and destroying him forever.

In Bombay, Gandhi resided at Mani Bhawan (the house of a close friend). Staying with him were the British anthropologist Verrier Elwin and a few others. They all slept on the roof. On January 4, 1932, Gandhi was arrested in the middle of the night. Elwin, in his book *Tribal World of Verrier Elwin*, wrote: "I was in deep sleep when there was a stir and a whisper: 'The police have come.' I saw what I shall never forget—a fully uniformed Commissioner of Police at the foot of Bapu's bed. Gandhi was just waking up. The Commissioner said: 'Mr. Gandhi, it is my duty to arrest you.' It was Monday—the day of silence for Gandhi. He scribbled a note for the commissioner. 'I shall be ready to come with you in half an hour...'" Gandhi was again taken to Yeravda Jail. Along with him, the entire Congress leadership was arrested and sentenced to long prison terms. As Fischer comments: "...again he was His Majesty's guest in Yeravda Jail. A few weeks earlier he had been the guest of His and Her Majesty in Buckingham Palace."

1932 *A painting capturing the emotions of Gandhi's supporters on his arrest soon after his return from the Second Round Table Conference in London.*

1932 *Dr. Bhimrao Ramji Ambedkar led a resolute struggle against untouchability and fought for the rights of Depressed Classes.*

AMBEDKAR AND GANDHI: YERAVDA PACT

On September 20, 1932, Gandhi woke up at 2:30 a.m. in Yeravda Jail to begin his fast in protest of the British government's decision to award a separate electorate to the Depressed Classes (Harijans) as advocated by Dr. B. R. Ambedkar. He wrote a letter to Tagore, whose approval he desperately sought. Then he ate his last meal: lemon juice, honey and hot water. Sardar Patel and Mahadev Desai were with him, as was Sarojini Naidu, who had been shifted from the women's wing. Outside, the negotiators were racing against time. Gandhi was over 60 years old, and the doctors feared for his life. Kasturba had been shifted from Sabarmati Jail to Poona. "Again the same old story," she said when they met.

On September 21, an extraordinary meeting was held in the prison to discuss the terms to be offered to Dr. B. R. Ambedkar. As the negotiations dragged on, Gandhi became weaker. Ambedkar's accumulated bitterness toward Hindus made him uncompromising. So determined was he to cut away from caste Hindus that he had separate parleys with the Sikhs, Jains and even Muslim leaders to merge his community of hundreds of thousands of untouchables with them. Ambedkar termed Gandhi's fast a "political stunt." The bargaining carried on.

On September 22, Ambedkar visited Gandhi and said he was ready to save his life by coming to some agreement, but added: "I want my compensation." By September 23, day four of the fast, doctors had declared Gandhi's condition extremely critical. That day, Ambedkar conferred with Hindu leaders and laid out his position. The MacDonald Award had given Depressed Classes 71 seats in the provincial legislatures while Ambedkar wanted 197. He met Gandhi again the next day and settled at 147 seats. Some last-minute glitches were smoothed over by C. Rajagopalachari without consulting Gandhi. The Yeravda Pact, also known as the Poona Pact, was signed the next day and ratified by Congress. It was signed by the leaders of both sides, but not by Gandhi himself. He refused to end his fast till the British ratified it as well. There was some delay in getting approval from London. Gandhi thought the end was near and instructed Kasturba on who

1933 *Gandhi convalescing after his release from Yeravda Jail.*

should get the few items lying around his death bed. Tagore arrived as Gandhi's health was deteriorating quickly. The two embraced each other with great emotion. Tagore sang a few songs that helped calm Gandhi's sinking heart. On Monday, September 26, 1932, the British government announced its approval. Finally, at 5:15 p.m. on the same day, Gandhi took a sip of orange juice from Kasturba to end one of his riskiest fasts.

The one and a half years in Yeravda Jail had severely weakened Gandhi. The outcome of his fast in the jail was the Yeravda Pact, which established the need for reserved seats for the Depressed Classes or untouchables (Gandhi called them Harijans, or people of God) in India's new constitution.

Following his release from prison, Gandhi toured extensively and visited many remote villages and districts, spreading his message against the practice of untouchability and collecting donations for the Harijan Fund.

1933 *Gandhi working on his box charkha (Yeravda charkha), after his release from Yeravda Jail.*

GANDHI LEAVES CONGRESS

Growing differences between Gandhi and Congress came to the fore during the Congress Working Committee meeting due to be held in Bombay in the last week of October 1934. On September 17, Gandhi had issued a press release to explain why he had decided to leave the party. The statement said that there was a growing "difference of outlook between many Congressmen and myself." He started with the fact that although he had put the spinning wheel and khadi to the forefront of the campaign against British rule, most Congressmen had not adopted them. He added that many Congressmen had been reminding him that he was responsible for the hypocrisy and evasion about the khadi cause. He reiterated that if India were to win independence, the spinning wheel and khadi "would have to be as natural to the educated few as to the partially unemployed and semi-starving millions." It was also felt that he had differences with Jawaharlal Nehru and his socialist-leaning friends. On October 23, the Subjects Committee discussed Gandhi's proposal to retire from Congress and reluctantly came to the decision: "...in as much as all efforts to persuade him (Gandhi) have failed, this Congress, while reluctantly accepting his decision, places on record its deep sense of gratitude..." Earlier, Gandhi had said that he was leaving Congress to lift the weight that had been suppressing it, so that it could grow and he in turn could grow with it. On October 30, Gandhi sent his official resignation to Rajendra Prasad, the party president at the time.

***

In December 1935, Gandhi agreed to meet Margaret Sanger. She was a birth-control activist in the days when contraception was not widely acceptable. A pioneer in the field, she had opened her first clinic in New York in 1917. As if waiting to discuss sex on equal terms, Gandhi poured his heart out to her in an interview that lasted two long days. Gandhi confessed that at 50 he had "nearly slipped" in a relationship that almost destroyed his marriage. So exhausting was this interview that Gandhi almost collapsed and was taken to a hospital in Bombay for a medical examination.

***

1935 *Gandhi with Margaret Sanger.*

1938 *Gandhi and Kasturba in the North West Frontier Province as guests of Khan Abdul Ghaffar Khan.*

As the guest of the popular Pashtun leader Khan Abdul Ghaffar Khan, popularly known as Frontier Gandhi, Gandhi visited Abbottabad twice in 1938, and then again with Kasturba in 1939. He visited villages where he was enthusiastically greeted by members of Khudai Khidmatgar (Servants of God)—Khan's famous pacifist political group founded in 1929.

Addressing Khudai Khidmatgars in the town of Tank in Dera Ismail Khan district, Gandhi famously said: "A small body of determined spirits fired by an unquenchable faith in their mission can alter the course of history."

FRONTIER GANDHI

There was another "Gandhi" in the Indian nationalist movement, Khan Abdul Ghaffar Khan, popularly called the "Frontier Gandhi." A Pashtun from the North West Frontier Province, he led the Khudai Khidmatgars (Servants of God), followers of Mahatma Gandhi's ideals of non-violence and non-cooperation. A brilliant exponent of satyagraha, he was neither a Hindu nor a religious leader, but a rich aristocrat, the son of a Pashtun chieftain, and a former soldier. He was built in a heroic mold typical of the wild, rugged, mountainous area, being tall and fiercely handsome with his hooked nose and grizzled beard. He presided over large areas of the North West Frontier. In October 1938, Gandhi toured the region in the company of Khan. They were an odd-looking pair, for Gandhi barely reached up to Khan's shoulder. Gandhi wandered among the Pashtuns like a child in a dream, scarcely able to believe that this warlike tribe had pledged non-violence. When the British arrested Ghaffar Khan in Peshawar, there were angry demonstrations, and the police abandoned the city to the Khidmatgars. Ghaffar Khan was ultimately released from prison. Three days later, two platoons of the Second Battalion of the 18th Royal Garhwali Rifles were sent in to establish order, but they refused to fire on the crowds of Muslims and broke rank. Never swerving from his faith in Muslim–Hindu friendship, non-violence and Pashtun autonomy, Khan died in 1988, at the age of 98.

Khan Abdul Ghaffar Khan with Red Shirt Movement volunteers.

Gandhi with Khan Abdul Ghaffar Khan, Sushila Nayyar and another associate Amtus Salam during their visit to the North West Frontier Province in 1938.

1938 *Gandhi joking with the grandson of Khan Abdul Ghaffar Khan. Standing behind are Pyarelal and Sushila Nayyar, who accompanied him on his visit to the North West Frontier Province.*

1938 *Gandhi, sharing a hearty laugh with the ruler of Dera Ismail Khan district, in North West Frontier Province.*

1938 *Kasturba with sons Devdas (standing, left), Ramdas (sitting, left) and Manilal (sitting, right) with Harilal's eldest daughter, Rami (standing, right) and his son Kanti (sitting in the middle).*

LETTER FROM SON TO A FATHER

Harilal to Mohandas Karamchand Gandhi

March 31, 1915

In the service of Pujya Pitaji,

A worm enters the body of a wasp and flies away having assumed the form of the wasp. I believe something similar happened to me. I have received much from you, I have learned much, I was formed by you and my character emerged unblemished. The only difference is that I lacked the patience and endurance of a worm and ran away even before I could become a wasp.

I separated from you with your consent. In so doing I followed the dictates of my conscience. This too I learned from you.

It is usually not possible to distinguish the Phoenix Institution from you and hence I left that too. We spoke much. You said much; you also did all that you could. I also said all that was possible for me to say. It was destined that we be separated.

When I experienced the desire to write to you at length, the following thoughts came to my mind. "Your life has been a public one. Even your personal life is no secret. All are naturally curious to know more about your life. Many would have asked you questions about the sudden change in me. I have been unable to say all that I wished to say to you." For such reasons I considered it proper to write a public letter to you.

The thoughts expressed in this letter are my own. Our differences are not of recent origin. We have had differences for the past ten years. They stem from one subject. You are convinced that you have given me and my brothers necessary education. You are convinced that you could not have given us a better education than what you did give us. In other words, you have given us necessary and sufficient attention. I believe that with your preoccupations and engagements you have unintentionally paid us no attention at all. It affected me and that is what I shall describe in this letter. I believe that due to your overwhelming desire to provide us education and care, you have experienced the illusion of having done so.

For ten years now I have been crying and pleading with you. But, for the wasp, the worm is insignificant. That is, you have never considered my sentiments. I believe that you have always used us as weapons. "Us" in this context means me and my brothers—Manilal, Ramdas and Devdas. I believe that to a lesser or a greater degree your conduct toward us brothers has been similar. You have dealt with us just as a ringmaster in a circus treats animals in his charge. The ringmaster may believe that he is ridding the animals of their beastly character because he has the welfare of animals in his heart.

If you have no knowledge of our sentiments, then there is no possibility of you paying any heed to what we have to say to you. You have oppressed us in a civilized way. You have never encouraged us in any way. The environment around you has become such that even a person who differs from you innocently and conscientiously is as good as dead. You have spoken to us not in love but always with anger. Whenever we tried to put across our views on any subject to you and engaged in a debate with you, with your permission, you have lost your temper quickly and told us, "You are stupid, you are in a fallen state, you lack comprehension. You think that you have attained the zenith of knowledge. You argue against me in everything. You will not know what is good. Such is your samskar." By saying such things you have shown your disdain and oppressed us. Thus oppressed I have remained melancholic, anxious and, as a result, sick. You have instilled fear in us, of you, even while we are walking, ambling, eating or drinking, sleeping or sitting, reading or writing, and working. Your heart is like vajra. Your love...I have never seen; so what can I say about it?

Under such circumstances what can people expect from your sons? Naturally they are disappointed. As you yourself said, after his first meeting with us, poet Shri Rabindranath Tagore used the term "ignoramus" to describe us. You also said that later he changed his opinion. It must be said, despite all the reverence I have for him, that he was being kind and generous. I remember one of the Phoenix inmates reporting that even Professor Gokhale had told you that our affection for you arose from fear. It is not as if I am drawing your attention to this for the first time. I have been pointing this out for years.

Whenever someone asks you about our education you reply that we study what our samskar allows us to. Forgive me, Pitaji, but it is not only our samskar which is to be blamed for the state of our education.

As your political life became full of hardships you have changed your ideas, and along with that you have also twisted our lives. I believe without any hesitation that our lives hitherto have been irregular and uncertain. You went from here to South Africa, came back, went again and came back once more. What we learned here we forgot there. We learned one thing for six months, something else for another six months and a third thing for another six months. Naturally, nothing came of it. We might be foolish; but allow me to add that you have kept us foolish. You have never considered our rights.

Here, I am reminded of the story of a father and his four sons. The father felt that he should initiate the sons in some profession.

He called each one and gave them the necessary encouragement. Each one was shown a path that suited his capabilities. What the father identified as the right path for one, he dismissed as the wrong choice for the others.

He called the first son (the father knew that this son desired knowledge) and told him, "Son, now you have reached an age where you should think for yourself and of your future. It is my advise that you should study further. Remember the shloka, 'Vidya nama narasya rupam adhika...vidya-vihina pasu.' People will revere you if you become knowledgeable. Only the wealth of knowledge stays with us, all the rest is false.

"Do not even think of business. You must have heard how many have become bankrupt and died in bankruptcy like Chunilal Sarriya. A businessman is worried all day long. He cannot even sleep with ease.

"Moreover, those who accumulate a lot of wealth endanger their lives. We have read about the son of a wealthy man in America who had to live in a golden cage because the father was afraid that his heir might be killed.

"Do not even think of agriculture. If you were a farmer and it does not rain for two years, you would have to bear huge losses. Government taxes would push you into debt. You, your laborers, your oxen—all would suffer. If you work with oxen, your intelligence would also become like theirs.

"You might have thought of service, but you know that among us service is considered most inferior among professions. One has to spend a lifetime converting fifty rupees into fifty-one rupees. Moreover, you will always have to be subservient.

"Therefore, my son, don't think of doing business, or agriculture, or taking up a service even in your dreams."

Then he called the second son (this son had the qualities of a businessman). Here, the father praised business and decried the pursuit of knowledge, "My son, I see the qualities of a Bania trader in you. I would be happy if you enter into some trade. There is immense wealth to be earned. You would also be famous. Remember the shloka by Bhartrhari, 'Yasyasti vitta sa nara kulina sa pandita...sarveguna kancanam asrayanti.' Look at Premchand Raychand! He built Rajabai Tower and his name is immortal.

"If you are considering further studies, read M.A. Banake Kyui meri Mim Kharab ki? Don't you see destitute B As? Who is willing to pay them even thirty rupees? To be educated means to be debauched. Therefore choose trade and commerce." (He denigrates agriculture and service.)

He called the third son (the father knew that this son wanted to be (a farmer) and told him, "Son, you have improved the condition of our farm. I went there earlier today. I think you are fond of agriculture. I am willing to buy you more land. Moreover, there is a saying among us that farming is the most superior of all occupations, after which comes trade, and service is the lowliest of all professions. And how simple is the life of a farmer? Have you ever heard of a farmer falling sick? His body is as strong as iron. No one prays to god as much as a farmer does. You select the land and we shall buy it." (As before, he denigrates the other occupations.)

Finally, the father called the fourth son. (He knew that this son liked administrative service. He presents the lowliest of professions as the most superior.) "Son, it would be good if you visit our ruler. He will give you a suitable position. Our forefathers have been administrators of this state. How can we give up our claims on it? You must have heard that one of our ancestors was a Divan. That grandeur will not come back to us without state service. We were the rulers. Son, I would like you to bring back the glory of our forefathers." (He denigrates other occupations.)

Pitaji, you have not paid any attention to us even when we sought it. God grants a newborn child mother's milk. If the child is given any other food, it has indigestion and falls incurably ill.

It is necessary to narrate my life story in support of what I have said earlier. The period to which I refer is from 1906 to 1911. In the end I ran away from you in 1911. This is the second time that a similar incident has taken place.

In 1906, at the age of nineteen, I implored and beseeched you, I made innumerable arguments and pleaded that I should be allowed to chart the course of my life. I wanted to study, to gain knowledge; I had no other desire. I demanded that I should be sent to England. I wept and wandered aimlessly for a year but you paid no heed. You told me that character building should precede everything else. I had respectfully submitted to you that a tree once fully grown cannot be bent in another direction. My character cannot be altered now. You would remember that you had gone to England at the age of nineteen against the wishes of all. Today you consider the lawyer's profession sinful! It is doubtful that you would be able to do what you do if you were not a lawyer.

Today, I do not consider my character altered. I do not think even others would claim that my character has been altered. The mistakes that I committed then, knowing them to be mistakes, were due to my weakness and I was helpless about preventing them. I cannot be held responsible for the mistakes that I did not consider to be errors and those which I did not commit. With time, having learned and understood some things, I do not repeat the mistakes of childhood. Therefore, some may very well say that my character has altered.

In order that my character be formed, using many arguments you proved that I was incapable of studying and that I first needed to acquire that capability. You made me adopt, not in Athens, but in today's world, in Johannesburg, the paths of Plato, Xenothon and Demosthenes—not with the guidance of any teacher but on my own. You asked me to drink milk not in the house of a cowherd, but in a pub. I am sorry that I am no Plato. It was proved that though I wanted to study I was incapable of it. All saw me with condescending eyes. You proved that I was utterly foolish. I had to accept your verdict.

I was told that I should leave Johannesburg and live in Phoenix to build my character. The *Indian Opinion* is published from Phoenix. Phoenix is regarded as a place for those desiring a simple life. No one can question the objectives of Phoenix. The value of nectar cannot be measured. But who got it? Who drank it? Allow me to remind you that Phoenix caused a dear friend of yours and an excellent electrician like Mr. Kitchin to run away. Phoenix also forced a gentleman and an excellent engineer like Mr. Liens to run away. There might have been other reasons in case of Mr. Cordes, but one particular reason was sufficient to drive him away. I can give other similar names. You believed (despite our warnings to the contrary) for many years that Murabbi Bhai Shri Chhaganlal would not leave Phoenix so long as even one tile of its roof held. You are aware that this belief has been proven false.

For the sake of Phoenix's future you decided to send Murabbi Bhai Shri Chhaganlal, as someone who had the finest understanding of the objectives of the Phoenix, to England in 1910 (this despite the fact that Dr. Mehta Saheb had requested you to send one of us to England at his expense). He fell ill there and returned to India in six months. You are aware that he decried Phoenix and praised the Servants of India Society. I was asked to build my character in a place like that. But who was I there? Was I of any consequence there?

So be it. But, the plight of my mother was much worse than mine at Phoenix. I saw that she was being insulted often. What I saw was like witnessing a thief admonishing the sentry. People brought complaints to you: "Mrs. Gandhi consumes too much sugar and hence expenditure has gone up." "What right does Mrs. Gandhi have to assign work to a worker of the press?" People said that Harilal does this and Harilal does that. If you had maintained records of all the complaints it would certainly fill a small notebook.

We would have preferred to be caned rather than be admonished by you every time a complaint was made. It is beyond my capacity to describe the hardships that my mother had to undergo. All this I could not bear. If we ever brought complaints to you, your response would be, "He is a good man. He desires your welfare. And such and such is a jolly fellow."

It was then the idea that you were using us as weapons took root in my mind.

In 1907 the satyagraha commenced. I joined the struggle. I had the opportunity to think freely while in jail. When I was out of prison I shared with you my ideas about how and what education we could acquire. But you deprecated my thoughts. I remained oppressed. I considered myself a lost cause. I stopped expressing my views.

Finally, after pleading with you for five years, in accordance with your teaching I obeyed my conscience and ran away after writing a personal letter to you. I thought that I would go back to India. That I would earn my livelihood and stay away from relatives and their temptations. I thought that I would live in Lahore. That I would study and manage to feed myself somehow. From Johannesburg I went to Delagoa Bay on my way to India. I requested the British Counsel there to send me back to India as a poor Indian immigrant.

I was delayed at Delagoa Bay, you came to know of my whereabouts and you caught up with me. Obeying your orders, I returned. I remained steadfast in my views. Therefore, instead of giving me a patient hearing you mutilated my thoughts and clipped my wings. You made me give up the idea of going to Lahore and instead made me stay in Ahmedabad. You promised to give me thirty rupees for monthly expenditure. You did not allow me to measure my capabilities; you measured them for me.

I stayed in Ahmedabad obeying your wishes. But my original objections were proved correct—relatives and social obligations to the family surrounded me. There were deaths in the family. After the death of my uncles I took ill. Only those who nursed me and the doctors of Ahmedabad could possibly give you an idea of my illness. In 1912 I failed the matriculation examination. How long could your daughter-in-law have stayed in her natal home? I was worried about this.

How could all the expenses be met in thirty rupees? I incurred debt. You say that mother's ornaments and those of your daughter-in-law should be sold and thus the debt be repaid. At the same time it is quite understandable that your present circumstances do not allow you to give money.

Despite leading an unhappy life in Ahmedabad I do believe that I learned much, I experienced much.

Now you have returned to India. I spent some days with you. My effort to rejoin the Phoenix Institution has failed. My views remain unchanged. You remain steadfast in the choice of your path and consider it to be just. When I complained to you that you did not allow me to go to Lahore and asked me to stay in Ahmedabad, you responded by saying, "Why did you not remain firm in your views then?"

Now I am firm in my views and will remain so. If I were to die doing so, I shall die a satisfied man. I know that my conscience is free of sin.

Under the circumstances that I have narrated, and with my wings clipped, I recommenced studies after seven years. I failed the matriculation examination for three years. I am not worried on that account. I consider it a sign of weakness to give up studies now. I will earn my livelihood, get through my education and become a servant of the country. Our differences on knowledge of letters are not new.

I consider it useful to study the subjects that are taught in our universities. I am aware that in the recent past the government universities have discarded some important subjects. The changes in the methods of imparting education are acceptable to me. I consider examinations to be important. I consider the awarding of degrees to be a form of encouragement to students. I see nothing wrong with schooling. Some reforms are required everywhere. I have no wish to claim credit by pointing them out. For me, even students living in a gurukul constitutes schooling.

You dismissed my desire to be a lawyer by saying that it was a "sinful activity," but you sent Bhai Sorabji to England for the very same purpose? This contradiction sows the seeds of the thought that you love us less. Bhai Sorabji is a good man. But, you would have tried to please even an ant at our expense.

Even after hearing and reading all this you would say only one thing, and that I know: "I have always loved my sons to the extent that I have not allowed them to do anything that I have considered wrong." Pitaji, the facts given above contain my response to your justification. One more thing remains to be said here. It is so subtle and delicate that it cannot be said fully, nor can it be expressed through words. Nevertheless, I consider it my duty to write about it.

You admonish me that I married "against your wishes." I accept that. Given my circumstances I feel that my action should be pardoned. I believe that no one could have acted differently under those conditions.

You know that I got engaged while I was still a child. This was arranged by Pujya Kala kaka in your absence. Thereafter at the age of seventeen I came to Rajkot severely ill. On hearing that I was on my deathbed you had written a letter of solace from South Africa. At that time I was staying with Murabbi Goki Phoi. There were no men in her house. Haridasbhai took me to his house. I was nursed and cared for in his house. I recovered my health. I stayed in his house for about two months.

I was not entirely unaware of the situation at that time. Haridasbhai's family was considered reformist. I knew that I was at my in-laws' place. Naturally, I desired to see what kind of girl was destined for me. I saw a photograph. A thought entered my mind that I was not engaged to an unsuitable girl, and that the in-laws' family is also good. After some days I desired to see the girl face to face. I saw her. Time did the rest. As we got more opportunities we talked and joked. The bond of love linked us.

After regaining my health fully I returned to our house. How were we to meet after that? We exchanged letters. Our affection for each other grew. It was time for me to leave for South Africa. What was I to do? It would be five or more years before I could return from South Africa. In Hindu society a girl who remains unmarried after a certain age is subjected to criticism. We decided to get married. I have the letter of 1915, which proves our reasons for the marriage. I am not reproducing the letter here. But I am willing to produce it whenever asked.

We got married in May 1906. Three months after our marriage I left India to be with you.

Please allow me to state that ever since the marriage, we have remained subject to your wishes. We have been married for nine years. We have spent six of those years pining for each other.

I dissociated myself from the Phoenix Institution which is now in Bolpur because I witnessed hypocrisy there. I consider the objectives of Phoenix to be most superior; but with respect to what I have seen, you are the only one who leads his life according to those objectives. It is my view that no one else is capable of following them. We all consider the ascetic life to be the most superior way of life, but all of us still lead the lives of householders—a practice which is inferior to the ascetic life.

No one can be made an ascetic. No one becomes an ascetic because others ask him to. A person becomes an ascetic of his own volition; only such asceticism can be and is sustained. If I recall correctly, during the time of Cromwell there was a group of Puritans. In those days reform was in the air. Those who did not join the Puritans were considered inferior to them. Many were shamed into joining the Puritans. When the winds changed direction it resulted in a "Puritan reaction." People withdrew from it with the same enthusiasm with which they had joined it. It is my humble belief that the same is true for the Phoenix Institution. The norms of the Phoenix Institution are the finest; but I am not willing to accept that those who stay in it follow the Phoenix path of their own volition.

At present, the Phoenix Institution has twenty-one members, young and old. Six of them have joined recently. Therefore, I am not counting them in. Of the remaining fifteen, I have known fourteen for many years. Phoenix was established six years ago. With affection for my younger brothers and respect for Murabbi Bhai, I must state that in these six years of following the ideals established by you and given their efforts, the change in them is not as great as it ought to have been. The apparent change is due to time—a man with an angry disposition does not remain the same after six years. It is extremely difficult to imbibe virtues of high morality. There should be no ill will for the Phoenix Institution. But, ill will toward the institution is quite apparent.

I cannot believe a salt-free diet, or abstinence from ghee or milk, indicates strength of character and morality. If one decides to refrain from consuming such foods as a result of thoughtful consideration, the abstinence could be beneficial. It is seen that such abstinence and asceticism is possible only after one has attained a certain state. By insisting on a salt-free diet and on specific abstinences at the Phoenix institution, you are trying to cultivate self-denial. It is my belief that before self-denial certain other qualities—non-possession, courage, and simplicity—have to be cultivated. I am skeptical whether those who are devoid of such qualities, but eat salt-free food or are fruitarians for the benefits offered by such diets, should be considered self-denying. Those who consume a salt-free diet because of such motives cannot be considered self-denying, as they have no ascetic qualities. Such persons promote hypocrisy by eating salt-free food. They think they have attained self-denial. They believe that godliness is manifest in them. They consider themselves superior, if not to everyone, at least to those who do not avoid consuming salt. It is well-recognized that among the Hindu families thousands of women and men observe rigorous vrata year-round. They observe fasts, but barring a few exceptions, they possess no sterling virtues; and good character is found also among those who do not observe any vrata.

After observing vrata, our women and men eat the usual roti and dal in large quantities; instead, if they were to follow a diet of fruits their vrata would certainly bear results. Those whose digestion is good keep good health. It is not as if the vrata observed by those who eat roti and dal does not bear results. Because, we know of many who eat roti and dal and yet observe the strictest of vows in the Jain upashrays. I wish to state that after the vrata, people tend to overeat. It is my experience that even the self-denying are not exempt from this. If my own experience or experiment of being a fruitarian for only twenty days has any validity, I speak with experience—I have also observed this characteristic among those who were fruitarians for six months— that people eat fruits and nuts far in excess to even those who overeat roti and dal. Therefore, indigestion is bound to happen. Under such circumstances I see no benefits in adopting a fruit diet.

It is my opinion that one should get accustomed to eating less food and, only thereafter, consider becoming a fruitarian. Eating less means being indifferent toward food and practicing abstinence. Then, issues of "I will not be able to give up this and that" do not arise. Only after attaining such a state do questions of what one should eat and what one should abstain from appear meaningful and beneficial. We are usually conscious of what we should eat and should not eat. In this age, the consumption of tea and condiments has increased greatly. No one can deny the need to be strict regarding their use. One can contend that it should be possible to eat less and be a fruitarian. I believe that this is not possible. Because while food that is considered good is being cooked and its aroma wafts up to you, and others are praising the cooking, doubts arise as to how, as a fruitarian, one could be indifferent to it. It is difficult to ascertain the precise quantity of food that one should eat. I believe that a fruitarian who eats within limits does not ever fall ill. If a fruitarian or someone who abstains from ghee, milk, etc. can show that he has not taken ill in ten years, I would accept that everyone should become a fruitarian. Exceptions must not be used to illustrate the success of this diet.

It is often asked, "Where are the restrictive impositions in the Phoenix Institution?" Such a contention is unacceptable to me. Because whatever I did there, and saw others do, I felt that their conduct was enforced by fear. It was as if everything was based on one principle: "Let the groom die, let the bride die, but do as Bapu says." And it is a fact, Pitaji, that those who believed so became dear to you and those who did not were despised. This was especially true for us; and among us, it was I who was so despised.

If one joined the Phoenix Institution with awareness of this rule, he should be willing to give his head when asked. If not his head, he should at least be willing to make sacrifices. The stated norm is that one should not do what appears wrong, that one should fight what is wrong, that one should be fearless. To then call those who are fearless and who oppose the wrong "ignorant" and "stupid," to withdraw affection from them, to refuse to even look at them, and to taunt them by saying "Ji" in response to their questions was unbearable for me, Pitaji. I have stated that all the members of the Phoenix Institution act out of fear. I felt that under such circumstances I would not become a servant of the country and my soul would not be enlightened. In the institution I saw everyone wanting to establish their own authority by belittling others. Generosity—I found lacking. I witnessed poisonous rivalries. I saw the sense of brotherhood decline. I found everyone lacking in public courage. I found each one covering up their views for the sake of their own interests. I wanted to learn fearlessness, but instead I saw myself benefitting through hypocrisy.

It is said that moral restrictions—even if they are labeled as fear—are natural. No one experiences fear over moral injunctions. (If one is not immoral.) If a man who drinks alcohol refrains from doing so either out of fear or shame, his behavior may be regarded as being attentive to a moral restriction. But to experience fear while eating sugar cannot be identified as observance of a moral injunction. This fear becomes coercion. Because a person who eats sugar would do so in the presence of others, but a drunkard would not drink alcohol in the presence of others; if those around him were also drunkards that would be quite another matter.

I am required to perform an unpleasant duty; but I do believe that I can perform this duty to completion.

Pitaji, whenever we told you "We do not benefit from the Phoenix Institution" or "We have not seen others gaining from the Phoenix Institution," you told us to follow the example of Murabbi Bhai Shri Chhaganlal and Murabbi Bhai Shri Maganlal. You have not said so but have indicated through your actions that we should follow Bhai Jamnadas. We should keep them as our ideals.

I have been bewildered whenever you have said so, because I have neither been able to bear it nor have been able to express what I have observed. They are my elder brothers and I am ready to serve them and press their feet. Bhai Jamnadas is for me like Bhai

Manilal. It is my duty that I should not hide my humble thoughts from you. Such is also your wish. I am performing such a duty by informing you of what I consider necessary.

Their example teaches us to nurture our self-interest. I do not intend to say that they have adopted both right and wrong means to further themselves. I have observed that their foundation is the maxim "Honesty is the best policy." I believe that for them abstinence from milk for the sake of it is secondary. I fail to see the significant sacrifices that they have made. Bhai Jamnadas, who is a part of your organization, could have sacrificed two or three years and refrained from encouraging child marriage. In Rajkot (it is necessary to remember here that you were prepared to break off my engagement) he created an impression that no one comprehends or practices your ideas as much as he does. You would say, "Should he not obey his parents?" If he had remained subservient to the conservative religious ideas of his parents, he could not have transgressed caste and community rules. Moreover, he got married, he enjoyed the life of a householder for three months and then he joined the Phoenix Institution by taking a vow of lifelong celibacy. All this appears to me very perplexing. I fail to understand what lesson I should derive from it.

If Bhai Ramdas were to follow his example, he could marry whenever he desires—perhaps immediately. Because after the son attains the age of sixteen, you consider him a friend and do not insist that he should act contrary to his own desires. He can not only get married, but after marriage he can directly join your institution.

Moreover, since there is no question of seeking deferment from you, it is asked, "What should we do, if we go there, to earn for ten years?" Based on such considerations, there is the answer "One cannot join your institution." Since I have touched upon the question of earning, I must say that the plan of Murabbi Bhai Shri Chhaganlal, Murabbi Bhai Shri Maganlal, and Bhai Jamnadas to earn a living from you is simple and superb. They have brought with them their characters. They use this character and keep you happy and pleased. They give their character to you and trade in the capital that is your character. In this transaction you have given them everything. But they can take only what their destinies allow them. There is an additional advantage of investing capital in your firm—there is no fear of losing out on the interest; each percent of the interest is calculated and paid.

But you have given us no capital. That is my quarrel with you. If you had given us some capital, we could have traded with some firm. What are the consequences of this? We trade without capital.

In business the norm that one must remember is that accounts must be calculated to the last paisa, even with a brother. Therefore, people mock us. "Go away, you freeloaders. You are eating out of your father's earnings. Why are you putting on airs?" (What airs? That I am a son of M.K. Gandhi.) What do you, with whom we could have traded, say? "Go away, stupid fool. I feed you but you don't even know how to eat?"

How can we feed off you? How could we possess a trader's cleverness? From where could we have gained the experience of such transactions that we could have become adept at them?

A dog that roams the farms belongs neither to the road nor to the village. Clever—It cannot be. Pitaji, you have kept us in such a condition. What example should we follow?

If Bhai Manilal were to follow the example of Bhai Jamnadas—he would not do so because I think the worm has become a wasp, but still—he could escape from the work that he now does at Shantiniketan—of cleaning the sleeping quarters of Mr. Andrews, making tea for him, etc. You have made all of us do such work. I have seen Bhai Jamnadas escaping from such work as he considers it lowly.

Bhai Manilal addresses me by my name because Bhai Jamnadas does that. Bhai Manilal is elder to Bhai Jamnadas both in age and relationship. But still, Bhai Jamnadas calls him Manilal. Vashisthaji used to address Vishwamitraji as "Rajarshi." I do not know if such is the case with them. I have no objection to it. But in our family and among us it is considered discourteous and insulting.

People wonder that if not much, something should have happened at the Phoenix Institution, some training in literacy should have been imparted. It is my view that no training in literacy has been imparted whatsoever. You admit that such training has not been imparted, but you also insist that such a sacrifice had to be made. We began making sacrifices around 1907. But many of us belong to the Phoenix from long before. All of us, and especially we brothers, have expressed our deep desire to acquire education, "but you have never paid any heed to us. It is doubtful if Bhai Manilal, Ramdas, and Devdas at the age of twenty-three have the knowledge of a fourth grader.

Pitaji, I have not been able to say even one-fourth of what I have to say. The letter has become very long. Printing is expensive. From where will I find the money to pay for it?

Before I conclude, Pitaji, if I have unknowingly expressed rash and immature ideas, I seek your forgiveness from the depths of my conscience. At the age of twenty-eight I have been forced to write to you like a young child; this pains me, but I had no other choice. My conscience dictated the letter and I merely wrote it. Whatever I have said about the Phoenix Institution I have said because of my blood relations with it. Therefore, I have pointed out only its shortcomings. The virtues of the Phoenix Institution are known to the world.

My entire letter stresses one point—you have never been generous and patient with our failings. You have never considered our rights and capabilities; you have never seen the person in us. Your life and actions are very harsh. I consider myself unsuitable for a life such as yours. To you a son and others are equal. If there be two accused—one of your sons and someone else—you have considered it unjust to regard the other as guilty. It is justice that a son must suffer, but unfortunately I have not been able to bear such suffering.

Moreover, whether it is right or wrong, I am married. God has granted me four children. I am caught in the web of worldly relations, in its delusions and enchantments; I cannot acquire the detachment of an ascetic and renounce the world like others. Therefore, I had to separate from you with your consent. I feel that I must earn my own livelihood. Even after this I am willing to join the Phoenix Institution at your command. You know that I have not disobeyed you on purpose. It is possible that my views are wrong. I hope that they prove to be wrong—if I realize that they are wrong, I shall not hesitate to reform myself. In the deep recesses of my conscience, my only desire is that I be your son—that is, if I am good enough be your son.

Your obedient son,
Harilal's Sashtang Dandvat Chaitra Sud Purnima
Samvat 1971
March 31, 1915
Mumbai

GANDHI AND HARILAL

Gandhi was 19 when his first child Harilal was born in Rajkot in 1888. The infant Harilal closely resembled his father in looks. Only a few months after Harilal's birth, Gandhi left for London to pursue his legal studies and came back to India three years later. Despite having worked in London, he did not find much success with his legal practice in India. His second son Manilal was born in October 1892. Gandhi had to leave behind his infants and doting wife when he sailed for South Africa in April 1893 to take up a position as legal adviser with Dada Abdullah & Co. His family missed his presence, especially Harilal. He was five now and had only a faint recollection of his father's face. Once assured of a steady income to support his family, Gandhi returned to India in July 1896 to take them to South Africa. In November 1896, Gandhi boarded *SS Courtland* with his wife, Kasturba, two sons, Harilal and Manilal, and nephew Gokuldas. With Gandhi and the boys attired in Western-style coats and trousers, the family arrived in Durban on December 12 to start a new life. Besides his legal work, Gandhi got involved in social and political work and was recognized as a leading activist among the Indians. Two other sons, Ramdas and Devdas, were born during this time in South Africa. Despite being closer to his mother, 13-year-old Harilal often supported his father's views, much to the annoyance of his beloved mother.

Upon their return to India, Gandhi had to choose whether Harilal or his nephew Gokuldas should be sent away for his higher education. In his eyes, both were equal and could not be discriminated against. The matter was decided by hiding two coins, one of one rupee and one of one paisa, in different parts of the house. Harilal and Gokuldas were tasked with finding the coins, and Gandhi decided that whoever found the rupee coin would be sent to further his studies. Gokuldas found the coin and was sent to Banaras, while Harilal remained in Gujarat. Harilal was once again denied formal higher legal education, this time in Britain, when Gandhi chose another nephew, Chhaganlal, over him. When Chhaganlal fell ill in Britain and had to cut short his education and return to South Africa, Gandhi organized an essay competition to select his replacement. Though being the sole adjudicator, Gandhi again favored a young Parsi associate over Harilal, despite his high score in the competition. For Gandhi, a clean image, clear of any form of nepotism, was of prime importance. But this left a deep scar on Harilal, who had blindly followed his father and was ready to sacrifice all he had, yet was deprived of the fruits of being a good son.

In 1904 Kasturba, along with her three sons Manilal, Ramdas and Devdas, sailed for South Africa to establish a household there. Sixteen-year-old Harilal was left behind to pursue his studies in India. Despite objections from Gandhi, Harilal got married to Gulabbehn, daughter of a fellow member of the prosperous business community from Rajkot, on May 2, 1906, aged 18. Gandhi thought Harilal was too young to get married and wanted him eventually to go back to South Africa to join him in his campaigns. Gandhi was not even consulted as they fixed a date for the wedding and a few weeks later, when he got to know of the marriage, he wrote a letter to his elder brother Laxmidas: "It is well if Harilal is married; it is also well if he is not. For present at any rate I have ceased to think of him as a son." Leaving behind his bride of three months, Harilal sailed for South Africa, following a call from his father. Gandhi could not keep the teenage couple apart for too long. Gulabbehn, too, joined her husband at the Phoenix settlement and soon they became the happy parents of a daughter, Rami. It was around this time that Harilal threw himself fully into the struggle against discrimination, broke government orders and was arrested twice and went to jail on the advice of his father, who thought: "...it will be part of Harilal's education to go to jail for the sake of his country." Gandhi's call for satyagraha was gaining momentum. Both father and son were arrested several times and shared the same jail. However, young Harilal's heart lay in the pursuit of higher education and becoming financially independent. Since he had been denied that opportunity and was possibly bearing a deep desire to be united with his wife, who had sailed back to India earlier and had given birth to their son, Harilal decided to run away from home. Before he could board the ship, Harilal received two telegrams from Gandhi pleading with him to come back. With a heavy heart, Harilal returned to Johannesburg and spent the night arguing his case with Gandhi, accusing his father of suppressing the family and putting Ba and the sons last. The next day Gandhi announced that Harilal would leave for India, and, along with some of his close associates, bid his son farewell. With tears in his eyes, Gandhi hugged him and said: "Forgive your father, if you think he has done you wrong." The father and son were not to meet again until January 1915—almost four years later. Gandhi's arrival in India did not mend the relationship between the two; on the contrary, it became worse.

A year after Gandhi landed in India, he learned that his younger son had loaned some ashram money to Harilal to continue his fledgling business. Gandhi admonished Manilal and threatened to go on a fast. A lamenting and sobbing mother and the youngest son Devdas had to intervene to dissuade him from doing so.

Two years later, in 1918, Harilal's wife died of influenza and his children were left without a mother. They were, despite Harilal's strong objection, left in the care of his wife's sister, who frowned upon Harilal as much as Gandhi did. Gandhi did not allow him to remarry even for the sake of his motherless children. That shattered Harilal completely. He took to drinking and womanizing. He failed in every business enterprise that he established, and lenders often wrote to Gandhi either complaining or demanding money that they had loaned to Harilal. He did, however, find tremendous success as a salesman for Godrej soap. So pleased was A. B. Godrej with the surge in sales that for four or five years after Harilal had left the company, Godrej still sent him money to sustain himself.

In 1925, Gandhi wrote a public letter clarifying his position regarding his son. It was a typical Gandhi letter that expressed his own mistakes in bringing up his firstborn and how much he still loved him despite keeping himself away from his son and his wrongdoings. He wrote: "There is much in Harilal's life that I dislike. But I love him in spite of his faults.... Men may be good, but not their children." In 1935, at 47, almost 17 years after the death of his wife, Harilal found a companion in Margarete Spiegel, a German Jew who was a close associate and ardent follower of Gandhi. Like Madeleine Slade, whom Gandhi named Mirabehn, Margarete, too, was given an Indian name, Amala. It seems Harilal and Amala fell in love and wanted to get married. Gandhi in his typical manner considered the matter and warned both sides. He wrote to Harilal: "How can I, who have always advocated renunciation of sex, encourage you to gratify it?" Much of the correspondence on this subject between Gandhi, Harilal and Amala is not easy to find, but what we know is that the liaison ended unsuccessfully. Commenting on Harilal's deep desire to remarry, Gandhi wrote: "I may accept his marriage, but I can't welcome or like it." Gandhi was also aware of his son's drinking and other habits. He warned Harilal: "Even if you die of hunger, do not beg, die of thirst but do not drink alcohol, become impotent but do not indulge in adultery."

C. B. Dalal, in his biography of Harilal, quotes Saraswati Gandhi, Harilal's daughter-in-law: "My father-in-law was very humorous, very generous, and a very hospitable man . . ." She quotes Gandhi, who once said: "Saru, the victory over Harilal, which was denied to me, has come to you." Harilal, who stayed for six months with his son Kantilal and Saraswati, dictated his last letter to Bapu, titled "My grievances against my father." The letter was never completed. One day, he asked his daughter-in-law about the cosmetics she used. Upon being told that she used inexpensive Pond's cream and powder because she could not afford better, he advised her to use Hazeline, which in those days was more expensive. He promised to get her better cosmetics. The next day Harilal gave her 1,000 rupees and asked her to buy Hazeline and other expensive cosmetics.

As feared by his son Kantilal, after spending six happy months with them, Harilal went back to his alcohol addiction and he left their home, quietly disappearing for a long time. In April 1936, Harilal met his parents, Gandhi and Kasturba, in Nagpur and demanded money to set up a business. Gandhi refused and this probably infuriated Harilal so much that he decided to convert to Islam. He announced his conversion on Friday, May 29, 1936, at Jama Masjid in Bombay. Gandhi was obviously hurt, but it was Kasturba who was most wounded. She wrote "An open letter from a mother to her son." She loved Harilal most among her four sons and could not bear the misery and the tragedy of his life. Widely published, this was a long public letter to a nearly 50-year-old son. Full of anguish and pain she wrote: "Think of the misery you are causing to your aged parents in the evening of their lives.... I am a frail old woman unable to stand the mental anguish you are causing.... I beseech you therefore to pause and consider and turn back from your folly." Harilal refused to believe that his uneducated mother was capable of writing such a letter, but it did touch his heart.

With deep affection for his mother, whom he possibly met in the interim, and under the influence of Arya Samaj, a Hindu reformist movement, Harilal reconverted to Hinduism at the Arya Samaj Hall in Bombay, ending his public speech with: "Lead kindly me to light, Om Shanti." But the reconversion did not change Harilal. He continued to borrow money, which was given to him in his father's name, drank heavily and wandered about from place to place. Intermittently, he was in touch with Kasturba. Once, upon hearing that Ba and Bapu would be journeying through Katni station by train, Harilal could not stop himself from catching a glimpse of Ba. He reached the station and while others were shouting "*Mahatma Gandhi ki jai*," he shouted "*Kasturba Ma ki jai*." Surprised on hearing her name, Ba looked out for the voice and found Harilal standing on the platform. Looking at his pathetic state, Ba could not control her tears. Her son was equally distraught. He took out an orange from his pocket and said: "Ba, I have brought this for you." Hearing this, Gandhi asked if he had brought anything for him. "No, this is for Ba. I want to tell you that you have achieved greatness because of Ba," he told his father. As the train started moving, the last words she heard from her beloved son were: "Ba, only you must eat the orange."

By the beginning of 1944, a sick Kasturba was sinking and the end seemed imminent. She asked for Harilal and he presented himself five days before her death. She was very happy to see him and requested that Harilal be allowed to see her every day like her other relatives, despite government orders restricting the number and frequency of visitors. A day before her death, Harilal came to see her in a totally inebriated state, and the distraught mother beat her chest in pain over her son. That was the last he saw her alive. Ba passed away the next day, on February 22, 1944. Harilal was present when she was cremated in Aga Khan Palace in Poona. The three brothers, Harilal, Ramdas and Devdas (Manilal was in

South Africa), had a meal together with Gandhi. Shared tragedies can often provide unforeseen family reunions, yet for a long long time the three never met again.

Harilal Gandhi, 1945.

Gandhi was assassinated at 17 minutes past five on January 30, 1948. According to Hindu custom, the eldest son lights the father's pyre, but Harilal was not to be found at the time of Gandhi's funeral. The ritual was performed by Gandhi's third son, Ramdas. There are a few differing accounts about Harilal's presence during Gandhi's cremation. Most of the records say that Harilal, carrying his bedding, arrived at Devdas' house four days after the funeral to share the family's grief. There are others who doubt this version. News of Gandhi's assassination had spread like wildfire all over the world and Harilal must have got the news at once, and, though estranged, most of the family members were in touch with him. He had been brought to Poona to meet Ba when she was dying, so how is it possible that he could not be located at this time? Was it the embarrassment that his presence would have created for the family? Was he too sick to travel? Was his absence due to his resentment against his father? Very unlikely. According to Gandhi's biographer Robert Payne: "Among the many visitors who came to the cremation ground that night was Harilal, the prodigal son. Thin and gaunt, suffering from tuberculosis that would soon carry him off, he mingled unrecognized with the crowd, and spent the rest of the night in the house of his brother Devdas, who had always loved him and never lost faith in him. Harilal was dead less than five months later." He died on Friday, June 18, 1948, in Bombay.

***

COMPASSION CURE

One quality that Gandhi had in abundance was compassion. One winter evening in 1939, he was taking his customary walk when the sight of a visitor brought sorrow upon his face. It was Parchure Shastri, a well-known Sanskrit scholar and poet who had spent time in prison with Gandhi at Yeravda in 1922. In the ensuing years, Parchure had contracted a virulent form of leprosy. Embarrassed and ashamed of his illness, he wished to disappear for good but before doing so, he wanted to have a last darshan (viewing) of the Mahatma. As he had not replied to Parchure's letter asking to visit him in the ashram, Gandhi was not only surprised but saddened to see his pathetic appearance. The visit was so sudden and unexpected that Gandhi had no time to discuss Parchure's visit with the others at the ashram. Sensing Gandhi's dilemma, Parchure offered to leave the ashram after delivering the yarn he had spun specially for him. But Gandhi asked the other ashram members to get food for him and had him sleep in a hut at a distance. Neither of them slept that night. In the morning, after explaining the risk of infection, Gandhi obtained the consent of the other members. He argued that it would be his life's challenge

Defying age-old beliefs, Gandhi nursed Parchure Shastri to health.

to nurse Parchure back to health and if he denied the latter refuge, Gandhi would compromise his conscience and therefore his relationship with God. The next day Parchure was moved to the hut right next to Gandhi's. In the midst of visits by top political leaders and the difficult political environment that Gandhi was in, he found time to personally clean Parchure's wounds at least thrice every day. Though it took years, with a combination of love, affection, diet and compassion, Gandhi nursed Parchure to health and the scholar became an intrinsic part of the ashram.

1939 *Gandhi nominated for the Nobel Peace Prize.*

Gandhi was nominated five times for the Nobel Peace Prize and shortlisted thrice. The first time he was nominated in 1937 and shortlisted too; then in 1938 and 1939 he was nominated but not shortlisted. His next nomination was in 1947 and the last, two days before his death, in 1948, led to him being shortlisted again. In 1937, Professor Jacob Worm-Mueller, in a report on behalf of the Nobel committee, made a somewhat critical observation on Gandhi's nomination: "He is a freedom fighter and a dictator... he is frequently a Christ but then, suddenly, an ordinary politician." As the years progressed, however, the reports on his nomination became more charitable. In 1948, he was assassinated before the award was decided. Even though there was no precedence of posthumous awards, the Nobel committee deliberated and came to the conclusion that: "Posthumous awards should not take place unless the laureate died after the committee decision had been made." That year, no one was awarded the Peace Prize as the committee could not find "a suitable living candidate."

***

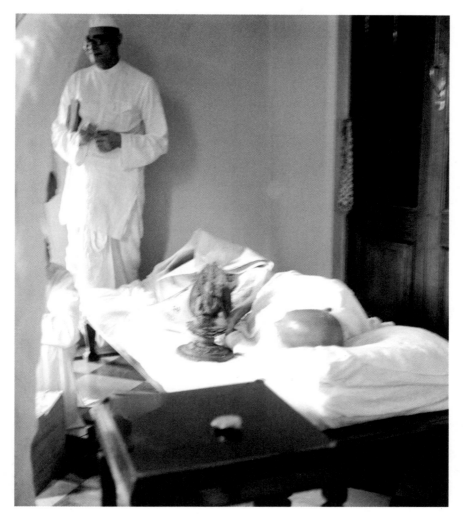

1939 *Gandhi resting, while his personal secretary, Mahadev Desai, stands in the background.*

Mahadev Desai, Gandhi's personal secretary for almost 24 years, joined Gandhi's ashram in 1917 and maintained a diary, in which he chronicled his life with Gandhi, from November 1917 till his own death in August 1942. He was an accomplished writer and translator, and regularly contributed to various Indian journals and newspapers.

```
                                        As at Wardha
                                        C.P.
                                        India.
                                        23.7.'39.

Dear friend,

        Friends have been urging me to write to you for the sake
of humanity.  But I have resisted their request, because of
the feeling that any letter from me would be an impertinence.
Something tells me that I must not calculate and that I must
make my appeal for whatever it may be worth.

        It is quite clear that you are today the one person in
the world who can prevent a  war which may reduce humanity to
the savage state.  Must you pay that price for an object
however worthy it may appear to you to be ? Will you listen to
the appeal of one who has seliberately shunned the method of
war not without considerable success? Any way I anticipate
your forgiveneas, if I have erred in writing to you.

Herr Hitler                        I remain,
Berlin
Germany.                       Your sincere friend

                                    M.K. Gandhi
```

1939 *Gandhi's undelivered letter to Adolf Hitler.*

Gandhi wrote two letters to Hitler. The one reproduced above, dated July 23, 1939, was censored by the government and never delivered. He again wrote to Hitler on Christmas Eve, 1941, this time a long public letter. Addressing Hitler as "Dear Friend," Gandhi wrote: "That I address you as a friend is no formality. I own no foes. Further, we resist the British imperialism no less than Nazism." Extolling the virtues of peace, he wrote: "In non-violent technique, there is no such thing as defeat. It is 'do or die,' without killing or hurting." There is no evidence to prove that Hitler read this letter, for Gandhi never got a reply.

THE WORLD AT WAR, INDIA DIVIDED

On September 3, 1939, Britain declared war with Germany. A day earlier, Viceroy Lord Linlithgow had invited Gandhi to Shimla, informing him that Britain was at war and asking for his support. Gandhi's sympathies lay with Britain, but he found himself isolated because of his stand. "I am sorry to find myself alone in thinking that whatever support was to be given to the British should be given unconditionally and non-violently." The Congress leadership was clear that it would not support the war without an assurance of independence after the war ended. The Congress Working Committee met in Wardha to review the crisis. On June 21, 1940, it declared that it would "not go the full length with Gandhi" on non-violence. Nehru would write in his autobiography: "Gandhi went one way and the Congress Working Committee another." The Congress reaction was also partly because Lord Linlithgow had told certain Congress leaders that if Congress did not support Britain's war efforts, then they would lean toward Muhammad Ali Jinnah and the Muslim League. India appeared divided as Jinnah, Ambedkar, the princely states and Congress each approached the viceroy with their own conditions for support, thus extracting their own pound of flesh. For the first time in 19 years, Gandhi's younger colleagues had voted against Gandhi. Linlithgow met Gandhi again, and indicated that Britain would not allow Congress to rule India without Muslim consent. This was the first time Muslims were given a veto on India's political future. The British had accepted the importance of the Muslim League and its leader, Muhammad Ali Jinnah.

"Here is a mantra, a short one that I give you," Gandhi told the Committee: *"The mantra is 'Do or die.' We shall either free India or die in the attempt."*

MOHANDAS KARAMCHAND GANDHI

1940-1946

Cripps Commission
Quit India Movement

GANDHI: CRIPPS COMMISSION "A POSTDATED CHECK ON A FAILING BANK"

Gandhi may have been sympathetic to the British and their situation with regard to Hitler, but he was determined to protest against the war and the manner in which Britain had involved India without consulting its leaders. He therefore launched a civil disobedience campaign in 1940, calling on Indians selected by him to defy the ban on protests against the war. Those selected included the mild, scholarly Gandhian Vinoba Bhave, who was promptly arrested. Gandhi next selected Nehru, who, too, was arrested and sentenced to four years in jail. Then came the turn of Sardar Patel, who

1942 *British War Cabinet minister Sir Stafford Cripps (left) with Maulana Abul Kalam Azad (center) and Pandit Jawaharlal Nehru outside the Viceroy House.*

1942 *Sir Stafford Cripps, on a special mission to India, sharing a light moment with Gandhi on the steps of Birla House in Delhi.*

was arrested even before he could make his official protest speech. Gandhi suspended the movement in December 1940 as a Christmas gesture of goodwill, but the British went ahead and arrested Maulana Azad, the then president of Congress.

Under pressure from all sides, with Burma having fallen to the Japanese, the British Prime Minister Winston Churchill sent Sir Stafford Cripps to New Delhi to begin negotiations with the Indian leadership. He carried proposals by the British government with the offer of full-fledged dominion status for India and the right to secede from the British Commonwealth. He arrived in Delhi on March 22, 1942, to begin talks with prominent leaders. There were some restrictions contained in the offer regarding the princely states and those with a Muslim-majority population. India would be split into nearly 600 separate sovereign states. Cripps met Jinnah, Nehru, Azad, Ambedkar and Gandhi. On April 9, Congress rejected the offer, as did the Muslim League, the Sikhs, the Hindu Mahasabha, the Harijans and other representatives. The Cripps Mission failed because it did not guarantee independence but offered only possible long-term benefits. Gandhi described the offer as "a postdated check on a failing bank."

ROOSEVELT AND CHURCHILL: DISCORD OVER GANDHI

Franklin D. Roosevelt

On August 14, 1941, the American President Franklin Delano Roosevelt and the British Prime Minister Winston Churchill met on board a ship in the middle of the Atlantic Ocean to jointly announce what came to be known as the Atlantic Charter. Consisting of eight significant points, it was to serve as a blueprint for the new world order after the Second World War. Clause three of the charter read: "They respect the rights of all peoples to choose the form of government under which they will live." However, a month later Churchill backtracked somewhat. Speaking at the House of Commons on September 9, he said: "The joint declaration does not qualify in any way the various statements of policy...about development of constitutional government in India..." Roosevelt was not very happy with this development.

Stories of Gandhi's non-violent struggle against colonial rule had crossed the seven seas and on reaching America had established him as a messiah of peace, a Mahatma, the great soul. Driven by immense media and public pressure, President Roosevelt and his administration tried to persuade the British government to allow the Indians at least an interim self-government.

Around this point in the war, the allied forces were witnessing some of the worst reverses in the Far East. The fall of Hong Kong, Singapore and Rangoon seemed imminent and reports from India were not very promising either. After a four-hour-long meeting with Gandhi, General Chiang Kai-shek, the undisputed leader of China—who had traveled to India to assess public opinion—reported to both Roosevelt and Churchill: "If the Japanese should know of the real situation and attack India, they would be virtually unopposed." Alarmed, President Roosevelt decided it was time to step into Britain's India affair, despite it being politically incorrect to interfere in the internal affairs of a close ally. Toward the end of February 1942, Roosevelt drafted a long letter to Churchill extolling the virtues of freedom, drawing parallels with the United States between 1783 and 1789, when it fought for freedom from British colonial rule, and bluntly advocating the "right of self-government to the Indians." This unusually long letter, personally composed by the president himself, was held back and never sent at the president's own discretion.

Roosevelt did, however, send a long cable to Churchill on March 10, 1942, a day before the British premier announced the departure of a high-level delegation led by Sir Stafford Cripps, urging at least stop-gap self-government. Then again in mid-April, following the receipt of information that the Cripps Mission had almost failed, Roosevelt wired Churchill suggesting the British delegation should not leave India unless some sort of working arrangement was finalized. A third message, conveyed through Lord Halifax, the British ambassador in Washington DC, was more humanitarian than political. Gandhi was by then on a life-threatening fast in detention, and Roosevelt appealed to Churchill to save Gandhi's life and not let him die in custody. Keeping diplomatic sensitivity in mind, Roosevelt would often end his dispatches by saying "India is none of my business." As Harry Hopkins, Roosevelt's closest adviser and speech writer, mentions in his memoirs: "It is probable that this was the only part of the cable with which Churchill agreed."

Persistent interventions by the Americans were understandably poorly received by the British government, particularly by Churchill, who simply despised Gandhi. He bluntly warned that any further interference by the American administration would result in "great embarrassment between the two governments." According to Harry Hopkins: "India was one area where the minds of Roosevelt and Churchill would never meet" and Gandhi was the prime reason.

By now Gandhi was well aware of his popularity with the American masses, who sent him dozens of letters every week, some of which carried invitations to speak. On July 1, 1942, less than a month before Gandhi was to announce the launch of the Quit India movement, he wrote to President Roosevelt (a portion of

Winston Churchill

Sevagram, Via Wardha
(India)

1st July 1942

Dear Friend,

I twice missed coming to your great country. I have the privilege
having numerous friends there both known and unknown to me. Many of my
countrymen have received and are still receiving higher education in America.
I know too that several have taken shelter there. I have profited greatly
by the writings of Thoreau and Emerson. I say this to tell you how much
I am connected with your country. Of Great Britain I need say nothing
beyond mentioning that in spite of my intense dislike of British Rule, I
have numerous personal friends in England whom I love as dearly as my o
people. I had my legal education there. I have therefore nothing but
good wishes for your country and Great Britain. You will therefore
accept my word that my present proposal, that the British should unreser
vedly and without reference to the wishes of the people of India immedia
withdraw their rule, is prompted by the friendliest intention. I would
like to turn into good will the ill will which, whatever may be said to
the contrary, exists in India towards Great Britain and thus enable the
millions of India to play their part in the present war.

My personal position is clear. I hate all war. If, therefore, I
could persuade my countrymen, they would make a most effective and deci-
sive contribution in favour of an honourable peace. But I know that all
of us have not a living faith in non-violence. Under foreign rule however
we can make no effective contribution of any kind in this war, except as
helots. ...

It is on behalf of this proposal that I write this to enlist your
active sympathy.

I hope that it would commend itself to you.

Mr. Louis Fischer is carrying this letter to you.

If there is any obscurity in my letter, you have but to send me
word and I shall try to clear it.

I hope finally that you will not resent this letter as an intru-
sion but take it as an approach from a friend and well wisher of the
Allies.

I remain,
yours sincerely
mkgandhi

dent Franklin D.Roosevelt

the letter is illustrated on the facing page). The letter was delivered by the American journalist Louis Fischer, Gandhi's future biographer. Precisely a month later, despite Churchill's objection, on August 1, 1942, President Roosevelt replied (see the full letter below). Gandhi was arrested on August 9, 1942, before the letter could reach him. It was finally delivered to him two years later, after his release from jail.

India gained independence on August 15, 1947. President Roosevelt, who died in state on April 12, 1945, did not live to see it.

August 1, 1942

My dear Mr. Gandhi;

I have received your letter of July 1, 1942, which you have thoughtfully sent me in order that I may better understand your plans, which I well know may have far-reaching effect upon developments important to your country and to mine.

I am sure that you will agree that the United States has consistently striven for and supported policies of fair dealing, of fair play, and of all related principles looking towards the creation of harmonious relations between nations. Nevertheless, now that war has come as a result of Axis dreams of world conquest, we, together with many other nations, are making a supreme effort to defeat those who would deny forever all hope of freedom throughout the world. I am enclosing a copy of an address of July 23 by the Secretary of State, made with my complete approval, which illustrates the attitude of this Government.

I shall hope that our common interest in democracy and righteousness will enable your countrymen and mine to make common cause against a common enemy.

Very sincerely yours,

FRANKLIN D. ROOSEVELT

Enclosure:

Copy of speech by
Secretary of State,
July 23, 1942.

Mr. M. K. Gandhi,
Sevagram Via Wardha,
Central Provinces, India.

GANDHI AND NEHRU

Gandhi and Jawaharlal Nehru shared a complex relationship. They admired each other but also had opposing views on many crucial issues. They first met in December 1916 during the Lucknow session of the Congress. In his autobiography, Nehru wrote: "He seemed very distant and different and unpolitical to many of us young men. He refused to take part in Congress or national politics then and confined himself to the South African Indian question. Soon afterward his adventures and victory in Champaran...filled us with enthusiasm." Nehru's open admiration for Gandhi did not go down well with his father, Motilal, who was opposed to his son being under the influence of Gandhi. In his book *Nehru: The Making of India*, M. J. Akbar writes: "No one is sure why Motilal changed, but it is clear from reading his letters that he had realized that if he did not stand by Gandhi at this vital juncture he would lose his son."

Nehru and Gandhi forged a relationship that was both political and personal. The Harrow- and Cambridge-educated Nehru was not a Gandhian like other Congress leaders. The two differed in their outlook on life and ideology but Nehru's loyalty to Gandhi and the latter's love and affection for the former never diminished. As Nehru writes in *The Discovery of India*: "And then Gandhi came. He was like a powerful current of fresh air that made us stretch ourselves and take a deep breath; like a beam of light that pierced the darkness and removed the scales from our eyes; like a whirlwind that upset many things, but most of all the working of people's minds."

When Gandhi called off his non-cooperation movement in 1922 after the Chauri-Chaura incident, Motilal and Jawaharlal felt let down. Yet, when Motilal died on February 6,

SOON AFTER GANDHI'S RELEASE FOLLOWING HIS APPENDICITIS SURGERY IN FEBRUARY 1924, AN INTERESTING INCIDENT TOOK PLACE ON THE SIDELINES OF A CONGRESS WORKING COMMITTEE MEETING. A MAN WITH A DECORATED BULL, KNOWN FOR ITS PREDICTIONS AND FORTUNE-TELLING ABILITIES, WAS ASKED BY GANDHI'S FRIEND, JAMNALAL BAJAJ: "AMONG US, WHOM DOES GANDHIJI LIKE THE MOST?" THE BULL DID A ROUND, SNIFFING AT EVERYONE, AND FINALLY STOOD BEFORE JAWAHARLAL NEHRU NODDING DECISIVELY! THE BULL'S PROPHECY WAS TO COME TRUE OVER TWO DECADES LATER.

Gandhi with Motilal and Jawaharlal Nehru walking out of a tent.

1931, Gandhi was inconsolable. In a message, he wrote: "My position is worse than a widow's. By a faithful life she can appropriate the merits of her husband. I can appropriate nothing. What I have lost through Motilal's death is a loss for ever." It was clear from letters written by Motilal that he had been pressing Gandhi for the election of his son as president of Congress, but Gandhi was reluctant. He wrote to Motilal on June 13, 1927: "Jawaharlal is too high-souled to stand the hooliganism that seems to be growing in the Congress." However, in 1936, Gandhi asked Patel to withdraw from the presidential election in favor of Jawaharlal. Dr. Rajendra Prasad lamented later in his memoirs: "Gandhiji had once again sacrificed his trusted lieutenant for the sake of glamorous Nehru." At the Congress session at Wardha in January 1942, Gandhi designated Nehru as his heir. He said: "Pandit Jawaharlal Nehru and I have had differences from the moment when we became co-workers, yet I have said for some years and say it now that not Rajaji (C. Rajagopalachari), nor Sardar Patel but Jawaharlal will be my successor." Those who witnessed the scene testify that Patel agreed reluctantly to support Nehru's candidature at Gandhi's nod. The die was cast! Nehru became the president of Congress, leader of the Congress party, and later the first prime minister of India.

1942 Left to right: *Sardar Patel, Gandhi and Acharya Kripalani share a laugh at a Congress meeting.*

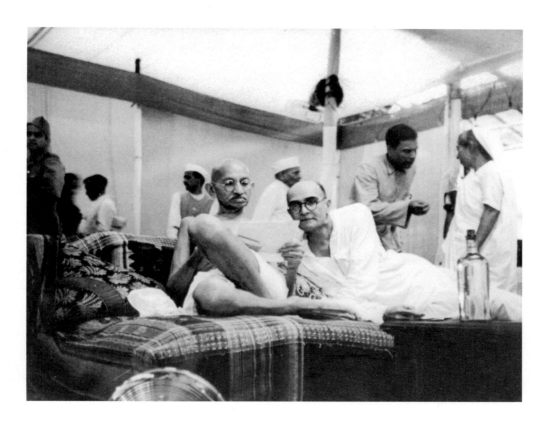

1942 *Gandhi with his secretary Mahadev Desai at the All-India Congress Committee meeting in August.*

MADELEINE SLADE (MIRABEHN)
(1892–1982)

Madeleine was the daughter of a British admiral, Sir Edmond Slade, and lived the fairly regulated life of the British elite. She was a fan of Beethoven, which is how she came into contact with the French intellectual and writer Romain Rolland, who had not only written extensively on the musician but also published a biography of Mahatma Gandhi. Fascinated by what she read, she decided to practice the Gandhian way of life and wrote letters sharing her experiences and asking for permission to visit his ashram. She was so committed to the Gandhian way that she took lessons in farming, gave up alcohol, turned vegetarian and started reading Gandhi's journal *Young India*. At the end of October 1925, she arrived in Bombay, and was in Ahmedabad a week later.

She describes her first meeting with Gandhi: "…As I entered, I became conscious of a small spare figure rising up from a white gaddi [seat] and stepping toward me. I knew it was Bapu, but, so completely overcome was I with reverence and joy, that I could see and feel nothing but a heavenly light. I fell on my knees at Bapu's feet. He lifted me up and taking me in his arms said: 'You shall be my daughter.' And so has it been from that day." Madeleine Slade was named Mirabehn. She went to jail several times and accompanied Gandhi to the Second Round Table Conference in London in 1931.

Around her early 40s, Mirabehn fell in love with a dashing Sikh, Baba Prithvi Singh, a nationalist revolutionary who was imprisoned by the British for ten years in 1915 but escaped mid-sentence and remained underground until the late 1930s when he met Gandhi. Though Gandhi was not entirely against their relationship, he liked to conduct the lives of his followers, especially when it came to love and marriage. Gandhi and Mirabehn's relationship became very acrimonious. He started to address her as "Dear Ms. Slade" as compared to the more affectionate "Chi Mira," and the fight degraded to money matters. However, her deep reverence and love for Bapu lasted throughout her life. She moved to the foothills of the Himalayas hoping that one day Gandhi, too, would move to an ashram she was creating there. After Gandhi's assassination she wrote: "For me there were only two. God and Bapu. And now they have become one."

NILA CRAM COOK
(1908–1982)

Nila Nagini, as she was known among the ashramites, was a hippie long before the term was coined. She fancied herself as Lord Krishna's gopi (devotee), lived with a swami in Mount Abu, and fell in love with a prince from Mysore. An American by birth, she was a true bohemian and perhaps the most difficult of Gandhi's disciples. She wrote to Gandhi in September 1932 from Bangalore, describing the anti-untouchability work she had been doing with a young man she was living with. They exchanged letters regularly and eventually met up in February 1933 in Yeravda Jail. Gandhi sent her to Sabarmati Ashram, and there, too, she started to have "special feelings" for a few members. Finding ashram life too claustrophobic for a liberated personality like herself, she fled and was later found in Brindaban, though she was subsequently deported to America by the government. She converted to Islam, translated the Koran, and became the director of the Iranian National Ballet and Opera.

SARALA DEVI CHOUDHURANI (1872–1945)

Highly educated, elegant and with a deep interest in music, languages and writing, Sarala was Rabindranath Tagore's niece. Gandhi was her guest in Lahore while her husband, Rambhuj Dutt Choudhuri, a freedom fighter and activist, was in jail. They became very close. Gandhi called her his "spiritual wife" and confessed later that his relationship with her almost wrecked his marriage. They traveled together throughout India promoting khadi. Her extreme attachment alarmed those close to Gandhi, while her possessiveness led to Gandhi calling off the relationship. She died a recluse in the foothills of the Himalayas.

SAROJINI NAIDU (1879–1949)

The first Indian female president of the Indian National Congress, Sarojini led the Salt Satyagraha after Gandhi's arrest. Said Sarojini of her first ever meeting with Gandhi in London: "…a little man with shaven head, seated on the floor on a black prison blanket and eating a messy meal of squashed tomatoes and olive oil out of a wooden prison bowl…I burst instinctively into happy laughter at this amusing vision of a famous leader…he lifted his eyes and laughed back at me saying 'Ah, you must be Mrs. Naidu! Who else dare be so irreverent? Come in and share my meal.' 'No thanks,' I replied, sniffing, 'what an abominable mess it is.' Thus began an enduring relationship."

RAJKUMARI AMRIT KAUR (1889–1964)

Of royal lineage, Rajkumari was the daughter of Raja Sir Harnam Singh from the state of Kapurthala in Punjab. Educated in England, she was one of Gandhi's closest satyagrahi, and he gave her much affection and respect. They exchanged hundreds of letters from 1934, after their first meeting. She was arrested during the Salt Satyagraha and again in 1942 during the Quit India movement, and she became independent India's first health minister. In their exchange of letters, Gandhi addressed her as "My dear Idiot and Rebel," while he himself signed off as "Tyrant."

MANU GANDHI (1928–1969)

Manu was in her teens when she came to serve Gandhi. She was the daughter of a distant relative, and Gandhi called her his granddaughter. Gandhi was fond of her, and they were closest during his Noakhali days. She nursed Kasturba in her dying days. Her diary and books have proven to be a valuable resource for researchers, especially on the last four years of Gandhi's life.

THE WOMEN WHO FOLLOWED GANDHI

DR SUSHILA NAYYAR
(1914–2001)

Sushila was the sister of Pyarelal, who became Gandhi's secretary after Mahadev Desai's death. Punjabi by birth, the sister and brother came to Gandhi despite initial resistance from their mother (who herself later became a staunch follower of Gandhi). After qualifying as a doctor, she became Gandhi's personal physician. With Manu and Abha Gandhi, she often rotated to serve as Gandhi's "walking stick." She was arrested along with Kasturba in Bombay during the Quit India movement and looked after her during her last days at the Aga Khan Palace in Poona. She participated in Gandhi's brahmacharya experiment and traveled with him during his Noakhali days. Together with her brother, she produced a ten-volume set of books on Gandhi that serves as one of the best references on his life.

ESTHER FAERING (1889–1962)

Danish by birth, Esther came to India in 1915 as a missionary and became a Gandhian soon after meeting Gandhi at the Kochrab Ashram. According to Thomas Weber, in 1916–1919 Gandhi wrote "more letters to Esther than to his own grown children." She married Kunhi Menon from Kerala, and had a son and a daughter. Her biography of Gandhi, written in Danish, was titled *Gandhi: A Sketch and a Portrayal*. Toward the end of her life, the exchange of letters between Gandhi and herself became less frequent. The Menons moved to London for Kunhi to complete a medical course, and Gandhi met her there in 1931 during his visit for the Second Round Table Conference. She died almost unnoticed in Denmark in the winter of 1962.

ABHA GANDHI (1927–1995)

A Bengali by birth, Abha was married to Kanu Gandhi, Gandhi's grandnephew. Abha used to sing bhajans at Gandhi's prayer meetings, while Kanu was a keen photographer who took many pictures of Gandhi in the 1940s. They traveled to Noakhali with him, spreading the message of peace between Hindus and Muslims. Along with Manu, she was one of Gandhi's two "walking sticks" when he was shot dead by Nathuram Godse.

SONJA SCHLESIN (1888–1956)

Sonja was barely 16 when, following an introduction by Hermann Kallenbach, Gandhi employed her as his secretary while he was in South Africa. Of Jewish-Russian origin and born in Moscow, she was just four when the family migrated from Russia to South Africa. She had a first-class diploma in shorthand and typing, and Gandhi wanted to pay her more than what his friend Kallenbach had suggested, but she declined in accordance with Gandhian principles. According to Thomas Weber: "One morning, Gandhi came into his office to find her 'sitting on the table, dangling her legs and smoking a cigarette.' He slapped her and threw away the cigarette. She burst into tears and apologized, promising never to do such a thing again, recognizing the love in his action." Gandhi later noted: "In a month's time, she had achieved the conquest of my heart." She got involved in the work of Gandhi's Phoenix settlement and took on a leading role when Gandhi and some of the other prominent leaders were in jail.

Gandhi and Sonja kept in regular touch even after he returned to India. She did not agree with the contents of Gandhi's autobiography, especially the sections relating to her; she was angry and made fun of the book, saying it would have been better if "the whole wretched thing were burned and you refrained from writing more autobiographical nonsense..." Although she complained about the misrepresentation in Gandhi's books, she remained a friend till the end. Gandhi was still hoping that she would one day set foot on Indian soil. She wrote to Gandhi suggesting that she could act as his secretary if he decided to attend the UN Peace Conference in San Francisco in 1945, but that never happened, and the two never met again after Gandhi left South Africa.

THE WOMEN WHO FOLLOWED GANDHI

MILLIE GRAHAM POLAK (1880–1962)

Millie was a Scottish Christian who met her future husband, Gandhi's friend Henry Polak, in London; following a brief courtship, they married in 1905. Gandhi had to reassure Henry's family—concerned that Millie's health was not robust enough for a life in the colonies—to get their consent for the marriage. He was the best man at their wedding in South Africa, which in itself was not an easy affair. Henry Polak always referred to himself and his friends as "we Indians," and having a colored best man did not help the matter either. The magistrate suspended the registration midway, suspecting it to be a mixed marriage. It was only after Gandhi's intervention that the marriage could be registered.

In her book, *Mr. Gandhi: The Man*, she describes her first impression of Gandhi, saying he "...was a medium-sized man, rather slenderly built, skin not very dark, mouth rather heavy lipped, a small dark mustache, and the kindest eyes in the world, that seemed to light up from within when he spoke...they were lamps of his soul."

The Polaks and Gandhis lived as one family under the same roof. Gandhi's family comprised Kasturba and their sons, along with two other followers. Said Millie: "My addition to the family completed its possibilities of accommodation"—meaning the house was now full. Gandhi was a loving and understanding elder brother to Millie and always signed off his letters to her as "Bhai," a brother. They were extremely close yet disagreed on many issues, especially when it came to family and the education of children. She was more outspoken and did not mince her words.

To quote Thomas Weber: "In the early years of their relationship, both Henry and Millie Polak helped shape Gandhi, the prototype Mahatma." They kept in regular touch even after the Polaks returned to Britain and Gandhi was back in India.

MARGARETE SPIEGEL (1897–1967)

Margarete was from a rich German merchant family and had a doctorate from Bonn University. It was her interest in Indian culture and philosophy, inspired by the writings of Rabindranath Tagore, that brought her to read books about and by Gandhi. Romain Rolland's biography of Gandhi fascinated her and she made plans to visit India and meet him in person. She did so at Yeravda Jail in April 1933 and remembered: "He was sitting in the courtyard of the jail under a mango tree, surrounded by a host of men and women. I thought of Jesus or Socrates...I felt the magic aura which a truly great man emanates. He, the prisoner, was master; the prison warden bowed to him." Gandhi allowed her to join the ashram, and gave her an Indian name, "Amala."

Margarete willed everything she had to Gandhi's ashram and offered her dead body to the Sassoon Hospital in Poona to meet her burial expenses. Harilal, Gandhi's eldest son, fell in love with her and wanted to marry her. Gandhi, though not very happy at the prospect, did not want to stand in the way. He advised both of them against any haste. In fact, he suggested that Harilal should drop the idea—which may have had something to do with Margarete's desire to have many children. For some time Margarete taught French in Santiniketan. Among her pupils was Nehru's daughter, Priyadarshini Indira, future prime minister of independent India.

SUCHETA KRIPALANI (1908–1974)

Born a Bengali, Sucheta married Acharya J. B. Kripalani, a Sindhi. Gandhi first tried to dissuade her from marrying, but later approved of the union and advised them to remain celibate. Indeed, they practiced brahmacharya, or celibacy, throughout their married life. Gandhi treated Sucheta as his daughter, and she and her husband accompanied him in most of his campaigns, notably in Noakhali, where Gandhi stayed for months and walked many miles to bring peace and harmony between Hindus and Muslims.

PRABHAVATI (1906–1973)

Prabhavati was the daughter of Braj Kishore Prasad, a well-known lawyer from Bihar who was with Gandhi during the Champaran campaign. Thanks to his forceful argument in the hearing of an official commission, he succeeded in getting wealthy planters in Champaran to return money they had extorted from poor indigo farmers. Prabhavati's first memory of Gandhi is when he visited their Darbhanga home in 1919. Since Gandhi had no daughter, he asked Prasad to send Prabhavati to his ashram to live with him and Kasturba as their adopted daughter. Around this time, Prabhavati, who was merely 14, married Jayaprakash Narayan (JP), who was four years her elder. Two years after the marriage, JP left for California University to pursue higher studies. In the meantime, Prabhavati, influenced by Gandhi's ashram environment, vowed to practice celibacy. Prabhavati, Gandhi and JP exchanged many letters between 1929 and 1936 on the subject. JP's letters were full of anger and frustration, yet he was logical. Prabhavati expressed helplessness and determination to keep the vow, while Gandhi's letters ranged from understanding to "ruthless logic," with him even suggesting that rather than forcing Prabhavati to sleep with him, JP should remarry. Their marriage, as a result, was never consummated. "They slept in the same room but on separate beds," is how Jayaprakash Narayan's biographer Sudhanshu Ranjan describes their relationship.

QUIT INDIA

The failure of the Cripps Mission in 1942 had created a groundswell of anti-British sentiment and it would give rise to a new slogan and a new movement that would resonate across the world. The slogan was "Quit India" and it was to mark the start of a new civil disobedience campaign by Gandhi. He had the full support of Congress, which announced that it would convert the current anti-British feeling into goodwill, but that this would be possible only "if India feels the glow of freedom." The threat was reinforced in Bombay at the Congress Working Committee session in August 1942 when Gandhi spoke as though he had suddenly discovered that the British were the enemy. "Here is a mantra, a short one that I give you," he told the committee, adding: "The mantra is 'Do or Die.' We shall either free India or die in the attempt." He concluded by stating that "this is an open rebellion."

Gandhi wrote to the U.S. president, Franklin D. Roosevelt, a strong ally of Britain: "British should unreservedly and...immediately withdraw their rule..." The letter was carried by his friend and biographer Louis Fischer. He knew that once the campaign was launched, all of the recognized Indian leaders would be arrested. He also suggested that there should be a widespread stoppage of work and businesses, a withholding of tax and land revenue, along with resignations from government jobs. Sardar Patel announced that this time Gandhi would not call off the agitation, even if the movement turned violent. "This time if a railway line is removed or an Englishman is murdered the struggle would not stop.... This is going to be an opportunity of a lifetime."

"DO OR DIE"

After the All India Congress Committee (AICC) meeting in Bombay, the delegates returned to their homes. Gandhi reached Birla House on August 8, 1942, where he was informed by Mahadev Desai about the rumors concerning his impending arrest. He was unperturbed. "They dare not arrest me. I cannot think they will be so

1942 *Gandhi discussing the Quit India concept with Jawaharlal Nehru.*

foolish. But if they do, it will mean that their days are numbered." Around midnight on the same day, the industrialist and nationalist G. D. Birla was informed that his guest at Birla House in Bombay was to be arrested immediately. He conveyed this to Gandhi, who still insisted that he did not believe it. He was woken up a few hours before sunrise, taken into custody and then shifted to the Aga Khan Palace Prison in Poona. Sarojini Naidu, Mirabehn, Mahadev Desai and Pyarelal Nayyar were also arrested and they shared his prison quarters. The next day, Kasturba courted arrest by announcing that she would address a meeting where Gandhi had been scheduled to speak. All members of the Congress Working Committee were arrested. While the press was placed under strict censorship, Congress was officially banned and all public meetings prohibited.

Gandhi's arrest would be a turning point in the freedom struggle; it removed the only obstacle to chaos and anarchy, and opened the gates to violence. Police stations and government buildings were attacked by mobs and set on fire, railroad and telegraph services were disrupted and government officials assaulted. A powerful underground movement started up, led by members of the Socialist Party and a segment of Congress. Leaders such as Jayaprakash Narayan and Aruna Asaf Ali marshaled the forces. Britain's writ did not run in large parts of the country and Indians set up independent village, town and district governments. In the two months that followed, violence erupted as leaderless mobs took to the streets and every symbol of British rule was attacked and torn down. The British called out the army and, by one estimate, as many as 568 people were shot dead. Over 100,000 Indian nationalists were jailed for indefinite terms and in a letter to the king, Viceroy Linlithgow termed Quit India "by far the most serious rebellion since that of 1857." The British even discussed the possibility of deporting Gandhi to Aden. There was just one slogan that resounded all around India: "Do or Die."

1942 From left to right: *Pyarelal, Mahadev Desai, Sardar Patel, Gandhi, J. B. Kripalani, Maulana Azad with Sarojini Naidu at the meeting of the Congress Working Committee in Sevagram, Maharashtra.*

1942 *Above: Women played an active part in the demonstrations during the Quit India movement.*
Facing page: Demonstrations in Bombay during the Quit India movement. Many people were injured in the nationwide protests.

"MAHADEV HAS DIED A YOGI'S AND PATRIOT'S DEATH"

Six days after Gandhi was arrested and lodged in the Aga Khan Palace Prison near Poona, he received news that visibly shook him. His secretary, Mahadev Desai, who had been arrested with him and was lodging in the same prison, had had a sudden heart attack and died. On hearing this, Gandhi cried out, "Mahadev, Mahadev." It was a tragic and also a deeply personal loss. "If only he would open his eyes and look at me, he would not die," Gandhi said. Even Kasturba was shattered. "Mahadev, look, Bapu is calling you," she cried. It was no use. Mahadev was gone. He was barely past 50 and had served Gandhi faithfully, devotedly and efficiently for the past 24 years as his secretary, adviser, chronicler, friend and son. He was cremated in the palace-turned-prison and his ashes were buried in the grounds there. Gandhi visited the spot every morning and evening to pray at the burial site. "Mahadev has died a yogi's and patriot's death," said Gandhi. In his telegram to Chimanlal Shah, manager of the Sevagram Ashram in Wardha, the ashram set up by Gandhi in 1936, he wrote: "Mahadev died suddenly. Gave no indication. Slept well last night, had breakfast, walked with me. Sushila (Nayyar), jail doctors did all they could but God had willed otherwise. Sushila and I bathed body....Only joy over such noble death. Cremation taking place front of me. Shall keep ashes."

GANDHI'S FIFTEENTH FAST...THIS TIME 21 DAYS

Under detention, on February 10, 1943, Gandhi went on a fast that almost ended his life. It would last 21 days and bring him closer to death than he had ever been. While he was in prison, the violence outside had disturbed him so much that he decided to fast. "If I cannot get a soothing balm for my pain, I must resort to the law prescribed for satyagrahis, namely a fast according to capacity." In his view, his capacity to fast was three weeks and he made his intentions clear to his close associates in jail. Sarojini Naidu was strongly against his decision and cautioned that this fast would be an act of violence against the people. However, Gandhi remained adamant and declared that his fast would commence on February 9 after

1942 *Mahadev Desai with Gandhi at Bardoli in Gujarat.*

breakfast and end on the morning of March 2. "My wish," he said, "is not to fast unto death but to survive the ordeal if God so wills."

There was an acrimonious exchange of letters between Gandhi and Lord Linlithgow. Before going on the fast, Gandhi wrote to Lord Linlithgow on December 31, 1942: "I have allowed many suns to set on a quarrel I have against you, but I must not allow the old year to expire without disturbing myself... what happened since the 9th of August last (arrest of leaders after the Quit India call) makes me wonder.... The law of Satyagraha knows no defeat... (it) prescribes a remedy in such moments of trial... crucify the flesh by fasting."

A letter was also sent to Gandhi stating that the government was reluctant to see him fast. If he proposed to do so, they would set him free for that duration. The fast, Gandhi wrote, had not been conceived by him as one undertaken by a free man. If he was released, there would be no fast. This response upset Viceroy Lord Linlithgow's plans, and he called it "political blackmail." The viceroy summoned his executive council to a meeting at 12:30 a.m., dragging them out of their beds. The meeting lasted three hours as they discussed whether Gandhi should be held in prison till he died, or released when in imminent danger of death. Many present felt that he should remain in prison till he died. The British secretly wished it, knowing his death would then be seen as self-imposed.

On February 10, Gandhi started his fast after a short prayer. When the news of the fast broke, thousands of prisoners in jails all over the country went on sympathetic fasts, industrial centers observed hartals (strikes) and exchange markets shut down for two weeks. In Ahmedabad 10,000 textile workers left the city. By February 20, Gandhi's condition had deteriorated alarmingly. The doctor attending to him, General R. H. Candy, the chief of prisons, told Gandhi that it was his duty as a doctor to tell him that he had reached the limit of his capacity to fast. He then burst into tears. Gandhi consoled him by saying that his life was "in God's hands. If he wishes to take me away, I shall go." So serious was the prospect of Gandhi dying because of the fast that Deputy Prime Minister Clement Attlee sent cables to many world leaders, including the prime ministers of Canada, Australia, New Zealand and South Africa, apprising them of Gandhi's deteriorating condition, seeking their understanding.

On February 28, Gandhi's health improved and he seemed cheerful. There was some speculation that the doctors had administered glucose while Gandhi was asleep. He woke up on March 2, the day he was to end his fast, at 4 in the morning. A prayer session followed a recitation from the Bhagavad Gita. After a massage, Gandhi was carried into another room. As soon as General Candy and the other doctors arrived, hymns were sung and Dr. B. C. Roy read out from Tagore's Gitanjali, the poem "This is my prayer to thee, My Lord. Strike and strike, cut the root of penury in my heart; Give me the strength..."

WESTERN UNION
(THE WESTERN UNION TELEGRAPH COMPANY)
(INCORPORATED IN THE STATE OF NEW YORK, U.S.A., WITH LIMITED LIABILITY.)

CABLEGRAM

ANGLO-AMERICAN TELEGRAPH CO., LD.   CANADIAN NATIONAL TELEGRAPHS

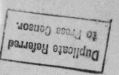

RECEIVED AT 22 GREAT WINCHESTER STREET, LONDON, E.C.2. (TEL. LONDON WALL 1234.)

869 WASHINGTON DC 323 1/58 22/836P

184D.

PRESS JOYCE INDIAOFFICE LDN=
WHITEHALL S. W.

(FOLLOWING BEEN REPEATED TO VICEROYS SECRETARY) SECOND CABLE
THOMPSON TEXT BEGINS BRITISH HAVE ACTED COMPLETELY RATIONALLY
STOP EYE CANNOT IMAGINE ANY GOVERNMENT INCLUDING AMERICAN IN
SITUATION WHEREIN IT FOUND ITSELF IN INDIA COULD HAVE OR
WOULD HAVE ACTED DIFFERENTLY STOP BRITISH ARE STILL FOLLOWING
ABSOLUTELY LOGICAL LINE STOP GANDHIS FAST IS BLACKMAIL PURE

Please send your Reply "Via WESTERN UNION"   You may telephone us for a messenger

---

WESTERN UNION
(THE WESTERN UNION TELEGRAPH COMPANY)
(INCORPORATED IN THE STATE OF NEW YORK, U.S.A., WITH LIMITED LIABILITY.)

CABLEGRAM

ANGLO-AMERICAN TELEGRAPH CO., LD.   CANADIAN NATIONAL TELEGRAPHS

RECEIVED AT 22 GREAT WINCHESTER STREET, LONDON, E.C.2. (TEL. LONDON WALL 1234.)

2/ 869 PRESS JOYCE 52=

ETSIMPLE STOP HES TACITLY SAYING TO HIS OWN PEOPLE QUOTE
BRITISH ARE GOING KILL ME UNQUOTE THIS IS NOT TRUE STOP
GANDHI IS COMMITTING SUICIDESIN AGAKHANA PALACE ETIS TELLING
WORLD HELL STOP COMMITTING SUICIDE IF BRITISH WILL YIELD STOP
BRITISH CONSIDER YIELDING TO BLACKMAIL IS END OF ANY KIND OF
AUTHORITY

Please send your Reply "Via WESTERN UNION"   You may telephone us for a messenger

1943 Telegrams sent out from India Office, London.

THE SAINT AND THE DEMAGOGUE

(After Edward Lear)

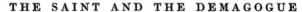

THE Saint and the Demagogue drifted to sea
  On a leaky swadeshi craft,
They had a mixed crew and a nanny goat too
  And a rudder both fore and aft,
The Saint sat and steered at the ' forrard ' end
  And moaned to an Indian guitar :
  " O Mahomed, my brother ! O Ali, my friend
  What an obstinate fellow you are
  You are
  You are
What an obstinate fellow you are ! "

At his steering post aft the Demagogue laughed
  And his answer was far from polite :
" It should be clear to you that your own stubborn vie
  Is solely the cause of our plight ;
You know in your heart that the course which I steer
  Is safer than yours, by far ;
O Mahatma, my love ! O Mohandas dear
  What a shocking old humbug you are
  You are
  You are
What a shocking old humbug you are !

A decade has gone and the wrangle goes on
  And the craft is still out in mid-ocean ;
Will they *ever* agree ?   Well, I too am " at sea "
  I haven't the ghost of a notion ;
But prophets discern in the arcuate moon
  A sign that they will before long,
O may the day dawn ! O may it be soon,
  But our prophets are often so wrong
  So wrong
  So wrong
Our prophets are often so wrong !

1944 *A satirical poem mocking the differences between two prominent leaders of the Congress and the Muslim League—Gandhi and Jinnah—Gandhi being referred here as a saint and Jinnah a demagogue.*

GANDHI AND JINNAH

Muhammad Ali Jinnah was a true aristocrat, quite the opposite of the ascetic Gandhi. According to Louis Fischer, he lived in a crescent-shaped marble mansion on Bombay's Malabar Hill. Jinnah was over 6 feet tall and extremely thin, with silver-gray hair combed straight back. Fischer described him thus: "The temples were sunken and the cheeks were deep holes which made his cheekbones stand out like high horizontal ridges. His teeth were bad.... He rarely laughed." Jinnah made an even more striking figure because of his dress. He often wore expensive Savile Row suits in the European style, or impeccably tailored Indian garments, sherwanis and kurtas with tight white pajamas that clung to his bony legs.

Curiously, he, too, was born in the Kathiawar peninsula, Gandhi's birthplace, though he was seven years younger. His native language was Gujarati, and Jinnah was actually a Hindu name; the family were recent converts to Islam. The son of a rich merchant, he was a Khoja Muslim. He was devoted to the cause of Muslims

1944 *Gandhi with Muhammad Ali Jinnah, Bombay.*

but was not himself a devout Muslim. Being somewhat Westernized in his outlook and appearance, he was not a regular attendee at mosque and knew very little Urdu, or even Arabic. He had married late, in his 40s, to a Parsi girl who was 18. Yet when his only child, a daughter, married a Parsi who had converted to Christianity, he disowned her.

Like Gandhi, he studied law in London; on his return to India, he built up a lucrative law practice in Bombay. His early political forays were attempts to unite Hindus and Muslims. All that changed once Gandhi was in his ascendancy. Jinnah became bitter and left Congress, an action that led to a steady deterioration in Hindu–Muslim relations. When differences came out in the open between him and the Congress leaders, Jinnah decided to stay on in England (from 1930 through 1934). He told Louis Fischer: "Gandhi does not want Independence.... Nehru does not want the British to go. They want a Hindu Raj."

These differences would impact the crucial talks between the two men in Bombay in 1944. Gandhi strongly believed that if Congress and the Muslim League forged an agreement, it would hasten the departure of the British from India. Gandhi arrived at Jinnah's house on September 9 for the first meeting, which lasted close to three hours. Jinnah had insisted on meeting at his home—Gandhi was staying down the road, at Birla House. Between September 9 and 27, Gandhi walked across to Jinnah's house on Mount Pleasant Road 14 times. They spoke in English, the only common language they had. After each meeting, they exchanged long letters, confirming and reaffirming the points discussed. Their frequent meetings were encouraging and raised expectations. Gandhi had even sent Jinnah to his naturopath, and on Eid, which fell during the talks, Gandhi sent him packets of wheat crackers. Yet the strains were evident. Asked after the first meeting what he had got from Jinnah, Gandhi replied: "Only flowers." At one of the meetings, Gandhi suggested he be allowed to address the executive council of the Muslim League, a suggestion Jinnah refused, calling it "most extraordinary and unprecedented."

The general belief was that the breakdown in their talks was over Jinnah's two-nation theory—his belief that India needed to be partitioned into two separate nations: one for Hindus and one for Muslims.

KASTURBA'S ARREST AND DEATH

Gandhi was arrested at Birla House in Bombay on August 9, 1942, a day before he was due to address a large public meeting. Expecting a massive turnout, the meeting was planned at the vast Shivaji Park. With Gandhi's arrest, the big question was who would replace him as the main speaker. No one could match Gandhi's stature. There was deep anxiety and tension in the camp as no substitute could be found.

"There is no need to despair," said Kasturba, "I will address the meeting."

This announcement from Ba took everyone by surprise. Not only was Ba unwell, she had rarely ever addressed a public meeting of this scale. Also, one thing was certain—if she went ahead with her decision, she, too, would be arrested.

Ba dictated a speech to Sushila Nayyar an hour before the meeting and then got into a car to go to Shivaji Park. The police inspector who was posted at Birla House with instructions to arrest anyone leaving the premises pleaded with Ba not to go. He did not have the heart to see her get arrested. He must have defied his duty for Ba to reach Shivaji Park.

Ba addressed a crowd of over 150,000 people—some shouting slogans, most with tears in their eyes. The atmosphere was emotionally charged. As soon as she finished her speech, she was whisked away by the police to Arthur Road Jail, along with Sushila. With triumph in her eyes, Ba said to Sushila: "I have a feeling, this time I will not come out alive." After being imprisoned in a dark cell meant for petty criminals for 30 hours, Ba and Sushila were transferred to Poona and incarcerated at the Aga Khan Palace Jail, where Gandhi had been brought earlier. This was going to be a long jail term for all of them, and no one knew how many would survive.

Gandhi turned 74 on October 2, 1943—his second consecutive birthday as a prisoner at the Aga Khan Palace. Fellow satyagrahis at the Aga Khan Palace had made elaborate preparations for the birthday celebrations a few days in advance. The otherwise reticent Ba decided, too, that this birthday should be special. She asked for the khaddar sari with a bright red border that her husband had woven for her. Ba had always been very sentimental about the sari—she had kept it carefully at Sevagram Ashram with instructions that she should be dressed in it when she was to be cremated. But she changed her mind and decided to wear the sari to show her affection and to celebrate the ushering in of Gandhi's 75th year. This was to be the last birthday that Gandhi and Ba would spend together.

Two months later, Ba developed acute bronchitis and had a heart attack followed by two more in January 1944. The series of heart attacks had weakened her greatly, and she was confined to bed. Gandhi spent most of his time nursing Ba, despite her gentle chiding. A small wooden table was made and placed on her bed for her meals. This became a parting memento for Gandhi, for he would carry this table with him everywhere after Ba's death and have his meals on it.

By mid-January 1944, Gandhi could see that Ba was sinking slowly. He wrote a series of letters to the authorities, including the inspector general of police and the home secretary, asking that he be allowed to consult his personal doctors as well as naturopaths and Ayurveda specialists. The permissions took a long time to come. Meanwhile, Ba's condition continued to deteriorate. Gandhi's letters got more desperate and angrier. On January 27, almost a month before Ba passed away, he wrote to the home department in Delhi requesting the services of Dr. Dinshaw Mehta and an Ayurveda specialist. He also requested that his grandnephew Kanu Gandhi be allowed to stay with Ba. Kanu had nursed Ba in the past and could soothe her by playing music and singing bhajans. Gandhi wrote again, this time asking for the services of Dr. Jivraj Mehta (of Yeravda Jail), Dr. B. C. Roy of Calcutta and Vaidya Raj Shiv Sharma (an Ayurvedic doctor) of Lahore. On February 3, Kanu was allowed to stay by Ba's side, but no other permission was granted. Ba's condition was getting worse—she was sleepless at night and in agony through the day. During Ba's last few nights, the Vaidya Raj camped outside the prison, sleeping in a car, in case there was an emergency. This came in handy when one night Sushila Nayyar had to wake up the prison doctor to seek his permission to call him, which was, on this occasion, granted. On the night of February 14, Ba was so ill that Gandhi attempted to summon the Vaidya Raj without permission from the authorities. On February 16, Gandhi wrote a letter at 2 a.m. to the inspector general of prisons in Poona asking permission for the Vaidya Raj to be in attendance for 24 hours, or to release Ba on parole so that she could receive proper medical care, or to release him from prison so that he would no longer be a helpless witness to her painfully deteriorating condition. Though the government gave in, it was too late. On February 18, after the Vaidya Raj gave up, Sushila Nayyar, Dr. Jivraj Mehta and Dr. Gilder resumed their efforts but did not succeed either. Gandhi had already given up and left it to God. In a last desperate attempt, Devdas arranged for penicillin to be flown in from Calcutta. Penicillin was then

1944 *Gandhi's partner in all his satyagrahas, Kasturba was cremated in the khaddar sari that Gandhi himself had spun for her.*

a new wonder drug. But when Gandhi was told that it was to be administered intravenously, he refused permission. He spent the next few days sitting by Ba's side, holding her hand. She asked for her sons. Harilal came, but his inebriated condition upset her so much that she beat her chest in agony. On February 22, seeing that the end was imminent, Devdas gave her a sip of Gangajal (water from the Ganges) at about 3 p.m.

Kasturba Gandhi died that evening at 7:30 p.m. There was a full moon on display, considered an auspicious sign by Hindus. Gandhi, joined by others, stood vigil throughout the night singing Ba's favorite bhajans. This may have helped him control his tears, but not his thoughts: "The best half of me is dead. What am I going to do now?"

Devdas, Pyarelal, Kanu and others cleaned the room where Kasturba lay. Gandhi, along with Sushila Nayyar and Mirabehn, gave her the customary last bath, combed a neat parting in her hair and wrapped her in the same sari with a red border that she had worn just a few months earlier to celebrate Gandhi's birthday. He then put a vermilion mark on her forehead. Every single flower from the palace gardens was used to make garlands for Ba. The five glass bangles that she wore on her right wrist throughout her married life were entwined together with flowers.

The funeral was planned for the next morning, but there were other matters to be resolved. The authorities did not want Ba's cremation to be a public event. Gandhi said: "Either the whole nation be allowed to participate in the funeral or no one." He told his sons Ramdas and Devdas (Harilal was in no condition to attend, and Manilal was in South Africa): "If people of India are not allowed to pay their respects to Ba, then you must suffer the same anguish."

Then there was the question of arranging the customary firewood for Ba's funeral pyre. Many of Gandhi's followers offered to send sandalwood, which he refused, saying he could not allow a poor man's wife to be cremated using expensive sandalwood. A prison official came forward and said the prison had bought sandalwood earlier, when they feared that Gandhi would not survive his last 21-day fast in February 1943. Gandhi agreed—if it was meant for his

1944 *Gandhi in mourning, with Kasturba's body lying before him.*

94   Re: Shri. Kasturba's funeral rites.
                      _____

(1)   " Body should be handed over to my sons and relatives which would mean a public funeral without interference from Government.

(2).   " If that is not possible, funeral should take place as in the case of Mahadev Desai and if the Government will allow relatives only to be present at the funeral, I shall not be able to accept the privilege unless all friends who are as good as relatives to me are also allowed to be present.

(3)   " If this also is not acceptable to the Government, then those who have been allowed to visit her will be sent away by me and only those who are in the camp (detenus) will attend the funeral.

        " It has been, as you will be able to bear witness, my great anxiety not to make any political capital out of this most trying illness of my life companion. But I have always wanted whatever the Government did to be done with good grace, which I am afraid, has been hitherto lacking. It is not too much to expect that now that the patient is no more whatever the Government decide about the funeral will be done with good grace."

(Gandhiji's reply taken down by the Inspector General of Prisons in writing from dictation at 8.7 p.m. on 22.2.'44 in answer to his inquiry on behalf of the Government as to what Gandhiji's wishes in the matter were).

          _____***_____

1944 *Gandhi's letter to the prison authorities dictated barely 30 minutes after Kasturba's death.*

1944 *Gandhi, photographed on the day of his release from Aga Khan Palace Jail, offering prayers at the samadhis of Kasturba and Mahadev Desai, memorials created on the spot where they were cremated.*

cremation, it could be used for his wife's. The next morning at 10 a.m., friends, relatives and detainees—over 150 of them in the end—finally gathered near the spot where Mahadev Desai's pyre was once lit. Ba's body was carried from the main building by Devdas and Ramdas, Pyarelal (Gandhi's secretary) and Gandhi himself. Passages from the Koran, the New Testament, Zoroastrian scriptures and the Bhagavad Gita were read. Devdas lit the pyre and Gandhi kept vigil under a tree until the last flame had died. "How can I leave her during her last moment on earth after we have lived for 62 years together? She would never forgive me if I did."

On the fourth day after the cremation, when her cold ashes were gathered by Ramdas and Devdas to be consigned to sacred rivers, they found the five bangles intact. It was a sign that she had lived and died a suhagini, that is, a woman who embodies the virtues of an ideal Hindu wife.

Born in the same year, Ba had been six months older than Gandhi. Their marriage had spanned more than six decades. Kasturba had always stood by her husband in his struggle for India's independence. Her death left Gandhi at a loss.

Six weeks after Kasturba's death, Gandhi fell seriously ill with a severe attack of malaria. He became delirious and his temperature touched 105. At first he refused to take quinine, but he later relented and his fever abated. On May 3, he was again in a life-threatening situation, suffering from anemia and a very low blood count. On May 6, he was released and went to his friend Shanti Kumar Morarjee's house in Juhu, Bombay. This was to be his last time in jail—he had spent a total of 2,089 days in Indian jails and another 249 days in South African prisons.

1944 *Gandhi walking along Bombay's Juhu beach with his supporters.*
Facing page: *A bereaved Gandhi convalescing with his son Devdas at Juhu Beach.*

THE WAVELL PLAN

The British government came up with a new plan for the transition from British rule to an independent India. It was broadcast on June 14, 1944, by Lord Wavell, and came to be known as the Wavell Plan. The viceroy announced the release of all Congress leaders, including Nehru and Maulana Azad. He summoned India's leading politicians to Shimla for a conference on June 25. Jinnah and Liaquat Ali Khan, one of the founding fathers of Pakistan and the country's first prime minister, represented the Muslim League, while Master Tara Singh represented the Sikhs, and N. Sivaraj the Harijans. Gandhi came in his private capacity but was consulted by Congress throughout the discussions. According to this plan, the viceroy and commander-in-chief would be the only Englishmen in the viceroy's Executive Council; the rest would be Indians, taking charge of foreign affairs, finance, the police and other responsibilities. The plan provided for equal seats for Muslims and Harijans. Congress objected since it was a much larger organization than the Muslim League, with many prominent Muslims and Hindus as members, but they eventually accepted the formula, looking at the bigger picture. When Wavell asked for their list of names, Jinnah refused to comply, saying that any Muslim in the council must be nominated by him alone. A stalemate then obstructed any agreement since Congress had Maulana Azad, a Muslim, as president and there were other prominent anti-Jinnah Muslims who could not be ignored. Jinnah issued a statement saying that Indian problems could be settled in minutes if Gandhi would agree that there should be a Pakistan. But Gandhi considered the division of India as blasphemy. Wavell then compiled his own list of Muslim leaders, but Jinnah again turned it down. In fact, he was single-handedly responsible for the failure of the Wavell Plan.

***

1944 *Gandhi and Jinnah after one of their many meetings.*

GANDHI'S AMERICANA

During the cold, dark South African winter night of June 7, 1893, Gandhi was pushed out of the first-class compartment of a train at the Pietermaritzburg station for being "colored" and a "coolie." After spending the night shivering at the station, he took a train to Pretoria in the morning, where he expected to be met by his hosts. But there was nobody to receive him. Stranded there alone and with no hope of getting a roof over his head, he was contemplating his next step when a friendly "American Negro" approached him with an offer of help, and took him to an inn owned by a fellow American, a white man called Mr. Johnson. Gandhi was given a room, but on the condition that he would not show himself and would have his dinner in his room. Gandhi waited impatiently for the waiter to bring his food. Instead, Mr. Johnson appeared: "I was ashamed of having asked you to have your dinner here," he said, "so I spoke to [the] other guests about you... they said they had no objection... please, therefore, come to [the] dining room... and stay here as long as you wish." This was Gandhi's first direct interaction with an American.

Gandhi never crossed the Atlantic but his reputation as a Mahatma, the great soul, had traveled far, and had made an impact in the United States. One of his earliest American admirers was a clergyman, Dr. John Haynes Holmes (1879–1964), "a social activist, pacifist who was born in Philadelphia and grew up in

the suburb of Boston." He went on to become a senior minister and later minister emeritus of the Community Church of New York. By all accounts, Holmes was the first American to mention Gandhi in a sermon in 1921 in New York, calling him the "greatest man in the world...a savior...when I think of Gandhi I think of Jesus." Gandhi returned the favor two years later, by sending Holmes

Dr. John Haynes Holmes

a Gandhi cap spun by his own hands. Holmes also acted as a mediator between Gandhi and his publisher, Macmillan, and helped ensure the smooth publication of Gandhi's autobiography in the West.

Dr. Eli Stanley Jones

But the book itself, *The Christ of the Indian Road* (1925), largely influenced by Gandhi and his philosophy and which sold over a million copies worldwide, was written by another American, the missionary Dr. Eli Stanley Jones (1884–1973). He followed it up by writing another book, *Mahatma Gandhi: An Interpretation,* first published in 1948. Dr. Jones was born in Baltimore, Maryland, and went to college in Wilmore, Kentucky. In 1907, aged 23, he was sent to India as a missionary by the Methodist Church. Greatly influenced by Gandhi and the Indian freedom movement, he divided his time between the U.S. and an ashram he set up in the foothills of the Himalayas. It was in Dr. Jones' book that Dr. Martin Luther King Jr. first discovered Gandhi.

In 1930, Gandhi embarked upon one of the most powerful movements in the Indian struggle for freedom, one that gave a severe jolt to the empire. Popularly known as the Salt Satyagraha, it had resonances with the Boston Tea Party, a precursor to the American War of Independence (1775–1783), which led to the formation of the United States of America. In America the import tax concessions given to the East India Company by the British rulers resulted in the company having a monopoly. Opposing this, the "Sons of Liberty," as the British settlers were called, dumped tons of tea imported from China by the East India Company into the seawater in Boston Harbor. This came as a big shock to the British Empire and what started as a trade conflict resulted in war, leading to the formation of the United States of America a decade later. Gandhi's Salt Satyagraha, almost a century and a half after that, also shook the empire and showed them at their brutal worst. Gandhi often compared the Boston Tea Party with his satyagraha. A year later, in

1931, in a meeting to sign what came to be known as the Gandhi–Irwin Pact, Lord Irwin (viceroy of India) asked Gandhi how he would like his tea to be served, with milk or sugar. "With salt…to remind us of the famous Boston Tea Party," Gandhi reportedly said.

Louis Fischer (1896–1970) was a Jewish American journalist born in Philadelphia into a family of fish peddlers. Professional duty brought him to India in the scorching heat of May 1942. He spent seven days with Gandhi in his ashram at Wardha, often sleeping outdoors under a tree to combat the heat, which nudged 110 degree F (43 degrees C). Gandhi spent a few hours with him every day and they became close friends. Fischer compiled his experiences in a book titled *A Week with Gandhi,* and it was he who carried the famous letter that Gandhi wrote to the American President Franklin Roosevelt in 1942. Three years after Gandhi's assassination, he published a definitive biography, *The Life of Mahatma Gandhi*, which became the basis for the Richard Attenborough film *Gandhi*, winner of eight Oscars. The book continues to be rated among the best accounts of Gandhi's life.

Another prominent American in Gandhi's life was Margaret Bourke-White (1904–1971), the Bronx-born daughter of a Polish immigrant father of Jewish descent and an Irish orthodox Christian mother, Minnie Bourke. Henry R. Luce, the legendary publisher of *Time* magazine, after having chanced upon some of her photographs, asked her to come to see him, whereupon he hired her to visually revamp the weekly magazine. Six years later she became part of another of Luce's ambitions, *Life* magazine, which would articulate the time through photographs. She loved troublespots and covered combat during the Second World War, photographing concentration camps in Germany as they were being liberated. She was also permitted to photograph Joseph Stalin, the first woman to do

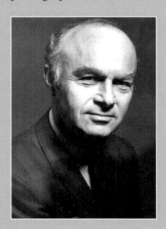

Louis Fischer

Margaret Bourke-White

so, inside the Kremlin. *Life* magazine sent her to India to photograph the setting sun over the British colony and to document the biggest migration in human history, the partition of India. Arriving in India in March 1946, she immediately tried to set a date to photograph Gandhi. First, the philosophy behind the charkha (spinning wheel) was explained to her, and she practiced the art of spinning without breaking the thread. When she was eventually permitted to see Gandhi, she discovered it was his day of silence, and that she was allowed to use only three flashbulbs. As Gandhi started his spinning, she pressed the shutter but it did not synchronize with the flashbulb. The first bulb was wasted. Though the second shot seemed perfect, she realized that she had forgotten to pull the slide. Mercifully, the third shot worked and she created the most iconic photograph of Gandhi, looking at papers sitting beside his charkha.

Affectionately named "torturer" by the Mahatma, Bourke-White became one of his favorites and was the last person to interview him, barely a few hours before he was assassinated. Ever the professional, she rushed back with a concealed camera. No photographers were allowed to photograph the scene of the crime and, as the bulb flashed, Feroze Gandhi, Indira Gandhi's husband, snatched the camera and pulled out the film, depriving the world of those last few historical moments.

Minutes after the shooting, it was another American, Herbert Reiner Jr., a diplomat serving his first posting in Delhi, who grappled with the killer, Nathuram Godse, and delivered him to the Indian police.

1945 *Gandhi photographed collecting donations for the Harijan Fund while aboard a train.* Facing Page: *Gandhi on his peace mission in Bengal.*

In December 1945, Gandhi toured the eastern part of Bengal to promote peace and harmony between Hindus and Muslims. He traveled by train and boat, and walked miles every day—on occasion, he was transported on wooden chairs carried by his supporters. In this image (facing page), Gandhi is on his way to Midnapore with his associates Sudhir Ghosh (on the left) and industrialist Ramkrishna Bajaj, younger son of Jamnalal Bajaj, businessman and Gandhi's friend, in the center.

THE CABINET MISSION FAILS

The next attempt by the British government to ensure a smooth transfer of power to independent India was to send a Cabinet Mission. The delegation was headed by Sir Stafford Cripps and reached India on March 23, 1946. Cripps had headed an earlier failed mission in 1942. The delegation met with Indian political leaders and other groups. Gandhi came to Delhi at their request and stayed in a Harijan colony. Lord Pethick-Lawrence, part of this 1946 Cabinet Mission, was the Secretary of State for India. Members of the Mission would often go to the Harijan colony in Delhi to meet the Mahatma. The talks dragged on because of the differences between Jinnah and Congress on a power-sharing arrangement between Hindus and Muslims. The Cabinet Mission offered a "smaller Pakistan" made up of divided Assam, Bengal and Punjab, along religious lines, but Jinnah refused to accept the proposal. He wanted Pakistan made up of six provinces—Punjab, Sindh, Baluchistan, the North West Frontier Province, Bengal and Assam. The Mission proposed its plan for the composition of the new government on May 16, 1946. It declared that a united dominion of India would be granted independence. It would be a loose confederation of provinces, with Muslim-majority provinces grouped together. The central government would be empowered to handle defense, economy and diplomacy. Gandhi declared: "My conviction abides that it is the best document the British could have produced in the circumstances." However, Jinnah remained stubborn. He refused to accept the proposal of a "smaller Pakistan." He called for "Direct Action" to get Pakistan and set the stage for a bloody confrontation.

1946 *Gandhi and Lord Pethick-Lawrence in Delhi.*

"I was convinced that the right solution for them would have been to keep a United India.... Mr. Jinnah made it abundantly clear from the first moment that so long as he lived, he would never accept a united India. He demanded Partition, he insisted on Pakistan."

LORD LOUIS MOUNTBATTEN

1946-1947

Communal Riots
India Partitioned
Independence

GANDHI TRAVELS INTO THE HEART OF TROUBLE

Calcutta had borne the brunt of the bloody communal clashes in 1946, following Jinnah's Direct Action call, leaving almost 5,000 dead. Gandhi decided to travel to the city, but for him any train journey across India was a taxing experience. He was given a special train to avoid any kind of disruption. People broke windows and tried to stop the train. At times the railway authorities had to use water cannons to disperse the crowds. Gandhi arrived in Calcutta five hours late, tired and saddened by the sight of houses and shops gutted. He toured the city with H. S. Suhrawardy, the Muslim prime minister of the state.

GANDHI IN NOAKHALI

Gandhi left for Noakhali, in the Chittagong division of Bengal, where Muslims had slaughtered Hindus in October 1946, forcibly converted many to Islam, burned Hindu homes and temples and raped and assaulted their women. "It is the cry of outraged womanhood that has called me to Noakhali," he said at one of his prayer meetings. "If necessary, I will die here, but I will not acquiesce in failure. If the only effect of my presence in the flesh is to make people look up to me in hope and expectation, which I can do nothing to vindicate, it would be far better that my eyes were closed in death."

Gandhi lived in 49 villages during his visit to Noakhali, to try and restore peace. He had reached Noakhali on November 6, 1946, saying: "All I know is that I won't be at peace with myself unless I go there." It was a remote, inaccessible place, located in the water-logged delta of the Ganges and Brahmaputra rivers. He stayed for months, declaring his mission was "Do or Die." It meant that he would make every effort to ensure that Hindus and Muslims lived peacefully together, or he would die in the attempt. He would rise at 4 a.m. and walk barefoot from village to village, spending a few days talking to villagers. He would stay in a hut provided by one of the villagers, usually a Muslim. While in Noakhali, he turned 78. Surveying the horrors of the violence, he discovered that new groups

1946 *A crowd gathered at a railway station in Kushtia (Bengal). This photograph was taken minutes before Gandhi's departure for Noakhali in Chittagong division.*

of murderers whose communal bloodlust knew no bounds had emerged. Their objective was to kill Hindus in a deliberate, planned massacre. Gandhi alone realized that the violence in Noakhali was a plague that could destroy India unless it was stopped. He set up a temporary ashram at Srirampur village and ordered his team, comprising Sushila Nayyar, Pyarelal, two women followers Bibi Amtus Salam and Sushila Pai, and Kanu Gandhi, among others, to go to different villages and spread the message of peace. Very few Muslims attended his prayer meetings, and he could sense their hostility. He would often see human excrement deliberately left on the pathways he used, and once a Muslim even spat on his face. He was horrified, but remained calm and moved on. He half expected to be assassinated and said he would welcome such an end.

An estimated 5,000 Hindus were killed during the Noakhali riots. Phillips Talbot, the South Asia correspondent for the *Chicago Daily*, traveled to Noakhali when Gandhi was on his peace mission and wrote: "Here, if I ever saw one, is a pilgrimage. Here is the Indian—and the world's idea of sainthood: a little old man who has renounced personal possessions, walking with bare feet on the cold earth in search of a great human ideal."

1946 *People gathered at Noakhali railway station to witness Gandhi's arrival.*

1946 *Gandhi on his peace march in Noakhali.*

"AN ANESTHETIC IS REQUIRED BEFORE THE OPERATION"

Lord Mountbatten and Lady Edwina arrived in Delhi on March 22, 1947, to draw the curtain on British rule in India. They were a handsome couple with royal connections and soon charmed everyone. Within 24 hours of his arrival as India's last viceroy, Mountbatten faced his first challenge when Jinnah

1947 Gandhi with Lord and Lady Mountbatten during their first meeting in Delhi.

announced in public that Partition was the only solution to the communal conflict. Mountbatten tried his best to bridge the strained relationship between Gandhi and Jinnah. He would later elaborate on his strategy during an address to the Royal Society in London in October 1948, after he had left India. He said that he had tried to get them together "to talk and to gossip." He got Gandhi to speak about his early life in South Africa while Jinnah spoke about his years in London. Jinnah, however, stubbornly stuck to his two-nation stand. In his London address, Mountbatten recalled: "I was convinced that the right solution for them would have been to keep a united India under the plan of the British Cabinet Mission. Mr. Jinnah made it abundantly clear from the first moment that so long as he lived, he would never accept a united India. He demanded Partition, he insisted on Pakistan." Mountbatten disclosed that the Congress leaders wanted an undivided India but accepted Partition to avoid a civil war. "When I told Jinnah that I had their (Congress) provisional agreement to Partition, he was overjoyed. When I said that it logically followed that this would involve partition of the Punjab and Bengal, he was horrified."

Mountbatten had a reputation for being strong-willed and logical, a man who could make daring decisions. Gandhi would prove even more daring. He suggested that Jinnah should be empowered to form a Muslim government to rule over the whole of India. Nehru and Congress shot down that proposal and when Congress eventually agreed to Partition, Gandhi issued a statement for all Indians saying: "Support your leaders." The determined Jinnah had the better of Gandhi but it would prove an expensive victory. Jinnah demanded a quick, surgical division, to which Mountbatten responded: "An anesthetic is required before the operation." The best Mountbatten could do was to try and ensure a peaceful parting of sides. But this was destined not to be.

1947 *Gandhi on his "healing mission" in Bihar.*

A "HEALING MISSION" IN BIHAR

While Gandhi was still in Noakhali, disturbing news from parts of Bihar shook him. In March 1947, he reached Bihar and rebuked Hindus for attacking Muslims in revenge for the Noakhali killings. His main concern was to reduce rioting prompted by the inevitable division of India. He visited village after village and urged people to live peacefully and work toward communal harmony.

The country was aflame with Hindu–Muslim riots. Gandhi could not avoid Partition but at the behest of Lord Mountbatten he agreed to sign a joint declaration with Jinnah to try and infuse some sanity into the situation. When

We deeply deplore the recent acts of
lawlessness and violence that have brought the
utmost disgrace on the fair name of India and
the greatest misery to innocent people,
irrespective of who were the aggressors and
who were the victims.

We denounce for all time the use of
force to achieve political ends, and we call upon
all the communities of India, to whatever persuasion
they may belong, not only to refrain from all
acts of violence and disorder; but also to avoid
both in speech and writing, any words which might
be construed as an incitement to such acts.

M.A. Jinnah 15/4/47 ... i e m... gandhi

1947 *A joint statement issued by Gandhi and Jinnah, in response to the nationwide riots.*

Gandhi suggested that he could get Acharya Kripalani, president of Congress party, to sign too, Jinnah objected. He wanted just two signatures—his and Gandhi's. While Jinnah announced the inevitability of Partition despite Gandhi thinking otherwise, Gandhi in a prayer meeting responded, saying: "Whatever happens, I have to spend my life with him" (Jinnah).

***

1947 *Gandhi with his followers in Delhi. He has his arms around Abha (wife of his nephew Kanu Gandhi) and Manu (his grandniece), whom he fondly called his "walking sticks."*

At the height of summer in 1947 in Patna, Gandhi's grandniece Manu developed a very high fever accompanied by vomiting. She was diagnosed with appendicitis and was immediately sent for an emergency operation. She was operated on at night and Gandhi, wearing a surgical mask, was inside the operating theater. Since Kasturba's death, Gandhi had accepted the use of penicillin and agreed that it could be administered to Manu by injection as she was having difficulty passing urine.

***

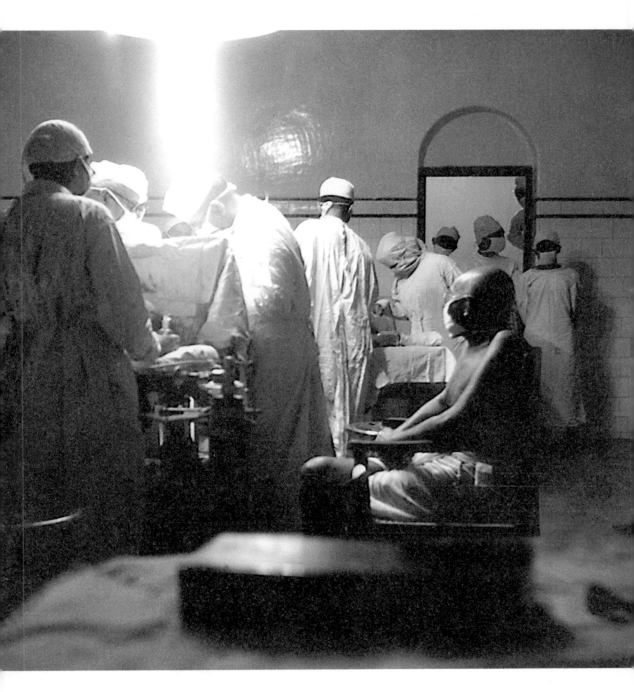

1947 *Gandhi in a surgical mask watches as his grandniece is operated on for appendicitis.*

1947 *One of the largest "exchange of populations" rendered millions homeless.*
Left: *Convoy of Sikhs migrating to East Punjab after Partition.*

With the division of the country into India and Pakistan, neighbors became foes overnight. The days of Partition have been among the bloodiest in Indian history, with an estimated 14.5 million people crossing the border from either side. It was considered the largest migration in human history.

Partition left millions of Hindus, Sikhs and Muslims homeless. People living in Punjab and Bengal bore the brunt of this division. Leaving their "desh" (homeland), hordes of Hindus crossed the eastern border with Pakistan looking for peace and security in the new states of West Bengal, Assam and Tripura.

GANDHI AND AUGUST 15, 1947, INDEPENDENCE DAY

The date August 15, 1947, was a historic day for millions of Indians. Yet, for the chief architect of the freedom movement, Mahatma Gandhi, it was special for different reasons. It was also the fifth anniversary of the death of his closest associate, Mahadev Desai. He awoke at 2 a.m., an hour earlier than usual, at Hyderi Manzil, an old run-down Muslim home in Beliaghata, Calcutta. Like every August 15 for the past five years, he fasted and had the entire Bhagavad Gita recited in memory of his late secretary. He had been invited to Delhi to participate in the celebrations by the newly formed Indian government, but he declined, preferring to stay in Calcutta and work for peace among Hindus and Muslims.

A day earlier, Gandhi had asked for armed guards to be withdrawn from Hyderi Manzil and replaced with Hindu and Muslim volunteers. His Muslim hosts had decorated the house with the Indian tricolor as thousands were expected to greet Gandhi. In the pre-dawn darkness, groups of young girls arrived singing Rabindranath Tagore's songs. According to Pyarelal, Gandhi's secretary and biographer: "...they came and stopped outside the window of Gandhiji's room.... Reverently they stopped their singing, joined the prayer, sang again, took darshan and departed. A little later another batch of girls came and sang songs...a beautiful beginning to the day..." He was mobbed when he went for his morning walk, and on his return found thousands more waiting for him. On seeing him they shouted "*Hindu Muslim Bhai Bhai*" (Hindu-Muslim are brothers). Hyderi Manzil was under siege the entire day and Gandhi had to come out every half hour to give darshan to the crowds. Cries of "Long live Mahatma Gandhi" were deafening. Later in the day, the new ministry led by Prafulla Ghosh paid a visit. Gandhi's advice to them was: "You wear a crown of thorns.... Be humble. Be forbearing...beware of power...power corrupts...you are in office to serve the villagers and the poor..." According to Pyarelal, the newly-appointed governor, Dr. Rajagopalachari, came and they embraced, and "exchanged sallies of wit, jokes and words of mellowed wisdom for over an hour."

1947 *Gandhi and his grandniece Manubehn at Hyderi Manzil in Calcutta, where he spent India's first Independence Day fasting, praying and spinning.*

In the afternoon Gandhi walked to prayer meeting at a nearby maidan (an open ground) in Beliaghata. Hindus, Muslims and people from all walks of life attended, shouting "*Hindu Muslim Ek Ho*" (Hindu–Muslim unite).

As Lord Mountbatten later said: "...in Punjab we have fifty-five thousand soldiers and large-scale rioting on our hands...in Bengal our forces consist of one man, and there is no rioting."

Gandhi saw August 15, 1947, not as Independence but as Partition Day.

"KILL ME, WHY DON'T YOU KILL ME?"

For a year, since Jinnah's Direct Action call to assert the Muslim League's demand for a separate Muslim state, Calcutta had seen bloody riots. On the night of August 31, 1947, while Gandhi slept, a gang of youths from the Hindu Mahasabha arrived and started shouting outside the Hyderi Manzil. They had brought a man who was heavily bandaged and claimed he had been stabbed by Muslims. They seemed determined to start a large-scale riot using the supposedly injured man as an excuse. Manubehn, Abhabehn and two servants were present with Gandhi at the time. The youths began throwing stones and forced their way inside. The two women faced the angry mob and told them that Gandhi was sleeping. Hearing the commotion, Gandhi went outside to confront them. He stood at the door with his hands folded, but the mob became more threatening. Gandhi was so angry that he shouted: "Kill me, why don't you kill me?" He tried to rush toward the crowd, but the two women held him back. Someone aimed a lathi at him and missed, another threw a stone that hit a Muslim by his side. Knowing he could do nothing, Gandhi returned to his room. Saddened by the incident, the dead bodies and the burned houses he had seen while touring the city, Gandhi decided to fast unto death unless sanity returned. Groups representing all faiths and communities promised there would be no more trouble. He asked for a written pledge and they obliged. From that day forward, even when communal violence flared elsewhere in the country, Calcutta was a haven of peace.

1947 *Gandhi arriving through a surging crowd for a prayer meeting at the Calcutta Maidan on August 26. Thousands of Hindus and Muslims congregated to listen to him during the meeting in celebration of Eid-al-Fitr.*

"If someone were to shoot me in the belief that he was getting rid of a rascal, he would kill not the real Gandhi, but the one that appeared to him a rascal."

MOHANDAS KARAMCHAND GANDHI

1948

Assassination
Funeral

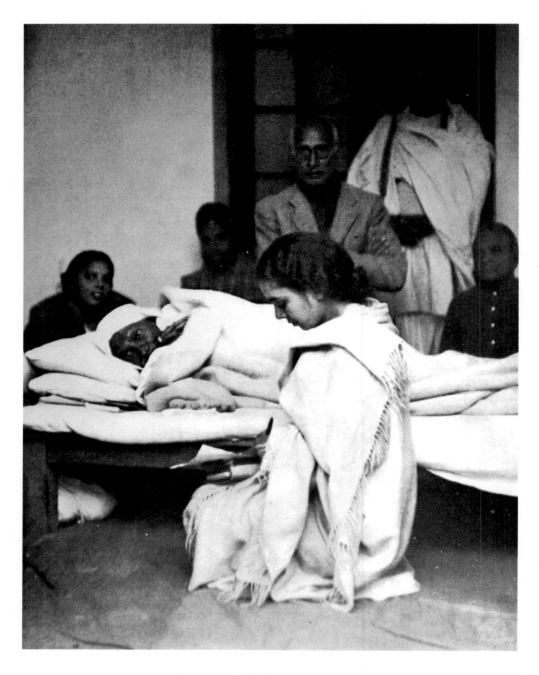

1948 *Gandhi on his last fast, Birla House, Delhi.*

GANDHI'S LAST FAST

Gandhi returned to Delhi from Bengal in September 1947. On January 12, 1948, he decided to go on a fast unto death. This was his last fast and one that incensed his would-be assassin. The only person Gandhi consulted was Lord Mountbatten, who agreed to the fast in the larger interest of improving the communal situation in both of the newly born countries of India and Pakistan. The other reason for the fast was to force the Indian government to transfer 55 crore (550 million) rupees, which was due to Pakistan, but was held up by the Indian government as Pakistan had waged war in Kashmir. Alarmed by Gandhi's failing health and fearing that he could succumb to the fast any day, warring communal groups of Hindus, Muslims, Sikhs and Christians assembled at Birla House, where Gandhi was fasting, on January 18 and signed a pledge of amity.

As soon as the news of Gandhi's fast and his insistence on the transfer of 55 crore rupees to Pakistan made headlines, a group of fanatical Hindus involved in the publication of *Hindu Rashtra*, a Marathi-language newspaper, decided it was time to get rid of Gandhi. In a loosely planned conspiracy, they made their first attempt on his life on January 20, 1948, but failed. The plot was to throw bombs, create panic and shoot him at close range. However, the plan's execution did not go beyond the explosion, and Madan Lal Pahwa, a Hindu refugee from Pakistan who threw the explosives, was arrested. In his interrogation he confessed: "*Woh phir ayenge*" (they will come again). And they did. This time on January 30, when Nathuram Godse killed Gandhi at point-blank range.

1948 *During his last fast, Gandhi became so weak that he had to be carried on his chair-turned-palanquin.*

THE FINAL HOURS AND A PREMONITION OF DEATH

Gandhi often talked about living up to 125 years or more, but on January 29, the day before his assassination, he was unusually eloquent about mortality and his own death. On that day, members of the Nehru family had arrived at Birla House around lunchtime. They included Jawaharlal's sister, Krishna Hutheesing, his daughter Indira, with her four-year-old son, Rajiv, as well as Sarojini Naidu. They headed straight for the garden where Gandhi was basking in the sun. Looking up at the approaching group, all wearing brightly colored saris, he greeted them, saying: "So, the princesses have come to see me." In winter, Gandhi enjoyed eating lunch in the garden at Birla House; he stayed there when he was in Delhi and held a daily evening prayer meeting. About her last meeting with Gandhi, Krishna Hutheesing later wrote: "Gandhi looked exceedingly well that day; his bare brown body was absolutely glowing." When Rajiv picked up flowers that visitors had brought for the Mahatma, and started wrapping them around Gandhi's feet, the Mahatma playfully pulled the young boy's ear, and said: "You must not do that. One only puts flowers around dead people's feet." They were followed by a group of villagers from Bannu who had suffered communal attacks and been rendered homeless. One agitated member of the group shouted at Gandhi: "You have done enough harm. You have ruined us utterly. Leave us alone and take your abode in the Himalayas."

That evening, while walking to his prayer meeting, he confided in Manubehn: "The pitiful cries of these people is like the voice of God. Take this as a death warrant for you and me." While speaking at the prayer meeting, he declared: "God will do what He wills. He may take me away. I shall not find peace in the Himalayas. I want to find peace in the midst of turmoil or I want to die in the turmoil." Finally, there was an uncharacteristic outburst of anger at having to take the pills his doctor had given him to cure his bad cough. "If I were to die of disease or even a pimple, you must shout to the world from the house tops, that I was a false Mahatma. Then my soul, wherever it may be, will rest in peace. But if an explosion took place or somebody shot at me and I received his bullets on my bare chest, without a sigh and with Rama's name on my lips, only then you should say I was a true Mahatma." If this was a premonition, it was so eerily accurate that it was prophetic. Just a few hours earlier, he said to Manubehn: "Who knows what is going to happen before nightfall or even whether I shall be alive?"

On January 30, Gandhi had awoken at 3:30 a.m. He had a long and busy day ahead. At 3:45 a.m., he asked, surprisingly, for a rendition of a Gujarati bhajan, *"Thake na Thake chhatayen hon, manavi na Leje visramo, ne jhoojhaje ekal Bayen, Ho manavi, na Leje visramo"* (Whether tired or not, O man do not take rest, stop not, your struggle, if single-handed, continues). Shortly after, he started to work on revising the draft constitution for the re-organization of the Congress Party.

Ominously enough, Nathuram Godse was also finishing the last piece he would ever write, his own will and testament. A covering letter was addressed to his co-conspirator, Narayan Apte, and stated: "My mental condition is inflamed in the extreme, so that it has become impossible to find... any reliable way out of the political atmosphere. I have therefore decided for myself to adopt a last and extreme step. You will of course know it in a day or two. I have decided to do what I want without depending on anyone else."

Gandhi, meanwhile, met Rajan Nehru, wife of Jawaharlal's nephew, R. K. Nehru, who was leaving for America that morning. At 8 a.m., it was time for his morning massage, during which he made some last-minute corrections to the draft of the new constitution for Congress before handing it over to his trusted secretary, Pyarelal. Then it was time for his daily Bengali lessons, both written and spoken, which he took from his grandniece, Abha Gandhi. His morning bath was accompanied by a check on his weight, which, that morning, was 109 pounds (49.4 kilos). He showed a healthy appetite for breakfast, which comprised exactly 12 ounces of goat's milk, a cup of boiled vegetables with radishes and ripe tomatoes, as well as a glass of orange and carrot juice. This was followed by a medicinal concoction of ginger, sour lime and aloe vera. After resting for a while, Gandhi got up and walked toward the bathroom. Manu said: "Bapu, how strange you look?" referring to the fact that he had not gone anywhere recently without his "walking sticks." Gandhi responded, quoting Rabindranath Tagore: *"Ekla chalo, Ekla chalo…"*

(Walk alone, walk alone). The last walk he would take alone had begun. Sometime later, Margaret Bourke-White, the famous American photographer with *Life* magazine, arrived for an interview. It would turn out to be his last one. Among her questions was: "Do you stick to your desire to live to the age of 125 years?" To this, Gandhi replied: "I have lost that hope because of the terrible happenings in the world." Gandhi also received the well-known French photographer Henri Cartier-Bresson, who presented him with an album of his photographs. His last meeting of the day was with Sardar Patel, which began at 4 p.m. Patel came with his daughter, Manibehn. The meeting was to sort out differences between Nehru and Patel. Two leaders from his home state, Kathiawar, had also arrived unannounced while Gandhi was in this crucial meeting with Sardar Patel. On being informed of their desire to see him, Gandhi said: "Tell them that I will see them, but only after the prayer meeting and that, too, if I am alive." Around the same time, Godse, with a loaded Beretta pistol, was on his way to Birla House from Connaught Place. His mission: to kill Mahatma Gandhi.

The meeting between Gandhi and Patel was an attempt to repair the damaged relationships between Nehru and Patel as well as between Patel and Gandhi. As was his style, Gandhi continued to use his spinning wheel while talking to Patel. He informed Patel that he would highlight the issue of unity in his post-prayer speech and also told him that he was meeting Nehru and Azad to discuss the issue after the prayer meeting that evening. While Patel was still with him, Gandhi had his last meal: 14 ounces of goat's milk, vegetable soup and three oranges. It was now 4:30 p.m. and the issue was still unresolved. His prayer meeting started punctually at 5 p.m., as Gandhi did not like to be late for any appointment. It was now close to 5 p.m., but the discussion with Patel had become so intense that no one dared disturb the two. Abha, in desperation, picked up Gandhi's pocket watch and tried to show it to him, but the two were so engrossed that nothing registered. Finally, Manibehn interrupted them. "It's ten past five," she announced. "I must tear myself away," was how Gandhi bade his final good-bye to Patel. Those would be his last words, apart from the ones that escaped his lips before he breathed his last, just a few minutes later. Since he was running late, Gandhi took a shortcut, walked briskly, faster than normal, to the waiting crowd and his assassin. Standing in front, wearing military-style khaki dress, was Godse, who greeted Gandhi with folded hands that hid a Beretta automatic pistol. Gandhi returned his greeting, which would be his last act on earth. In a swift movement, Godse fired three bullets into Gandhi. The Mahatma fell with folded hands and the exclamation "Hey Ram" on his lips. His body crumpled as Manu held him in her lap. There was a shocked silence before the enormity of what had happened began to sink in. The assassin did not try to flee. In the melee, no one had really noticed the man who had fired the fatal shots. Even as Godse was apprehended, Gandhi's blood spread across the white shawl he had spun himself. The pocket watch that he wore was shattered. It stood frozen at 5:17 p.m.

Gandhi's closest aides, Manu, Abha and Pyarelal, were in shock immediately after the bullets were fired. A young female doctor, a close friend of Sushila Nayyar, took over and placed Gandhi's head on her lap. His body was quivering and still warm, his eyes half shut. She did not have the courage to announce his death, but she could tell he had passed away. The news of the assassination spread like wildfire. Patel, who had barely reached his home after meeting Gandhi, rushed back to Birla House with his daughter, Manibehn. He clasped Gandhi's wrist, hoping to find some signs of life. Finally, Dr. B. P. Bhargava, a close friend of Gandhi's aides, who was present at the prayer meeting, pronounced that Gandhi had been "dead for ten minutes."

"WHO KNOWS BAPU MAY WAKE UP"

Lord Mountbatten rushed to Birla House as soon as he heard the news. With thousands clogging the gates, he could barely find a way to get in. "It was a Muslim who murdered him," shouted an angry young man. "You fool," retorted Mountbatten with his usual presence of mind: "It was a Hindu," for he knew that if it was indeed a Muslim, the country would witness another bloodbath, this time of unimaginable magnitude. Only later did he discover that it was indeed a Hindu, a maharashtrian Brahmin, who had killed Gandhi. That evening, both Nehru and Patel addressed

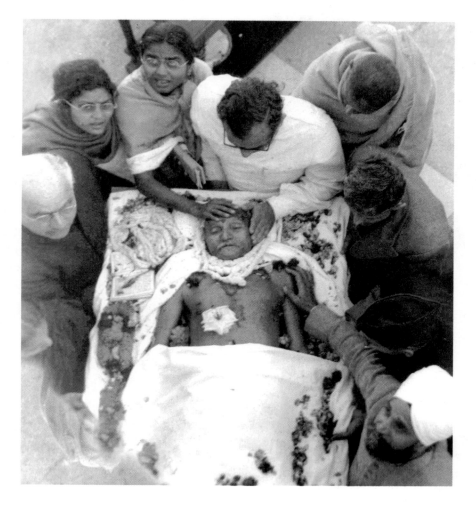

1948 *The last darshan of the Mahatma.*

the nation on All India Radio. "The light has gone out of our lives…" said Nehru, in a phrase that would become entwined with Gandhi's death forever. A distraught Patel, generally a man of few words, managed to say: "My heart is aching…my tongue is tied…the occasion demands not anger but earnest heart searching from us…" Gandhi's body was taken to the first-floor balcony of Birla House for his countrymen to have a final darshan (a last viewing) of their departed leader. At one point, distraught and completely lost, Nehru told Manubehn: "Let's go and

Regd. No. S-1028. Vol. VII No. 30. Price: ANNAS TWO

DAWN

Founded by Quaid-i-Azam Mohammad Ali Jinnah

Karachi, Saturday, January 31, 1948
19 Rabi-ul-Awwal, 1367

Editor: Altaf Husain

MAHATMA GANDHI A MARTYR TO ASSASSIN'S BULLETS

HIT BY FOUR SHOTS AT CLOSE RANGE: WORLD SHOCKED BY NEWS OF DELHI OUTRAGE : ASSAILANT ARRESTED

Manager's Notice

The offices of Dawn will remain closed today (Saturday) as a mark of respect to Mr Gandhi's memory.

The next issue of Dawn will be published on Monday.

Prayer meeting tragedy: 'Bapu is finished': dramatic Birla House announcement

Body to be cremated today: embalming was against his wish

Dawn regrets to announce:-

NEW DELHI, JAN 30: MAHATMA GANDHI WAS SHOT BY A MARATHA HINDU, AT ABOUT 5-10 P.M. ON FRIDAY. LIFE WAS EXTINCT AT 5-40 P.M.

MAHATMA GANDHI WAS SHOT AT FOUR TIMES WHILE HE WAS WALKING TO THE PRAYER GROUND. HE WAS HIT IN THE CHEST AND IMMEDIATELY COLLAPSED. HE WAS REMOVED TO BIRLA HOUSE WHERE HE DIED HALF AN HOUR LATER AT 5-40 P.M.

The name of the man arrested in connection with Mahatma Gandhi's assassination is stated to be Nathuram Vinayak Godse. He is a well educated 35-year-old Maratha Hindu.

Mahatma Gandhi came out of Birla House at 5-5 p.m. and walked towards the prayer meeting ground supporting himself on the shoulders of his two grand daughters. As he approached the platform the congregation which numbered about 500 broke into two parts leaving a passage for Mahatma Gandhi to pass.

A man probably between 30 and 35 in a khaki tunic, who was in the congregation, fired four shots from a revolver at a range of about two yards as Mahatma Gandhi was approaching.

Mahatma Gandhi was hit in the stomach and immediately collapsed. His grand daughters, Ava Gandhi and Manu Gandhi who were supporting him held him and started crying. The incident was so sudden that no one in the congregation realised what had happened. The assailant was immediately pounced upon by some members of the congregation and seized. A part of the congregation ran in panic while others closed upon the spot where Mahatma Gandhi had been shot.

Mahatma Gandhi who was bleeding profusely was removed to Birla House where doctors were immediately summoned. Visitors were prohibited entry into the room where Mahatma Gandhi was lying.

About half an hour later at 5-40 p.m. a member of Gandhi's camp came out of the room and said "Bapu is finished".

The crowd which was anxiously waiting to hear some news of Mahatma Gandhi's condition was stunned.

LAST MOMENTS

Within a few minutes the doctor announced the death of Mahatma Gandhi, a hushed silence prevailed inside Birla House.

By his bedside were Mr Devdas Gandhi, his wife and children, who presumably came after Mahatma Gandhi had expired. Lord Mountbatten, Pandit Nehru, Sardar Patel, (who had an intimate talk with Mahatma Gandhi a few minutes earlier) and

Continued on Page 4, Col 4

Rioting in Bombay: eleven persons killed

BOMBAY, Jan 30: Eleven persons were killed and 47 were injured tonight in central mixed localities of Bombay in clashes and stray stabbings—attributed in police circles to misapprehensions regarding the identity of Mahatma Gandhi's assassin.

The police, who were on the alert, opened fire several times and brought the situation under control by 9 p.m. after which no further incidents were reported.

The affected areas were Golpitha, Null Bazaar, Pydhonie and Dongri. In the Golpitha area the police picked up eight dead bodies with stab wounds.

Curfew was imposed on the localities, and armoured [illegible] were seen patrolling all potential trouble centres.

Mr Morarjee Desai, the Home Minister, accompanied by the Commissioner of Police, toured the areas tonight.

As attempts were made by demonstrators in crowded localities to stop trams and buses and to attack them, the BEST Company ordered immediate withdrawal of all trams and buses from the streets for tonight.—API.

Quaid-i-Azam's tribute to Mahatma Gandhi: "loss to India is irreparable"

"I was shocked to learn of the most dastardly attack on the life of Mr Gandhi, resulting in his death," said Quaid-i-Azam Mohammad Ali Jinnah, Governor-General of Pakistan, on hearing the news of the death of Mr Gandhi.

He added: "There can be no controversy in the face of death. Whatever our political differences he was one of the greatest men produced by the Hindu community and a leader who commanded their universal confidence and respect.

"I wish to express my deep sorrow and sincerely sympathise with the great Hindu community and his family in their bereavement at this momentous, historic and critical period so soon after the birth of freedom for Hindustan and Pakistan.

"The loss to the Dominion of India is irreparable and it will be difficult to fill the vacuum created by the passing away of such a great man at this moment."

Universal tributes to Gandhi

"The tragic news of Gandhiji's assassination has come as a terrible shock to me," said Mr Liaquat Ali Khan, Prime Minister of Pakistan, in a statement.

He added: "It is a most dastardly act and I am sure it will be condemned unreservedly in the strongest terms by everybody.

"He was a great figure of our times and was working unceasingly to bring back sanity to the people and to establish communal harmony. His loss will be felt and mourned by all.

"For the last many years he had been the soul of the Congress Party and it would be no exaggeration to say that he was the Father of the Congress.

"It is a strange irony of fate that a man who had been preaching all his life the doctrine of non-violence should himself be made the tragic target of violence.

"His recent efforts for communal harmony will be remembered with gratitude by all lovers of peace. His removal from the stage of Indian politics at this juncture is an irreparable loss.

"I send my sincere and heartfelt sympathy to his relations and to all those who mourn him."

When the news of Mahatma Gandhi's assassination was received in Karachi, the Prime Minister of Pakistan was in conference with Mr Ghulam Mohammad, Pakistan's Finance Minister, and with the Premier of East Bengal, Khwaja Nazimuddin, and East Bengal's Finance Minister, Mr Hamidul Haq Chowdhry.

An API correspondent who waited

(Continued on back page)

Gandhi's death casts gloom over Karachi: news stuns the City

By Dawn Special Correspondent

The news of Mahatma Gandhi's tragic end cast a thick pall of gloom over the capital of Pakistan on Friday evening. As the news spread, newspaper office telephones rang constantly and anxious voices asked: "Is it true?" Everybody seemed stunned by the news and the first reaction was not to believe it.

Most of the city's newspapers, including Dawn (English and Gujrati) published special bulletins carrying the first flashes of the dire news.

People gathered in groups in public places discussing the news. Streets of the city were unusually crowded till late in the night with people coming out to buy the Special News Bulletins.

Gandhiji's assassination evoked expressions of genuine horror from officials and non-officials, Hindus and Muslims. The Indian High Commissioner, Mr Sri Prakasa, broke down completely with grief. He could only speak in mono-syllables to the Pressmen and others who went to see him in the evening.

To the man in the street, the news came as a blow and a shock. A Muslim car driver exclaimed: "Why did this happen? This is terrible. I can hardly believe it. What is coming over the world?"

The Government of Pakistan and the Sind Government have ordered the closing of their offices on Saturday as a mark of respect to the memory of Mahatma Gandhi.

All schools and colleges and the Municipal Offices will also remain closed today.

Qazi Fazlullah, the only Sind Minister present in the capital, passed orders that all flags on Sind Government buildings should be flown at half-mast on Saturday throughout the province.

Press Communique

All offices under the Government of Pakistan will be closed on Saturday, January 31, 1948 as a mark of respect to the memory of Mr Gandhi, says a Press communique issued by the Ministry of Interior, Government of Pakistan, last night.

Lahore

An API report from Lahore says: A thick cloud of gloom suddenly descended on Lahore as the grim news of Mahatma Gandhi's death flashed like lighting throughout the West Punjab capital.

Social gatherings all over the city instantaneously broke up, people drowned in deep sorrow and regret and unable to comment on the colossal tragedy ever enacted in history only whispered to each other their heartfelt sorrows.

Cinema shows for the evening have been cancelled and all newspapers are closing down for saturday as a mark of respect for the great Indian leader.

Eye-witness account of assassination

An API correspondent, who was present when Mahatma Gandhi was assassinated, says: "The congregation of about 500 was anxiously waiting for Mahatma Gandhi to arrive at the prayer meeting when it was 5 o'clock. Mahatma Gandhi was delayed five minutes. He emerged out of Birla House being supported by his grand daughters Ava Gandhi and Manu Gandhi and walked briskly, as was his custom, to the prayer platform.

"As he approached the congregation they split into two parts to make a passage for him to reach the platform.

When Mahatma Gandhi was 15 yards from the platform I heard a shot fired about two yards ahead of me. I spotted the man who fired the shot and saw him holding revolver in his right hand at right angles. Three more shots followed in succession.

I saw Mahatma Gandhi collapse. He appeared to be hit in the stomach and I was shocked to see blood oozing out and staining his white dhoti. There was immediate panic. For a minute I was dazed.

ASSASSIN SEIZED

Immediately, those who were behind the assailant overpowered him and seized him by the wrist. His revolver dropped to the ground. The assailant was dressed in khaki shirt of military design and in a pair of trousers. The police who were on sentry duty took hold of the man. I rushed to the spot where Mahatma Gandhi had fallen.

I saw Mahatma Gandhi bleeding. His eyes were closed and his head bent. His hand were folded as if in prayer. He was held up in a sitting posture by his grand daughters.

Mahatma Gandhi was immediately carried by four of five persons into Birla House. The doors of the room where Mahatma Gandhi was laid to rest were closed and no per-

Continued on Page 4, Col 5

Nehru appeals to Indian people to end conflicts in face of great disaster

NEW DELHI, Jan 30: The Prime Minister, Pandit Jawaharlal Nehru, in a broadcast tonight on the assassination of Mahatma Gandhi, said: We must hold together and all our petty troubles, difficulties and conflicts must be ended in the face of this great disaster.

The best prayer that we could offer him and his memory is to take a pledge to dedicate ourselves to the truth and to the cause for which this great countryman of ours lived and for which he has died.

The Prime Minister, in a voice quivering with emotion, said: "Friends and comrades, the light has gone out of our lives and there is darkness everywhere. I do not know what to tell you and how to say it. Our beloved leader, Bapu as we called him, the father of the nation, is no more. Perhaps I am wrong to say that. Nevertheless, we will not see him again as we have seen him for these many years.

We will not run to him for advice and seek solace from him and that is a terrible blow not to me only but to millions and millions in this country. And it is a little difficult to soften the blow by another advice that I or anyone else can give you.

The light has gone out, I said, and

Continued on Page 4, Col 5

King shocked at death of Gandhi

LONDON, Jan 30: His Majesty the King has sent the following message to Lord Mountbatten: "The Queen and I are deeply shocked by the news of the death of Mr Gandhi. Will you please convey to the people of India our sincere sympathy in the irreparable loss which they and, indeed, mankind have suffered."

The King is at his country home at Sandringham, in Norfolk.—Reuter.

1948 *News of Gandhi's assassination spread worldwide. Young women, members of London's Indian and Pakistani population, photographed outside India House reading a newspaper bearing the headline: "Gandhi shot dead."*
Facing page: Newspapers in Pakistan carrying the news of Gandhi's assassination expressed equal shock. Dawn, *founded by M. A. Jinnah, devoted the full front page to the story, treating the assassination as a shared tragedy.*

ask Bapu what arrangements must be made..." making everyone present burst into tears. At about 2 a.m., Gandhi's body was brought down and given the last ritualistic bath by the family, with water brought from the Jamuna river. As Devdas removed Gandhi's clothes one piece at a time, those present could see three clear bullet marks: the first one, on the right side of his abdomen, was two-and-a-half inches above the navel; the second was an inch to the right; and the third, the fatal shot, had made a hole an inch above the right nipple. The first two bullets had pierced the frail body and come out of the back. While the body was bathed, these two bullets were found lodged in Gandhi's shawl. The third was embedded in his lungs and was recovered 27 hours later, when the ashes were being gathered from the cold pyre. Emotions continued to run high as the group cleaned the blood from the body to prepare it for the final journey. A red tilak (marking) was put on Gandhi's forehead and sandalwood paste was applied all over his body. Using flowers and leaves, the words "Hey Ram" were fashioned near his head and the sacred "Om" near his feet. His body was covered with a white khadi cloth, possibly spun by Gandhi himself. The body was then covered with flowers and rose petals, except for the chest. "I asked for the chest to be left bare. No soldier ever had a finer chest than Bapu's," said Devdas. At one point, Nehru came to Manu and said: "Sing louder.... Who knows Bapu may wake up." By now, thousands of people had surged toward Birla House in the heart of the part of Delhi known as Lutyens' Delhi, to have the last darshan of their beloved Bapu. The body was once again placed on the balcony for a short while for them to view. It was brought down the next morning, draped in independent India's tricolor, and placed on a gun carriage decorated with flowers. Two hundred hand-picked men from the Indian army, navy and air force pulled the vehicle, using ropes, while Nehru, Patel and close family members sat next to the dead body.

It was a sad day, never to be forgotten by those who witnessed it, when India bid adieu to "Bapu," a man whose life left an indelible mark on the history of the world.

1948 *Mourners crowding around Gandhi's body during the funeral procession.*

1948 *Gandhi's funeral pyre, with police holding back the distraught crowd.*

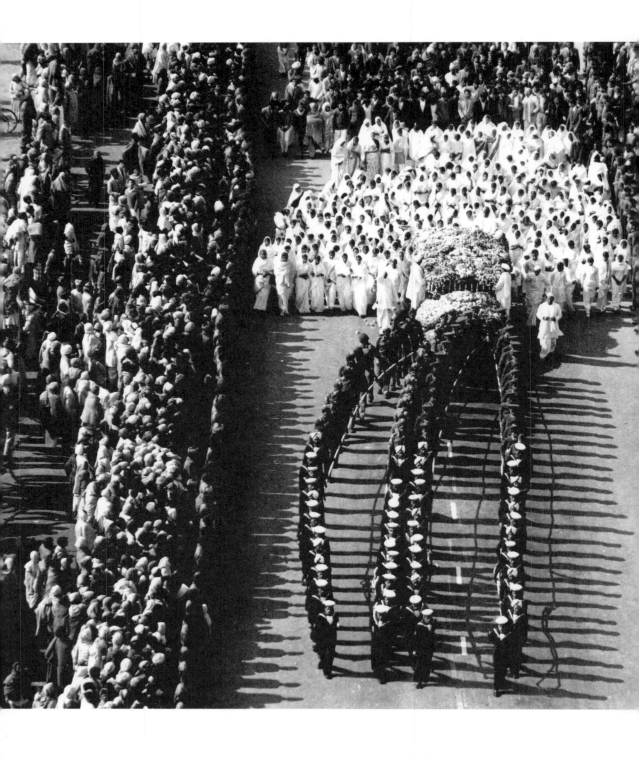

THE LAST JOURNEY

Melville De Mello, with his deep baritone, was a legend of his time thanks to his All India Radio (AIR) broadcasts. Working for AIR, De Mello's seven-hour commentary of Gandhi's funeral is etched into the minds of those who heard it that day. This is an excerpt from his reminiscences of the day:

"It was the morning of the cremation. I reached Birla House at 6 o'clock to take Bapu's darshan...there lay the great Mahatma, his fine broad chest uncovered. I shuddered when I saw the bullet-wounds—dark ominous patches of hate and madness. And then I saw his face. What a wonderful face it was in death!

"It was during the State funeral cortege. My radio-van crawled slowly along Queensway to Raj Ghat. Just behind us, slowly moved the trailer on which lay the body of Mahatma Gandhi, exposed to public gaze. Around the body, like figures in marble, stood Pandit Nehru, Sardar Patel, Devdas Gandhi, Sardar Baldev Singh, Acharya Kripalani and Dr. Rajendra Prasad. Millions lined the route—millions sang his favorite hymns—millions shouted his name—and all wept—nowhere did I see a dry eye.... Dakotas streaked across the sky and showered rose petals and garlands on the bier.

"I reached Raj Ghat five minutes before the funeral cortege arrived...I scrambled onto the roof of the van to get above the crowds.... Then the cortege arrived, and

1948 *Gandhi's funeral procession shows a naval guard escorting the coffin.*

MAHATMA GANDHI ASTHI SPECIAL
NEW DELHI—ALLAHABAD
WEDNESDAY, FEBRUARY 11, 1948

Instructions to Passengers

1. All accommodation is third class, in keeping with Gandhiji's practice of travelling third.

2. There is no charge for the special ticket. The Railway Board is running the train on behalf of Government.

3. The train is due to leave at 6-30 a.m. from the ceremonial platform, New Delhi Railway Station.

4. Passengers due to travel by the train must be on the platform not later than 4 a.m. This is necessary because large crowds are expected to come for Darshan and it may be difficult for passengers to get access to the train if they arrive later than 4 a.m. Those coming after 4 a.m. may get left out.

5. Cars carrying passengers will enter by the State Entry Gate, Connaught Circus, and drive right up to the porch of the ceremonial platform. The Special Tickets will have to be shown to the Police at the gate.

6. Each passenger will be conducted to his coach and seat.

7. Only persons specifically authorized will enter or travel in the coach carrying the urn.

8. Pressmen and photographers will have a reserved compartment. They will be permitted by turns to travel in the coach carrying the urn.

9. No one travelling by the train in any capacity will smoke or eat pan during the journey.

1948 *Special printed instructions were issued to passengers who traveled (by invitation only) on the Asthi special train carrying Gandhi's ashes.*

a great wailing went up from the millions that had packed themselves tightly.... The sun went down as the first flames leaped skywards from the sandalwood pile. A great moan went up from the crowds as they surged forward. It was as if a storm had broken over Raj Ghat.

"Many would have been happy to mix their ashes with the Apostle of Truth and Nonviolence...I suddenly felt a lump in my throat...I made a few incoherent remarks—put the microphone above my head...I felt one with the heart-broken, tragic millions that groaned to the Heavens...

"I sat on the hood of my van many hours after the commentary was over. By this time, I was in strange company. A woman, who had fainted, and also a little girl and a boy who had almost been trampled to death. And then, I noticed a hand trying to take hold of the edge of the hood. I looked over and saw it was the prime minister—Pandit Nehru—I grasped the groping hand and lifted him to the roof of the van, 'Have you seen the Governor-General?' he asked. 'He left half an hour ago,' I replied. 'Have you seen Sardar Patel?' he asked. 'He left a few minutes after the Governor-General,' I replied. I soon realized that in the general chaos, friends had lost friends."

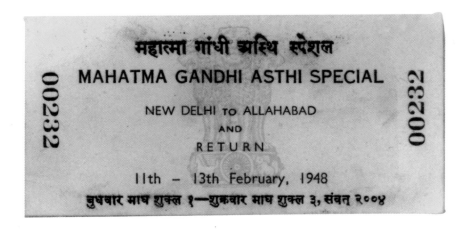

1948 *A ticket from the Gandhi Asthi special train. In accordance with Gandhi's wishes, his ashes were collected in 20 urns and sent to different parts of India to be immersed in sacred rivers.*

1948 *The gun that killed Gandhi.*

The nine men accused of plotting Gandhi's assassination, led by Nathuram Godse, were put on trial, the proceedings of which began on May 24, 1948, held in a special court created in the historic Red Fort in Delhi. All except Veer Savarkar were found guilty. The police could not establish any connection between Savarkar and the assassins, and he was acquitted. Vishnu Karkare, Madanlal Pahwa, Shankar Kistayya, Gopal Godse and Dattatraya Parchure were given life sentences. Nathuram Godse and Narayan Apte were given death sentences: "To be hanged by the neck till dead."

SELECT BIBLIOGRAPHY

Adams, Jad, *Gandhi: Naked Ambition*. London: Quercus, 2011.

Akbar, M. J., *Nehru: The Making of India*. New Delhi: Roli Books, 2002.

Amin, Shahid, *Event, Metaphor, Memory: Chauri Chaura 1922–1992*. New Delhi: Oxford University Press, 1995.

Attenborough, Richard, *In Search of Gandhi*. New Jersey: New Century Publishers, 1982.

Azad, Abul Kalam, *India Wins Freedom*. Calcutta: Orient Blackswan, 1959.

Bhattacharya, Sabyasachi, *The Mahatma and the Poet, Letters and Debates Between Gandhi and Tagore (1915–1941)*. New Delhi: National Book Trust, 1997.

Bose, Nirmal Kumar, *My Days with Gandhi*. New Delhi: Orient Blackswan, 1974.

Bose, Sisir Kumar, *Netaji Subhas Chandra Bose*. New Delhi: National Book Trust, 2001.

Bose, Sugata, *His Majesty's Opponent: Subhas Chandra Bose and India's Struggle Against Empire*. New Delhi: Penguin Books, 2011.

Chablani, S. P. and Preet Chablani (Editor), *Motilal Nehru: Essays and Reflections on His Life and Times*. New Delhi: S. Chand & Co., 1961.

Chandra, Bipan, *Communalism in Modern India*. New Delhi: Vikas, 1984.

Dalal, Chandulal Bhagubhai, *Harilal Gandhi: A Life*. New Delhi: Orient Blackswan, 2007.

Das, Durga, *India: From Curzon to Nehru and After*. New Delhi: Rupa & Co., 1981.

Dawarkadas, Jamnadas, *Political Memoirs*. Bombay: United Asia Publications, 1969.

Desai, Mahadev, *The Diary of Mahadev Desai*. Ahmedabad: Navajivan Publishing House, 1953.

Doke, Joseph J., *Gandhi: A Patriot in South Africa*. New Delhi: Publications Division, 1992.

Erikson, Erik H., *Gandhi's Truth*. New York: Norton, 1969.

Fischer, Frederick B., *That Strange Little Brown Man Gandhi*. New Delhi: Orient Blackswan, 1970.

Fischer, Louis, *The Life of Mahatma Gandhi*. London: Harper Collins, 2010.

Gandhi, Arun, Sunanda Gandhi with Yellin Carol Lynn, *The Untold Story of Kasturba: Wife of Mahatma Gandhi*. Mumbai: Jaico Publishing House, 2000.

Gandhi, Kanu, and Abha Gandhi, *Bapu Ke Sath* (Hindi). New Delhi: Publications Division, 2005.

Gandhi, Mahatma, e-version of *The Collected Works of Mahatma Gandhi* (volume 1 to volume 97). New Delhi: Publications Division, 1960–1994.

Gandhi, Manu, *Bapu Ki Ye Baaten*. Ahmedabad: Navajivan Publishing House, 1969.

Gandhi, Manu, *Last Glimpses of Bapu*. Agra: Shiv Lal Agarwala, 1962.

Gandhi, Manubehn, *Bapu My Mother*. Ahmedabad: Navajivan Publishing House, 1949.

Gandhi, M. K., *An Autobiography, The Story of My Experiments With Truth*. New Delhi: Prakash Books, 2009.

Gandhi, M. K., *Hind Swaraj or Indian Home Rule*. Ahmedabad: Navajivan Publishing House, 1938.

Gandhi, M. K. (Compiled and Edited by S. B. Kher), *The Law and Lawyers*. Ahmedabad: Navajivan Publishing House, 1962.

Gandhi, M. K., *My Early Life: An Illustrated Story*. New Delhi: Oxford University Press, 2012.

Gandhi, M. K., *Ruskin Unto This Last* (A Paraphrase). Ahmedabad: Navajivan Publishing House, 1956.

Gandhi, Rajmohan, *The Good Boatman: A Portrait of Gandhi*. New Delhi: Viking by Penguin Books, 1995.

Gandhi, Rajmohan, *Mohandas: A True Story of a Man, His People and an Empire*. New Delhi: Penguin Books, 2007.

Gandhi, Rajmohan, *Rajaji: A Life*. New Delhi: Penguin Books, 1997.

Gandhi, Tushar A., *"Let's Kill Gandhi!" A Chronicle of His Last Days, The Conspiracy, Murder, Investigation and Trial*. New Delhi: Rupa & Co., 2007.

Ghosh, Sudhir, *Gandhi's Emissary*. New Delhi: Rupa & Co., 1967.

Green, Martin, *Gandhi: Voice of a New Age Revolution*. Mount Jackson: Axios Press, 1993.

Guha, Ramachandra, *Gandhi Before India*. New Delhi: Allen Lane by Penguin Books, 2013.

Guha, Ramachandra (Editor), *Makers of Modern India*. New Delhi: Penguin Books, 2010.

Harvani, Ansar, *Gandhi to Gandhi: Private Faces of Public Figures*. New Delhi: Gyan Publishing House, 1996.

Hasan, Mushirul (Editor), *India's Partition*. New Delhi: Oxford University Press, 1993.

Hasan, Mushirul and Margrit Parnau (Editor), *Regionalizing Pan-Islamism, Documents on the Khilafat Movement*. New Delhi: Manohar, 2005.

Heller, Keith, *The Woman Who Knew Gandhi*. New York: Mariner Books, 2003.

Herman, Arthur, *Gandhi and Churchill: The Epic Rivalry that Destroyed an Empire and Forged Our Age*. London: Arrow Books, 2009.

Hofmeyr, Isabel, *Gandhi Printing Press, Experiments in Slow Reading*. London: Harvard University Press, 2013.

Jain, Jagdishchandra (compiled by James Campbell), *I Could Not Save Mahatma Gandhi, Untold Stories from a Witness's Diary*. Kolkata: Frontpage, 2010.

Jayakar, M. R., *The Story of My Life*, Volume I (1873–1922). Bombay: Asia Publishing House, 1958.

Jayakar, M. R., *The Story of My Life*, Volume II (1922–1925). Bombay: Asia Publishing House, 1959.

Kakar, Sudhir, *Mira and Mahatma*. New Delhi: Viking by Penguin Books, 2004.

Kalarthi, Mukulbhai, *Ba and Bapu*. Ahmedabad: Navajivan Publishing House, 1962.

Kripalani, Krishna, *Gandhi: A Life*. New Delhi: National Book Trust, 1982.

Kripalani, Krishna, *Tagore: A Life*. New Delhi: National Book Trust, 1986.

Kripalani, J. B., *Gandhi: His Life and Thought*. New Delhi: Publications Division, 1970.

Krishna, Balraj, *Great Indian: Surendranath Banerjea to Gandhi*. New Delhi: Rupa & Co., 2010.

Krishnadas, *Seven Months with Mahatma Gandhi*. Ahmedabad: Navajivan Publishing House, 1961.

Kumar, Girja, *Brahmacharya: Gandhi and His Women Associates*. New Delhi: Vitasta, 2006.

Kumar, Girja, *Mahatma Gandhi's Letters on Brahmacharya, Sexuality and Love*. New Delhi: Vitasta, 2011.

Lapierre, Dominique and Collins Larry, *Freedom at Night* (New Edition). New Delhi: Vikas Publishing House, 2004.

Lelyveld, Joseph, *Great Soul: Mahatma Gandhi and His Struggle with India*. New Delhi: Harper Collins, 2011.

Marcello, Patricia C., *Mohandas K. Gandhi: A Biography*. Mumbai: Jaico, 2009.

Matthews, Roderick, *Jinnah vs. Gandhi*. Gurgaon: Hachette India, 2012.

Nanda, B. R., *Mahatma Gandhi: A Biography, Complete and Unabridged*. New Delhi: Oxford University Press, 1996.

Nayyar, Sushila, *Fundamental Works: Mahatma Gandhi, Volume IV, Satyagraha at Work*. Ahmedabad: Navajivan Publishing House, 1989.

Nayyar, Sushila, *Fundamental Works: Mahatma Gandhi, Volume V, India Awakened*. Ahmedabad: Navajivan Publishing House, 1994.

Nayyar, Sushila, *Fundamental Works: Mahatma Gandhi, Volume VI, Satyagraha: The Watershed*. Ahmedabad: Navajivan Publishing House, 1995.

Nayyar, Sushila, *Fundamental Works: Mahatma Gandhi, Volume VII, Preparing for Swaraj*. Ahmedabad: Navajivan Publishing House, 1996.

Nayyar, Sushila, *Fundamental Works: Mahatma Gandhi, Volume VIII, Final Fight for Freedom*. Ahmedabad: Navajivan Publishing House, 1997.

Nayyar, Sushila, *Fundamental Works: Mahatma Gandhi's Last Imprisonment, The Inside Story*. New Delhi: Har Anand Publications, 1996.

Nayyar, Sushila, *Kasturba: A Personal Reminiscence*. Ahmedabad: Navajivan Publishing House, 1960.

Nehru, Jawaharlal, *The Discovery of India*. New Delhi: Penguin Books, 2004.

Pande, B. N. (Editor), *A Centenary History of the Indian National Congress, Volume I: (1885–1919)*. New Delhi: Academic Foundation, 2011.

Pande, B. N. (Editor), *A Centenary History of the Indian National Congress, Volume II: (1919–1935)*. New Delhi: Academic Foundation, 2011.

Pande, B. N. (Editor), *A Centenary History of the Indian National Congress, Volume III: (1935–1947)*. New Delhi: Academic Foundation, 2011.

Pande, B. N. (Editor), *A Centenary History of the Indian National Congress, Volume IV: (1947–1964)*. New Delhi: Academic Foundation, 2011.

Pande, B. N. (Editor), *A Centenary History of the Indian National Congress, Volume V: (1964–1984)*. New Delhi: Academic Foundation, 2011.

Payne, Robert, *The Life and Death of Mahatma Gandhi*. New Delhi: Rupa & Co., 1997.

Prasad, Rajendra, *Autobiography*. Bombay: Asia Publishing House, 1957.

Pyarelal, *A Pilgrimage for Peace: Gandhi and Frontier Gandhi Among N. W. F. Pathans*. Ahmedabad: Navajivan Publishing House, 1950.

Pyarelal, *The Epic Fast*. Ahmedabad: Navajivan Publishing House, 1932.

Pyarelal, *Mahatma Gandhi* Volume II, *The Discovery of Satyagraha: On the Threshold*. Ahmedabad: Navajivan Publishing House, 1997.

Pyarelal, *Mahatma Gandhi* Volume III, *The Birth of Satyagraha*. Ahmedabad: Navajivan Publishing House, 1986.

Pyarelal, *Mahatma Gandhi: The Early Phase* Volume I. Ahmedabad: Navajivan Publishing House, 1965.

Pyarelal, *Mahatma Gandhi: The Last Phase*, Volume IX (Books 1&2). Ahmedabad: Navajivan Publishing House, 1956.

Pyarelal, *Mahatma Gandhi: The Last Phase*, Volume X. Ahmedabad: Navajivan Publishing House, 1958.

Rajagopalachari, C., *Gandhi-Jinnah Vartalaap*. New Delhi: Hindustan Times, 1944.

Ramagundam, Rahul, *Gandhi's Khadi: A History of Contention and Conciliation*. New Delhi: Orient Blackswan, 2008.

Ray, Anuradha, *The Making of Mahatma (A Biography)*. New Delhi: Diamond Books, 2012.

Ray, Bharati (Introduction), Malavika Karlekar, *The Many Words of Sarala Devi: A Diary and the Tagores and Sartorial Styles, A Photo Essay*. New Delhi: Social Science Press, 2010.

Scarfe, Wendy and Allan Scarfe, *J. P. His Biography*. New Delhi: Orient Blackswan, 1975.

Sheean, Vincent, *Lead, Kindly Light*. New York: Random House, 1949.

Shirer, William L., *Gandhi: A Memoir*. New Delhi: Rupa & Co., 1993.

Shourie, Arun, Prannoy Roy, Rahul Bedi and Shekhar Gupta, *The Assassination and After*. New Delhi: Roli Books, 1985.

Shrimannarayan, *Builders of Modern India: Jamanalal Bajaj*. New Delhi: Publications Division, 1976.

Shukla, Chandrashanker, *Gandhi's View of Life*. Bombay: Bharatiya Vidya Bhavan, 1968.

Singh, Anita Inder, *The Partition of India*. New Delhi: National Book Trust, 2006.

Singh, Neerja (Compiled by), *Gandhi-Patel, Letters and Speeches, Differences within Consensus*. New Delhi: National Book Trust, 2009.

Singh, Neerja (Editor), *Nehru-Patel: Agreement within Differences, Select Documents and Correspondences (1933–1950)*. New Delhi: National Book Trust, 2010.

Sinha, Sarojini, *A Pinch of Salt Rocks an Empire*. New Delhi: Children's Book Trust, 1985.

Sitaramayya, Pattabhi, *The History of the Indian National Congress, 1935–47*. Bombay: Padma, 1947.

Suhrud, Tridip, *An Autobiography or The Story of My Experiments With Truth, A Table of Concordance*. New Delhi: Routledge, 2010.

Suhrud, Tridip and DeSouza, Peter Ronald (Editor), *Speaking of Gandhi's Death*. New Delhi: Orient Blackswan, 2010.

Tendulkar, D. G., *Gandhi in Champaran*. New Delhi: Publications Division, 1994.

Tendulkar, D. G., *Mahatma: Life of Mohandas Karamchand Gandhi* (Volume 1–8): Publications Division, 1951.

Varma, Ravindra, *Gandhi in Anecdotes*. Ahmedabad: Navajivan Publishing House, 2001.

Weber, Thomas, *Gandhi at First Sight*. New Delhi: Roli Books, 2015.

Weber, Thomas, *Gandhi, Gandhism and the Gandhians*. New Delhi: Roli Books, 2006.

Weber, Thomas, *Going Native: Gandhi's Relationship with Western Women*. New Delhi: Roli Books, 2011.

Weber, Thomas, *On the Salt March: The Historiography of Mahatma Gandhi's March to Dandi*. New Delhi: Rupa & Co., 2009.

Yagnik, Indulal, *Gandhi as I Know Him*. New Delhi: Mahal, 1943.

INDEX

PHOTO CREDITS